45880.

P9-AQK-005

5

William Cowper

and the

eighteenth century

by Gilbert Thomas

Verse

BIRDS OF PASSAGE
THE WAYSIDE ALTAR
THE VOICE OF PEACE
THE FURTHER GOAL
TOWARDS THE DAWN
POEMS: 1912–1919
MARY OF HUNTINGDON
THE INNER SHRINE

Essays

THE GRAPES AND THE THORNS:
  Thoughts in Wartime
THINGS BIG AND LITTLE
SPARKS FROM THE FIRE
CALM WEATHER
THE MASTER-LIGHT:
  Letters to David
TIMES MAY CHANGE

Criticism

JOHN MASEFIELD
  (*Modern Writers Series*)
BUILDERS AND MAKERS:
  Occasional Studies

General

AUTOBIOGRAPHY: 1891–1941
PADDINGTON TO SEAGOOD:
  the Story of a Model Railway

WILLIAM COWPER

From the portrait by Romney.

William Cowper
and the
eighteenth century

by

Gilbert Thomas

*new and revised
edition*

London
GEORGE ALLEN & UNWIN LTD.

FIRST PUBLISHED IN 1935
REVISED SECOND EDITION 1948

PRINTED IN GREAT BRITAIN
in 12 point Walbaum type
BY T. AND A. CONSTABLE LTD., EDINBURGH

To

E. E. Kellett

Master and Friend
for
many years

FOREWORD TO FIRST EDITION

THE AIM AND scope of this book are suggested in the first chapter. Here I need only say that, while the volume covers biographically the whole of Cowper's life, and while I trust it will serve to reveal anew the charm of his personality, it strives, as the title hints, to see him in relation to his time. Less even than most figures can Cowper be understood apart from his historical setting. In particular he cannot be understood apart from the Evangelical Revival. Yet previous biographers have very superficially treated this aspect of their subject: so much so, indeed, that, without immodesty or exaggeration, I can claim that this is the first attempt to survey in adequate detail the dominating influence in his life.

I have allowed him, wherever possible, to speak directly for himself, and have withstood the temptation of weaving purple passages of my own by paraphrasing his letters. For much biographical detail I am under obligation, as every worker in the same field must be, to Mr. Thomas Wright. One may not always agree with Mr. Wright's judgments; but his exhaustive research merits more acknowledgment than it has sometimes received. References to my other authorities appear as footnotes.

For the impulse to undertake this work with special regard to the religious background I am indirectly indebted to Mr. R. Ellis Roberts. For their kindness in reading the manuscript, and for much encouragement and help, I offer warm thanks to Mr. W. H. Balgarnie, M.A., and Mr. E. E. Kellett, M.A. The brief sketch of eighteenth-century Berkhampstead is based upon material graciously supplied by Mr. G. H. Whybrow, a local antiquarian. The Rev. Frederick C. Gill called my attention to the fact that Blake salutes Wesley and Whitefield by name; and it is to Mr. Gill that I owe this important reference. For the loan of not easily accessible books, or for assistance in various other ways, gratitude is offered to the Librarian and trustees of Dr. Williams's Library; to Mr. Charles W. F. Goss, F.S.A., F.L.A., Librarian to the Bishopsgate Institute; to Mr. Ormond Harris; to Mr. Roger Ingpen; and to the Rev. Leonard S. Shutter. For permission to embody or adapt certain passages in Chapters Two and Seven, which originally appeared in articles contributed to their respective journals, I wish to thank the editors and proprietors of the *Contemporary* and the *Quarterly* Reviews.

Had not Miss Mary Kyle, in typing the work, shown great patience and almost infallible skill in producing order out of chaos, my labour would have been much increased. Finally, the task would never have been accomplished at all but for the persistent encouragement and the help, both direct and indirect, of my wife.

G. T.

Christmas, 1934.

FOREWORD TO NEW EDITION

The kind reception given to this book when it first appeared in 1935, and the fact that there are signs of continued interest in it after it has been out of print for several years, owing to wartime conditions, suggest that there may be room for this new edition. In the absence of fresh evidence, I have seen no reason to make important changes. The text, though slightly abridged, remains substantially unaltered. I have merely removed certain passages or references that now seem to have lost what topical or other interest they may originally have possessed.

March, 1946.

CONTENTS

CONTENTS

Chapter One

INTRODUCTORY

I

ON JULY 5TH, 1796, Charles Lamb, aged twenty-one, wrote to Samuel Taylor Coleridge, aged twenty-three. The letter was headed "Let us prose"; but it included a copy of some verses which Lamb addressed "To the poet Cowper," who, then sixty-four, had temporarily emerged from the spiritual gloom of his declining years. Cowper is described as being "of England's Bards, the wisest and the best." With characteristic sympathy, Lamb wished to please the elderly and ailing poet; and if ever flattery were permissible it was surely in such a case. Later in the same letter to Coleridge, however, Lamb adds: "I fear you will not accord entirely with my sentiments of Cowper as *expressed* above (perhaps hardly just), but the poor gentleman has just recovered from his lunacies, and that begets pity, and pity love, and love admiration; and then it goes hard with people, but they lie."

Lamb, in his cooler moments, was a sound critic, and he was peculiarly fitted by his own temperament to understand Cowper. If Lamb be the poet among our essayists, Cowper is certainly the Elia among our poets. Cowper was the pioneer of a more natural style in verse, while Lamb's prose was studiously archaic. Yet the two men were fundamentally akin, as their letters—among the best in our language—testify. Both of them possessed the lovable whimsicality emanating from that hypersensitiveness which holds extreme sanity and extreme morbidity in precarious equipoise. In both their natures exquisite fun danced upon the edge of melancholy. Both of them were apparently born for domestic felicity, though it is just arguable that Lamb at least was happier single than he would have been in wedlock. At all events, marriage was denied them—Cowper through his own mental affliction, and Lamb through that of one dearer

11

to him than his own life. Finally, both of them transcend any mere literary stature, and survive for us even more as personalities than as writers. When Lamb said of Cowper that his condition "begets pity, and pity love, and love admiration," he might have been speaking of himself. He was certainly stating one of the main reasons why, a century and a half later, the author of *The Task* is still a living figure, though the bulk of his poetry be little read.

As the link between Pope and the Romantic Revival, between conventionality and nature, Cowper will always hold his place in literary text-books. But an insufficient exercise of historical imagination may blur the full extent of his achievement. His poetry seems so old-fashioned to-day that a genuine effort is needed if we are to appreciate how strikingly novel it was at first, just as when we gaze at a landscape of Constable, who cheered his later years by reading Cowper, it is difficult to realise that by painting Dedham Vale in its natural colours the artist did something so unprecedented that many of the sanest of his contemporaries thought him mad. Nor, though we now read Cowper mainly for his descriptions of Nature, was it as a Nature poet that he chiefly appealed to eighteenth-century readers. It is among my principal aims to see him against the background of his own age, and to show how many-sided was his contemporary influence.

If his historical importance be obscured, Cowper's present literary position is also underestimated in some quarters. Few people probably read his longer poems in their entirety, and his translation from Homer—his most sustained enterprise and the one that brought him the greatest financial reward—has long been gathering cobwebs upon neglected shelves. But portions of *The Task* are still familiar to us all: and, for that matter, how many of us are much more fully acquainted with the longer poems of Dryden, Keats, or Wordsworth? Each poet has his little band of devoted scholars, but most poets—the fact must candidly be faced—survive mainly through anthologies, in which Cowper holds his small but unassailable place. Moreover, the best of his hymns continue to be sung. "God moves in a mysterious way," "Oh for a closer walk with God!": these, and at least half a dozen others, are universal and imperishable. Cowper's influence as a writer remains not only alive but—whatever Hazlitt might say to the contrary—widespread.

Hazlitt was a fount of vital curiosity, and, when his anti-Bourbon prejudices were not involved, could speak as sensibly about poetry as about most other things. He spoke the more sensibly about poetry, indeed, because, himself being versatile, he saw it in relation to life, and not as a cult. He had one limitation. He could not recognise

" The strength that walks in ways of quietness."

And so impregnable are most of his verdicts that Cowper has had to pay the penalty of one of this master-critic's few misjudgments. Despite Macaulay, Leslie Stephen, and a host of other eminently virile witnesses against it, the legend of Cowper's "effeminacy" persists. Even Hazlitt found a masculine strength in the stanzas on the loss of the *Royal George*, and admitted that "the story of John Gilpin has perhaps given as much pleasure to as many people as anything of the same length that was ever written." But he said of Cowper as a whole that he "shrinks from and repels common and hearty sympathy." Had he forgotten Cowper's lines on his mother's portrait, or his verses to Mary Unwin? Where in our tongue are there poems of wider—even of manlier—appeal? And, apart from Shakespeare, have many poets coined more proverbs or phrases that have passed into general currency? My own copy of the moral satires and *The Task* is heavily scored with such passages. The "common man" in his daily speech still often quotes, or slightly misquotes, Cowper, though he might be amazed if you told him so.

Cowper the writer is not a spent force. Nevertheless, it is Cowper himself who to-day exercises the more potent spell. For every student who thinks of him in terms of literary history, or for every serious reader of his poetry, a dozen people grapple the man himself to their hearts, and live with him, in imaginative intimacy, through the medium of his letters. Fashions come and go. Simplicity alone is never permanently outmoded. As Sir Arthur Quiller-Couch said, the most deeply rooted instinct in man, for all his warring lusts, is his "perennial and pathetic curiosity about virtue." The best and longest biographies are usually those of people whose lives, by objective standards, were least eventful and exciting. Wesley, it is true, supplies an exception to the rule. That spiritual Colossus, whose frail physical figure is increasingly seen to dominate the century which his life nearly spanned, managed to combine superhuman activity with an unrelaxed hold upon principle. Most men of action become the slaves of predatory ambition.

> " *A life all turbulence and noise may seem*
> *To him that leads it, wise, and to be praised;*
> *But wisdom is a pearl with most success*
> *Sought in still water, and beneath clear skies;*
> *He that is ever occupied in storms*
> *Or dives not for it, or brings up instead,*
> *Vainly industrious, a disgraceful prize."*

In any case, the recital of mere deeds becomes staler with every repetition. But the more one contemplates quiet virtue, the greater becomes its charm. Familiarity only enhances the spell.

Nor is it merely a matter of charm. Quiet virtue is, after all, a more potent constructive influence than the set programmes of politicians. Even when spirituality is "extramundane," as it largely was with Cowper, it is still the most vital agent in promoting the common good. "It must be admitted," said Goldwin Smith,

"that while the wealth of Establishments, of which Burke was the ardent defender, is necessarily reactionary in the extreme, the tendency of religion itself, where it is genuine and sincere, must be to repress any selfish feeling about class or position, and to make men, in temporal matters, more willing to sacrifice the present to the future. Thus it has come to pass that men who professed and imagined themselves to have no interest in this world have practically been its great reformers and improvers in the political and material as well as in the spiritual sphere."

That is why we cannot know too much about Cowper, and why, with a more fundamental (if subconscious) instinct than that of mere pleasure, we like to revive in fancy those long evenings of domestic and spiritual companionship in the lamp-lit parlour at Olney, where he who sang "the Sofa" and "the cups that cheer but not inebriate" read to Mrs. Unwin as she wound the wool from his hands, while Bess, Tiney, and Puss enjoyed their gambols on the Turkey carpet. Cowper, like Lamb, is among that select company of writers whose prime appeal is to the heart, and about whom, if we care for them at all, we never tire of reading. And that is why I make no apology for this book in so far as it may be but a re-enacting of familiar rites.

II

I have long promised myself this labour of love: for I confess that, when I conceived the project, it was as a simple labour of love that I regarded it. Subsequent study, however, has modified my earlier point of view. All the critics are agreed upon Cowper's charm, and about that there is nothing new to be said or desired. Another biographer can only invite his readers to bask afresh in the sunshine, while he culls for them some of the flowers in Cowper's garden that most attract himself. That is all I originally intended to do. My book was to have been little more than a personal anthology of Cowper. It may still be something of that. But the deeper one's affection for a person becomes, the more one's curiosity is engaged. We ask nothing of casual friendships save their obvious rewards. In the give-and-take of normal intercourse, we accept people as we find them, and do not pry too closely behind the scenes. It is different when love is awakened. Then—though we sometimes do it at the peril of cherished illusions—we must needs probe to the core of intimacy. When every hope of further knowledge is exhausted, we must summon conjecture to our aid. And when, no longer satisfied with Cowper's companionship for its own sake, we seek to fathom the deeps of his life and incidentally to discover the source of his periodic madness, conjecture has unfortunately to be invoked.

While we have in Cowper's own letters a full and intimate chronicle of his later years, the data for reconstructing his earlier career, which holds the clue to his recurrent madness

or melancholy, is correspondingly meagre. There are few
historical figures of whom, provokingly, we know at once so
much and so little. Yet the available details of his earlier life
are not too scanty to refute the common impression of the
poet as one whose insanity was needlessly aggravated, if not
actually caused, by Evangelicalism, and whose evil angel was,
in particular, John Newton. This view, though it has found
doughty opponents such as Augustine Birrell and Clement
Shorter, has, on the whole, so prevailed as to become a popular
legend. One biographer and critic after another, from Sir
J. G. Frazer down to Mr. Hugh I'Anson Fausset [1] and Lord
David Cecil,[2] has helped, in varying degree, to perpetuate
a theory that lacks historical warrant and can be contradicted
by a careful study of dates and documents.

Oddly enough, however, that careful study has never been
made. It can be shown, for example, not merely that
Cowper's first attack of insanity occurred before he had
espoused Evangelicalism—this *has* sometimes been admitted
—but that he was, even in youth, a "diligent inquirer" into
religion, and that, long before he met Newton, he had con-
sorted with several Calvinistic divines and had become, like
them, a stricter Calvinist than Newton ever was. Yet even
where these facts have not been overlooked, their implication
has completely been missed.

I confess that I approached my present task with the conventional prejudice against Newton; nor do I now suggest
that he was the ideal friend for Cowper. Nevertheless, the
evidence has convinced me that, on balance, Newton's influence was broadening and beneficent. At all events, it is
crystal-clear that, whoever or whatever else may have been
the cause of Cowper's malady—and, though final proof eludes
us, I lean to Goldwin Smith's view [3] that it was constitutional
in origin—Newton must be held blameless; and it is time for
the stigma to be removed from the memory of one whom all
general historians have agreed in recognising as a great, good,
and eminently "human" man.

[1] *William Cowper.* By Hugh I'Anson Fausset. 1928.
[2] *The Stricken Deer : or a Life of Cowper.* By Lord David Cecil. 1929.
[3] *Cowper.* By Goldwin Smith. *English Men of Letters.* 1880.

Some biographers, like Mr. Fausset, who seeks to explain the riddle of Cowper in terms of modern psychology, hold that Evangelicalism was entirely harmful to the poet. Others take a less extreme view. Thus, Lord David Cecil allows that Evangelicalism was at first a blessing to Cowper, who needed a warmer religious faith than could be found in the latitudinarian Establishment of the period. Only in Evangelicalism could one side of Cowper's nature have found satisfaction. Nevertheless, Evangelicalism was too crude a spiritual vintage for one who, on a contradictory side of his character, was an eighteenth-century gentleman, with, even for that age, an excess of sensibility and refinement. The tragedy of Cowper's life, as Lord David sees it, lay in the fact that, while Evangelicalism failed to heal him, there was nothing else that could have done so. Evangelicalism was the best form of religion the time could offer him: but it was not good enough.

This view incidentally ignores the fact that Calvinism was by no means confined to Evangelicalism, and that, whether within the ranks of Evangelicalism or without, it found many of its strongest adherents among the socially select. That Cowper was a "gentleman" predisposed him towards Calvinism. But something more fundamental has been forgotten. It is remarkable that, of all Cowper's biographers, Goldwin Smith alone mentions—though he does not draw what seems the obvious deduction—the split within eighteenth-century Evangelicalism itself. A wide gulf of spiritual vision and values lay between the Calvinistic and Arminian branches of Evangelicalism—between the predestination in which Newton avowed belief (if in practice he was less rigorous than others of his creed) and the mellower gospel of Wesley. The whole period was rife with controversy between two sets of protagonists who shared the name Evangelical, but who often had little in common save their zeal for religion itself.

"Evangelicalism" did not necessarily mean predestination. For Cowper, had he come within the direct orbit of the Wesleys' influence, it might have meant healing and light. Indeed, Cowper—that sensitive mirror of so many aspects of the life of his day—reflected in himself the two opposing Evangelical camps. One element may have intensified,

B

though it did not *cause*, his morbidity. The other element, even while his mind disowned allegiance to it, warmed and enlarged his heart. His brain and his breeding kept him theoretically, and stubbornly, on the wrong side; but his heart, as we shall see, repeatedly triumphed. For this reason we shall find that, even as things were, Evangelicalism was more of a blessing to him than a curse. The view that his malady was merely constitutional hypochondria, aggravated by environment, may possibly be too simple: it is at least tenable. The attempt to equate "Evangelicalism" with Calvinism, and then to saddle it with the major responsibility for the poet's insanity, is not less simple: and it is, if Evangelicalism be properly understood, absurd.

III

But why this preoccupation with Cowper's madness? The motives that prompt us to dwell upon it have their roots, of course, in our very affection for the man. We want to know everything about him, and are thwarted by a mystery. Without understanding the nature of his melancholy, we cannot understand him as a whole. Moreover, the tenderness he awakens tempts us to shield him—even at the cost of finding a scapegoat. For myself, I believe that only the now unlikely emergence of new evidence will ever enable us to solve the problem of his madness, and so to draw a soundly finished portrait. Meanwhile, the effort to shield him is not only unfair to the scapegoat: it has the effect, which is far from being its aim, of misrepresenting the Cowper we actually know. While still agreeing with Lamb that Cowper "begets pity, and pity love, and love admiration," I am nevertheless convinced that we have allowed the heart to be excessively indulged. My affection for Cowper remains what it was: my pity, while still keen, has been modified.

During the greater part of his life—for a period longer than Byron's whole existence—Cowper was quite sane. He was sometimes quintessentially sane. Sanity, as distinct from the mere common sense of the market-place, is proverbially akin to madness. Inspired sanity demands an exquisitely balanced sensibility, which any severe physical or nervous strain may cause to tumble over the fine edge. Something or other disturbed, from time to time, the balance of Cowper's mind: but, even if there were some predisposing physical complaint, inherited or acquired, his mind itself suffered merely from a functional disorder, and in its moments of weakness displayed the obverse aspect of normal strength. In one of his letters, written during a fit of melancholy, he said that he had not lost his senses, but the use of them. They were in themselves very good senses; and even to-day, after a century and a half of unprecedented change, there is much widsom in his poems and letters which might with benefit be allowed to speak to our condition.

Cowper was not only sane during the major part of his life: he had, surely, a reasonable degree of happiness. Few people have more than that, though to read certain books on Cowper one might suppose that some element of tragedy were not the normal lot of mortal man. It is true that, in Cowper's ledger, the early loss of his mother weighs heavily on the debit side. Yet many lives have registered a similar debit entry without corresponding credit items. He had—he must have had—a sound physical constitution. Delicate, in the sense of being finely wrought, it may have been. But, for all his debility, there must have been essential vitality in one who, despite his mental troubles and the crude medical treatment to which he was sometimes subjected, reached, for his period, the advanced age of sixty-eight. During many of those years he had a congenial environment and congenial occupation. His poetry brought him at length fame and success, which meant less, indeed, to him than they do to most writers, though he *did* own to some vanity.[1] As for friendships: had ever a man more devotees who were ready to give him not merely their love and sympathy, but their time, their labour, and their money? That his own capacity for affection elicited and merited these blessings is beside the point. The deserving do not always, in this world, receive their deserts.

[1] " Oh, popular applause ! what heart of man
Is proof against thy sweet seducing charms ? "
The Task, Book II.

But of what real benefit, it will be asked, could such good fortune be to one whose mind harboured a fixed and terrible delusion? I suggest, in answer, that biographers have tended not only to select for quotation Cowper's gloomier utterances, but to take him, even in his darker moods, too much at his own word. They have made insufficient allowance for his merely habitual use of Calvinistic terminology. I do not mean that he consciously exaggerated: still less that he was insincere. I am not implying that certain episodes in his life were not "terrible," though even here the theory of compensation might be invoked, with the possibility that madness provides in some measure its own anaesthetic. Nor do I deny that Cowper's belief in his eternal damnation was "fixed" in the sense that, so long as he lived, it periodically recurred. But I think it is easy to misrepresent the degree to which it really overshadowed his career. There can, I suggest, be no such thing in human experience as even a relatively *settled* despair extending over so long a period as that during which Cowper is sometimes said to have been substantially bereft of hope. Such despair, continued for a much briefer time, would provide its own anodyne in the form of death or of incurable lunacy, which is more horrifying to the onlooker than to the person concerned. Only at occasional intervals was Cowper mad to the point of being helpless to express his despair, and so in large measure to resolve and belie the very gloom expressed.

A religious idiom, once adopted, becomes second nature, and Cowper, especially in his letters, wrote spontaneously. Even if he always weighed his words, we need not suppose that his words always weighed too heavily on him. In the Evangelical background of my youth, I knew many men and women whose professed preoccupation with the next world in no way seriously interfered with mundane concern and enjoyment. Nor, fundamentally, were they hypocrites. Though creeds are not unimportant, and though ideally our creeds and practice should correspond, religious experience, at the best, eludes precise definition, and most people fall back upon the terminology of their own age and environment. For Cowper, with his hypersensitiveness and innate logic,

Calvinism did sometimes assume the grimness of reality. Even in his case, however, we must make allowance for a merely casual use of Calvinistic imagery. The more may we discount his self-expressed melancholy when, as is often the case, we find it forming part of a letter otherwise brimming with mirth. Sadness and humour are compatible: they are, indeed, natural consorts. Real despair is a different matter.

It seems extraordinary to me that most critics, except Goldwin Smith, take even *The Castaway* at its face value. It is a morbid poem—or, at least, it reflects a morbid creed. But, as Goldwin Smith says, "the despair which finds this vent in verse is hardly despair. Poetry can never be the direct expression of emotion; it must be the product of reflection combined with an exercise of the faculty of composition which in itself is pleasurable." There is much insight into Cowper in those few lines. Two sides of his nature were often apparently at odds with each other; but the length of his life, with its variety of interests and activities, should alone convince us that, whatever he may have said about himself, his gloom was in fact but intermittent.

The neat division of Cowper's life into periods will not stand the test of the data, and all attempts at such theoretical precision—attempts that contradict one another according to the theory on which each is based—distort our whole view of him and his work. Never, unfortunately, did the spiritual and rational sides of his nature find lasting harmony. Yet a light did sometimes surprise him while he sang; the Lord did rise for him with healing in His wings; and his soul did know many

> *"a season of clear shining*
> *To cheer it after rain."*

His mind was often clouded; it was often caged within the cast-iron creed of his adoption. He wrote many hymns that are mere rhymed Calvinism. Yet he also wrote "Hark, my soul! it is the Lord"; and in *The Task* predestination and his own innate Christian radiance are found in strange juxtaposition. A mingling throughout his work of incongruous elements sufficiently disproves the view that he was ever consistently happy or miserable for long at a time. His poetry and letters reveal a life that was always, in his own words, "a chequer-board of joy and sorrow." The darkness was sometimes black indeed; but the sunshine was warm and generous when it broke through. His native vitality was such that it often escaped from bondage, and his utterance had then the strength and tenderness that are the inseparable elements of true manhood—which is not the synonym for mere force, but its very negation.

Cowper combined in himself two characteristics which in eighteenth-century society were sharply divided. To the "polite" world of his day religious enthusiasm was anathema; to the religious zealot anything that savoured of the world suggested the flesh and the devil. Cowper needed a faith that would have enabled him to make, in the true sense, the best of both worlds. His story might have been different had he come under the influence of Arminianism instead of Calvinism. As it was, he failed, as we of the twentieth century see the matter, to reconcile the claims of God and man; he oscillated, it appears to us, uneasily between the two. But it will be found on closer analysis that this seeming duality is traceable to the limitations of his time rather than to any fundamental conflict in himself.

He cannot, again, be understood apart from his age. Because mere *gleams* of a synthesis came to him when a happy combination of moods stimulated his inner light, we are more conscious of the measure of his failure than of the measure, historically viewed, of his success. We are tempted to regard him as a potentially great creative artist, who, through timidity, remained unnecessarily prisoned by his era: whereas the truth is that he was temperamentally a critic whose vocation, splendidly accomplished, was to serve his own day, but who in the process became sometimes a prophet and a creator in spite of himself.

Chapter Two

AN "EXTRAMUNDANE" AND HIS WORLD

I

"IT IS HARDLY possible for a man to interest himself less than I do in what passes in the political world. I have my own reasons for discharging myself of that burthen, and such reasons as I believe no man ever had but myself. Had I dropped from the moon into this system eleven years ago, the concerns of a world to which I did not naturally belong, would not have engaged me much; and just as little engaged I feel myself under a persuasion which nothing has yet shaken, that I am an extra-mundane character with reference to this globe of yours, and that, though not a native of the moon, I am not, however, made of the dust of this planet."

Thus, in 1784, Cowper, then fifty-two, started a letter to Newton. Perhaps even here we must allow somewhat for whimsicality; but, divorced from its context, as it sometimes has been, this passage, with its reflection of Cowper's belief both in his spiritual doom and in his own singularity in that respect, might be read as evidence of a wholly disordered mind. Yet there follows, in the same letter, a closely reasoned discussion of the causes and effects of the rejection by the House of Lords, under pressure from George III, of Fox's India Bill. We may accept or reject Cowper's arguments on the matter: they are, at any rate, well thought out and stated with perfect lucidity. "Extramundane," to some large degree, Cowper certainly was. But his character, as this single letter serves to show, lacked the consistency that can be summarised in a word.

He was a Calvinist whose innately ethical religion often overflowed the narrow channel of his creed. He was, again, both retiring and sociable. He passed nearly the last half of his career in a corner of Buckinghamshire, making no journey of any length between 1767 and 1792, when Hayley, who must have had remarkable powers of persuasion, took him to

Sussex. Yet his hermitage was no mere escapist's sanctuary. If his nervous constitution needed settled repose, and if the mere thought of travel would threaten him with panic, no man was less a solitary by nature. "Though my life has long been like that of a recluse," he wrote in 1781, "I have not the temper of one, nor am I in the least an enemy to cheerfulness and good humour." His claim was substantiated by the facts. The very hypersensitiveness that restricted his own movements accentuated the charm which made him a magnet to draw the most diverse friends to him. Your true hermit resents any intrusion upon his solitude. Cowper liked having guests under his roof, and through their visits, and the correspondence which ensued, maintained contact with the world. Moreover, he vicariously enjoyed travel and adventure through reading Cook's *Voyages* and other records of contemporary discovery. And, while he said that "God made the country, and man made the town," he did not refuse some of the amenities that came from the modern Babylon, including the *St. James's Chronicle*, the *Monthly Review*, and the *Gentleman's Magazine*.

"As when the sea is uncommonly agitated, the water finds its way into creeks and holes of rocks, which in its calmer state it never reaches, in like manner the effect of these turbulent times is felt even at Orchard Side, where in general we live as undisturbed by the political element as shrimps and cockles that have been accidentally deposited in some hollow beyond the water-mark, by the usual dashing of the waves."

So Cowper would write of his seclusion; while, in another mood, he might say, in reference to the contemporary political discontents, "well—all will be over soon. The time is at hand when an empire will be established that shall fill the earth. Neither statesmen nor generals will lay the foundation, but it shall rise at the sound of the trumpet." Yet, despite both his banter and his Calvinism, he followed current events with considerable interest. His deductions were often wrong, and many of his prophecies, like those of other votaries of the perilous art, have been disproved. But his reflections on public affairs were always intelligent; even through the least persuasive of them there ran a vein of sapience; while on the question of slavery he raised, from his platform as a poet, a bold and definite voice in favour of abolition.

His interest in the larger world grew with the years. This fact supports the contention that his later life was not one of relatively settled gloom. It also reflects the more dramatic change in national events after 1774. The "eighteenth century" of popular imagination—a period of placidity, reason, and formal elegance—is false to the deeper realities. But, if the conventional view has a veneer of truth, the "eighteenth century" began with the landing of William III at Brixham in 1688—a revolution that was merely consummated by the bloodless accession of the Hanover dynasty in 1714. When Cowper was born in 1731, this "eighteenth century" was well established. Not only was it mature; the seeds of its decay, while not suspected, were already at work. Walpole's long regime of sound finance and pacific foreign policy had still a decade to run; but the first cracks in his "system" were there, and in 1739 he was forced by popular opinion into war with Spain. In 1742 he resigned, and the next thirty-three years were coloured by the more brilliant, if less calculable, genius of Chatham. Change, however, took longer to make its effects visible than it does now. The Spanish War became merged in the War of the Austrian Succession. Neither that struggle, nor the Seven Years' War which opened in 1756, affected at home the "eighteenth-century" repose. There might be flaws in the foundations; but the Georgian structure still stood, solid, comfortable, and apparently unshakable.

With the outbreak of the War of American Independence, followed by the French Revolution and the gathering of storm clouds all over Europe, we enter a very different political atmosphere. Goethe said that the cannon of Valmy in 1792 proclaimed the opening of a new age and a new world. The shadows of coming events were discernible fifteen or twenty years earlier, and to the society which beheld them they suggested rather the close of an epoch than the beginning of another. Cowper, no more than most men of his age, could see all the new factors—though some of them had actually been gathering momentum throughout his own lifetime—that would enable England, with a solid array of active or potential enemies arrayed against her in 1780, to pass soon through two decades of conflict, and to emerge not only restored to power, but, despite the expenditure involved by warfare on a then unparalleled scale, increased in national wealth. Writing in December 1780, he could truly say of England:

> " *The nations hunt: all mark thee for a prey,*
> *They swarm around thee, and thou stand'st at bay.*"

In 1780, as their eyes gazed across the Atlantic, it seemed to others, as to him, that in losing her American colonies—bone of her bone, and flesh of her flesh—England might lose her own life: that "the mother might die with the child." The more did this gloomy outlook seem justified because France had taken the opportunity to launch a blow against her old enemy—a move in which Spain and Holland soon joined.

News, in those pre-railway and pre-telegraph days, travelled slowly:

"It is reported among persons of the best intelligence at Olney —the barber, the schoolmaster, and the drummer of a corps quartered at this place—that the belligerent powers are at last reconciled, the articles of the treaty adjusted, and that peace is at the door. I saw this morning, at nine o'clock, a group of about twelve figures very closely engaged in a conference, as I suppose, upon the same subject. The scene of consultation was a black-smith's shed, very comfortably screened from the wind, and directly opposed to the morning sun. Some held their hands behind them, some had them folded across their bosom, and others had thrust them into their breeches pockets. Every man's posture bespoke a pacific turn of mind; but the distance being too great for their words to reach me, nothing transpired. I am willing, however, to hope that the secret will not be a secret long, and that you and I, equally interested in the event, though not, perhaps, equally well informed, shall soon have the oppor-tunity to rejoice in the completion of it."

That is how, as described to Newton, Cowper gleaned the first rumour of the temporary European peace in 1783. News might travel slowly: but, sooner or later, it reached even Olney. And throughout the last twenty years of Cowper's life, which ended in 1800, it was mostly disturbing news. The political sky was full of threatening portents. There was one other bright interlude. The Bastille fell in 1789; and young William Wordsworth found it bliss then to be alive. But Cowper, who had five years earlier anticipated it with almost prophetic insight, also welcomed the event, ageing—and a Calvinist—though he was. But hope was followed by deeper gloom after the excesses of the Paris mob and the execution of Louis XVI. The times, from 1774 onwards, were out of joint. The old sense of stability had gone. The "eighteenth century" had ended.

II

But though Cowper lived during the birth-throes of a new era whose developments were beyond the dreams of the most clear-sighted men of his own generation, and though the trend of public events after 1774 moved him to a concern hardly compatible with his professed unworldliness, he remained, after all, a detached observer. "I find the politics of times past," he said, "more intelligible than those of the present." There speaks a philosopher rather than a man of action. Writing in 1788 to his cousin, Lady Hesketh, about the trial of his old schoolfellow Warren Hastings, he said: "The style of a criminal charge of this kind has been an affair settled among orators from the days of Tully to the present; and like all other practices that have obtained for ages, this in particular seems to have been founded originally in reason, and in the necessity of the case." Then, with elfish glee combined with a realistic view of average human nature, he proceeds to show his cousin why the man of affairs, "lest he should be suspected of fiction, or of precipitancy, or of a consciousness that after all he shall not be able to prove his allegations," must inevitably be "vehement, energetic, rapid"; must call his opponent "tyrant, and traitor, and everything else that is odious, and all this to his face, because all this, bad as it is, is no more than he undertakes to prove in the sequel," and because otherwise he might seem to "have trifled with the tribunal to which he has summoned him."

The letter then proceeds:

"And now, my dear, though I have thus spoken, and have seemed to plead the cause of that species of eloquence which you, and every creature who has your sentiments, must necessarily dislike, perhaps I am not altogether convinced of its propriety. Perhaps, at the bottom, I am much more of opinion that if the charge, unaccompanied by any inflammatory matter and simply detailed, being once delivered into the court and read aloud, the witnesses were immediately examined, and sentence pronounced according to the evidence; not only the process would be shortened, much time and much expense saved, but justice would at least have as fair play as now she has. Prejudice is of no use in weighing the question guilty or not guilty? and the principal aim, end, and effect of such introductory harangues is to create as much prejudice as possible. When you and I therefore have the sole management of such a business entrusted to us, we will order it otherwise."

This passage, for which many parallels can be found, shows Cowper's gift for seeing two sides of a question: his capacity for stating a case before proceeding to destroy it. This faculty does not tend to make its possessor a man of affairs. It may make him a lawyer; Cowper, indeed, had legal blood in his veins and was himself trained in early manhood for the law. But, without animus against that profession, we may suggest that Cowper's fastidious moral sense, apart from his nervous disability, would have made distasteful to him a calling that often necessitates the pressing of an argument which, however clearly seen and understood, does not carry personal conviction. And, though even Cowper could sometimes espouse a crusade, as in the case of slavery, the very capacity to see both sides of a problem makes a definite cause more difficult, as a rule, to find. Fairness, justice, reason: these were Cowper's watchwords in politics, so far as he had any at all. They are indeed the professed ideals of most actual politicians; though the method too often belies the profession. Cowper was right: the man of action must be galvanised by a touch of vehemence

and fanaticism.   The history of affairs is the history of a
balance maintained between conflicting prejudices.

Cowper, though he enjoyed watching their antics, could
never take politicians and other busybodies quite seriously.
One of the most humorous and famous of his letters is that
which describes the cold reception accorded to the "extremely
seducing" Parliamentary candidate who once found his way
to Orchard Side, and had, with his retinue, to be admitted
through the back-door, as Puss, one of the three famous hares,
had temporarily escaped from her box and so rendered impossible the opening of the "grand entry." Cowper was not
"extramundane" in the sense that he took no lively and
thoughtful interest in worldly affairs.   He was "extramundane" only in not taking practical folk at their own
valuation.

> "Forgive him, then, thou bustler in concerns
> Of little worth, an idler in the best,
> If, author of no mischief and some good,
> He seek his proper happiness by means
> That may advance, but cannot hinder, thine.
> Nor, though he tread the secret path of life,
> Engage no notice, and enjoy much ease,
> Account him an encumbrance on the state,
> Receiving benefits, and rend'ring none.
> His sphere though humble, if that humble sphere
> Shine with his fair example, and though small
> His influence, if that influence all be spent
> In soothing sorrow and in quenching strife,
> In aiding helpless indigence, in works
> From which at least a grateful few derive
> Some taste of comfort in a world of woe,
> Then let the supercilious great confess
> He serves his country, recompenses well
> The state, beneath the shadow of whose vine
> He sits secure, and in the scale of life
> Holds no ignoble, though a slighted, place."

It is true that, while he eschewed partisan prejudice or
rhetoric, he called himself a Whig.   He was, indeed, essentially a child of the "eighteenth century" that closed with the
American War.   His roots were in the solid Whiggism that
gave England an interval for peaceful consolidation after the

dissensions of the Stuart epoch. On his father's side he came
of the Whig legal nobility. Whiggism, when he was born,
was still a constructive force, and remained sufficiently vital,
during his youth and early manhood, to give its own stamp to
his nature. Through his mother there entered a very different element into his blood. But so far as he took political
colour from his own age, it was from Whiggism in the full
flower of its maturity. And since the period was one of many-
sided development at home rather than of expansion or
adventure abroad, it may be well, by way of preparing a
frame for his portrait, to glance briefly at English social life
in his day.

III

A number of factors combined to make the "eighteenth
century" a period of relative tranquillity. The Toleration
Act of 1689 both reflected and further promoted the growth
of intellectual and spiritual freedom. The Act still imposed
many restrictions on Nonconformists, and offered no legal
relief to Roman Catholics, among whom Jacobitism remained
strong and to be feared. But liberty of worship for every kind
of religious body was now established as a rule seldom in-
fringed. The Union with Scotland, in 1707, brought its own
advantages; while, six years later, the Treaty of Utrecht laid
the basis of a peace that left England comparatively undisturbed until the French Revolution and its sequel made
France again predominant in Europe. Another ameliorating
influence was, strangely enough, the ignorance of George I
of English language and customs. Certain Royal prerogatives
were allowed to slip into the hands of a Whig oligarchy.
Walpole, actuated by love of personal power rather than by
liberal ideals as we understand them, became in fact, while
declining the name, our first Prime Minister. We may trace
through the eighteenth century the characteristically fortuitous growth of our modern Cabinet system. It is doubtful, as
Dr. Trevelyan says, whether the nobles and squires would
have yielded greater powers to the House of Commons if they

had thought of it as a really popular body.[1] To them it was merely a house of gentlemen, many of whom were relatives or nominees of the Peerage. It was "the best club in London," or, when more seriously viewed, "'the Roman Senate,' to which the highest interests of the country could safely be committed." Democracy, as we know it, was yet unborn, and it was with no prevision or conscious design that Whiggism forged the weapons with which the cause of Reform was later to be fought and won.

Aristocracy was still in the saddle, and that fact has made us think of the "eighteenth century" largely in terms of Strawberry Hill, Ranelagh, and "the Bath"; of Lord Chesterfield and Horace Walpole; of Chippendale chairs and Adam decorations; of White's Chocolate House and St. James's Coffee House; of the *beaux* and *belles* painted by Reynolds, Romney, or Gainsborough. Our thoughts may turn also to Dr. Johnson, Gibbon, Garrick, and their illustrious company—not forgetting poor Goldsmith—at the Mitre or the Cheshire Cheese. But, while the aristocracy still saw an unbridgeable gulf between itself and the "meaner" part of mankind, and while the horizon of Dr. Johnson and his associates was bounded by politics, religion, and the arts, economic changes, already foreshadowing the Industrial Revolution, were at work. There was rapidly rising a new merchant *bourgeoisie*, recruited largely from the ranks of religious dissent. The English middle class was, indeed, beginning to evolve, and, however gradually, to dispute the power of the nobility, landowners, squires, and clergy. It has been well said that the Puritan of one age was Cromwell; of another Bunyan; and of the next Defoe.

Defoe died in 1731, the year of Cowper's birth. Among the later works of that "true-born Englishman" and founder of modern journalism, who lightly tossed off *Robinson Crusoe* as a "pot-boiler," was his *Tour* of Great Britain. Defoe had been employed by Harley, in Queen Anne's reign, as a confidential spy, whose function it was to report on the state of opinion in all parts of the country. He played no small part

---

[1] *History of England.* By George Macaulay Trevelyan, O.M. 1926. See also *England under Queen Anne: Blenheim.* 1930.

in the negotiations that led to the Union with Scotland in 1707. His *Tour*, based on material gathered during journeys made some years before its publication in 1724, was ostensibly a guide-book. It had to compete with the type of volume then popular, in which the natural or historical "wonders" of our island were gushingly described. His heart, which was given to commerce, was not in this part of his task. We can, as it were, hear him groan as he approaches Oxford, Winchester, or Glastonbury, and is faced with the necessity of "mugging up" antiquarian authorities, and of exhibiting some show of enthusiasm for scholarship or tradition. He is too resourceful a journalist to fail in the attempt, and his naturally reflective style—he was fundamentally religious—helps him. When contemplating, for example, the ruins of the once prosperous but now submerged city of Dunwich, he knows how to fill up space, and to create an atmosphere, by interpolating a moral disquisition.

Not always, however, will the man in him yield to the journalist. Thus, in traversing the "howling wilderness" of the Peak, he pays lip service to some of its "wonders," and is moved to genuine astonishment at Eldon Hole. But many of the Peakland "miracles" acclaimed by other contemporary travellers are in his opinion "poor things to wonder at." For himself the crowning miracle in this part of England is that of a poor lead-miner and his wife, living, patiently and cheerfully, in a cave "one hundred and fifty yards underground, or in a hole as deep in the earth as the cross upon St. Paul's cupola [1] is high out of it." He finds one other source for "real wonder" in Derbyshire. That is "the Duke of Devonshire's fine house at Chatsworth," and the marvel is "not that so noble and magnificent a palace should be built, but that it should be built in such a situation, and in such a country so out of the way, whoever sees it must take a journey on purpose."

Defoe, the utilitarian, differed from the "polite" society of his own and the next age in having no respect for the glory of tradition as embodied in church, college, or castle. He did not differ from it in having no feeling for Nature. Dr.

---

[1] Wren's Cathedral, finished in 1710.

Johnson expressed the prevalent view of his time when he said that one field was just like another.   It is significant that Richard Wilson lived and died in neglect, while Gainsborough, who won popularity as a portrait painter, though his heart was less set upon that side of his profession, left over forty unsold landscapes.   The eighteenth-century aristocrat might hunt or shoot or fish in the country: for its charm of form and colour, or the interplay of light and shade as the wind drove the clouds along our incomparable English skies, he had no vision at all.   Nor was England, as a whole, quite so beautiful as it was soon to become, and to remain until the Industrial Revolution began to sprawl its smoke and sordidness across the landscape.   In the south-east, where civilisation was of older date, the chess-board pattern of the countryside had long been familiar.   Elsewhere the process of enclosure was going on throughout Cowper's life, and was not quite completed even at the end of George the Third's reign.   The economic aspect of enclosure, which still engages rival schools of thought, need not concern us here.   About its aesthetic result there can hardly be two opinions.

While hedgerow and orchard were increasingly appearing, England was also being beautified through the agency of men who had no thought of beauty.   The passion for sport inspired many aristocrats besides the Duke of Devonshire to build stately homes in the country and to lay out extensive parks. It is questionable whether even the architects whose services were enlisted, and whose work to-day contrasts so vividly with the Victorian pseudo-Gothic revival and the later anarchy, entertained deliberate ideas of "beauty."   Dignity combined with a then spacious conception of utility were doubtless their aims.   Their taste was the purer on that account.   "The fusion of classic grace with vernacular energy" characterises eighteenth-century architecture, alike in town and country. The eighteenth-century gentleman may merely have wished to enjoy rural sport, while at the same time taming "the inhospitable terror" of hill, forest, or heath.   By so doing he promoted that "perfectly beautiful equilibrium between man and nature" which gives the English countryside its distinctive charm.

C

Hazlitt said of Cowper that

> "with all his boasted simplicity and love of the country, he
> seldom launches out into general descriptions of Nature: he
> looks at her over his clipped hedges, and from his well-swept
> garden-walks; or if he makes a bolder experiment now and
> then, it is with an air of precaution, as if he were afraid of being
> caught in a shower of rain, or of not being able, in case of any
> untoward accident, to make good his retreat home."

The charge is too severe, even when the historic background
is forgotten. It is seen to be grossly misleading when that
background is recalled. We may legitimately find amusement
in Cowper's statement, describing his journey to Eartham in
1792, that he was "a little daunted by the tremendous height
of the Sussex hills." But ridicule is another matter. Not
only, as the poet explained in the same letter, did the Sussex
hills dwarf by comparison all that he had seen elsewhere: he
lived in a day when wild Nature repelled the robustest gaze.[1]
If he looked at her "over his clipped hedges," he was the first
eighteenth-century writer, and, if we except Shakespeare and
Milton in certain moods, the first in the whole succession of
English poets, to look at Nature simply and unaffectedly at all.
He had partial rivals in Thomson, Gray, and Collins; but,
more fully than they, he broke through the tinted haze of
the Augustans, and peopled his landscape with flesh-and-blood
characters instead of the stock figures of a moribund Arcad-
ianism.

> *"Scenes must be beautiful which, daily viewed,*
> *Please daily, and whose novelty survives*
> *Long knowledge and the scrutiny of years."*

That was a new vision in Cowper's time. And if the scenes
were homely, was his love of them less manly on that account?
Is not greater rather than less vitality required to see beauty
not merely in the grandiose but in the commonplace? It is
of the gentler scenes, in which man and Nature are partners,
that we instinctively think when speaking of England; and it
was, perhaps, by a happy accident that Cowper and Constable,

---

[1] Dr. Johnson, speaking of Dovedale and of Wales, said that " every emergence
from these hills is an *escape*."

who broke through the traditionally formal treatment of
Nature in poetry and art, both lived by placid lowland
streams.

IV

All these things were hidden from the forward-ranging
vision of Defoe. They would in any case have bored one for
whom a thriving fish-market held more romance than an
Oxford quadrangle. The establishment of a Penny Post in
London, in competition with the General Post Office, fired
his enthusiasm more sincerely than the noblest cathedral or
the greatest "natural wonder." He liked the very things that
roused, a century later, the spleen of Cobbett, for whom "the
Wen" spread, like doom, across the face of England. In his
own earlier day, Defoe, who graphically contrasts the part of
the old City left by the Great Fire with the reconstructed
areas, rejoiced to see London developing so "prodigiously"
that Deptford, Islington, Mile End, Newington Butts, Lam-
beth, and Chelsea were—among other outlying villages—
being absorbed. He glowed with fervour when noting the
number of merchants and tradesmen who were making their
homes outside the city, thus causing the rapid growth of select
suburban hamlets like Stratford, Walthamstow, and "Layton
Stone."

The great centres of population were in the south, the
southern midlands, and East Anglia, though the wool industry
was growing fast in the West Riding, the coal trade well
established on the Tyne, and Lancashire already assuming
importance. Manchester had become "the greatest meer
village in England," while "Liverpoole," with its rapidly
rising buildings of freestone and brick, its beautiful new
church "on the north side of the town," and its pioneer wet
dock in the "Mersea," constructed at "an immense charge,"
was beginning to rival Bristol; and "what it may grow to in
time," adds the complete English tradesman, "I do not
know." "Hallifax," "Bradforth," and "Huthersfield" were
already making cloth, and "a noble scene of industry and
application is spread before you here, and which, joined to
the market of Leeds, where it chiefly centres, is such a sur-

prising thing, that they who have pretended to give an account of Yorkshire, and have left this out, must betray an ignorance not to be accounted or excused."

While the north was developing, manufacture was still largely concentrated around or near the coast. The making of canals began only in the reign of George III, and it was not until then that the new turnpike roads became common. Cowper spoke of the good roads at Huntingdon in 1765. His standards were comparative. It then took four days, even along the Great North Road, to travel from London to York; and much later in the century, as Cowper's correspondence from Olney and Weston Underwood reveals, the lesser roads, despite the rumour of "turnpikes," were mere ruts and often, in the winter, impassable quagmires. Pack-horses were still the chief means of transport for lighter goods; lumbering waggons, drawn by four or six horses, delivered, in their own good time, the heavier merchandise to its consignees. Sedan-chairs were still fashionable in the towns. The Thames was London's most popular highway. Passengers travelled longer distances by heavy coaches without springs. Cowper and his suite made their memorable journey to Sussex in a privately hired coach "with four steeds to draw it." His "terrors" of anticipation, while happily belied, were not without reason. Mishaps were common; delays frequent and lengthy. Dick Turpin had been hanged at York when Cowper was a boy, but his race was not extinct. Though Cowper died only thirty years before the Liverpool and Manchester Railway was opened, he never knew the light and swift coaches made possible by McAdam and driven by the senior Weller and his peers. The Pickwickian age was glorious but brief.

Until the roads were improved, industry, wherever possible, remained near the sea. In the eighteenth century the south coast and East Anglia were dotted with little ports, to which the merchandise of the interior came largely by river. Many of these ports had their own trade with foreign lands, but most of them were chiefly engaged in coastwise shipping, radiating to a remarkable extent upon

"opulent, enlarg'd, and still
Increasing London,"

which, relatively to the rest of the country, was even larger than it is now.[1] It is difficult for us, says Mr. Cole,[2] to appreciate the economic significance which that coastwise traffic had in Defoe's day. Its continued importance is attested, a century later, by a letter from Cowper to Joseph Hill in 1793. "As to the canal that is to be my neighbour," the poet writes,

"I hear little about it. . . . When it is finished, the people of these parts will have to carry their coals seven miles only, which now they bring from Northampton or Bedford, both at the distance of fifteen. But, as Balaam says, who shall live when these things are done? It is not for me, a sexagenarian already, to expect that I shall. The chief objection to canals in general seems to be, that, multiplying as they do, they are likely to swallow the coasting trade."

It is from the opening decades of the eighteenth century that there date the first recorded agricultural patents. Thereafter numerous devices—specialised ploughs, threshing machines and the like—began to appear. Until middle life, at any rate, Cowper probably saw labourers using much the same kinds of implement as those represented on Roman altars or mediaeval missals. Agriculture was still the main activity in eighteenth-century England, and underwent a great revival. But industry—especially the woollen industry —was widely extending its domain, and was altering the face of the country. The iron trade, again, was leaving its native stronghold in Sussex, being driven thence by the exhaustion of timber some time before the process of smelting iron with coal was discovered. There were, too, changes of industrial method. The "domestic system," under which skilled operatives worked in their own houses, still flourished, and Defoe gives us a vivid idea of how quiet by day, when the inhabitants were so engaged, a city like Norwich could be. The "domestic system" lingered in Cowper's time; his description of

[1] In 1700 England and Wales contained about five and a half million inhabitants, of whom 674,350 resided in the Metropolitan Area and about 200,000 in the City. By 1800 the population had risen to nearly nine millions.
[2] Introduction to *A Tour Through England and Wales*. By Daniel Defoe. *Everyman* Edition. 1929.

the poor lace-workers of Olney, toiling by winter candle-light
in their own cottages, will be recalled. But small masters or
capitalists were springing up in the country as a whole,
organising the business of production in workshops attached
to their houses. The invention of steam may have brought
the factory system to fruition: the shoots of it are clearly
discernible even in Defoe's pages.

V

The eighteenth century can now be recognised as having
been a period of relatively quick transition from an England
still almost feudal to the beginnings of England as we know
it to-day. Few people, however, saw the process of transition
at the time, because few people travelled and few could read.
Defoe and (a little later) Wesley are isolated figures. Through
constant journeying, they surveyed Britain more or less as a
whole. The average man seldom left his own town or village,
where change was too gradual to impress him forcibly. There
were none of the unifying and standardising influences
through which the Welsh miner, the Lincolnshire farm-
labourer, and even the Hebridean lightkeeper now share to
some extent a common consciousness. The outlook of the
eighteenth-century man was bounded as a rule by his own
immediate environment, which might differ widely from that
of another man of his own class some thirty or fifty miles
away: the more so because the Government, during the
earlier part of the century, adopted a policy—mainly wise,
perhaps, for the time—of *laissez-faire.*

The Revolution, which had risen out of indignation against
abuses of the Royal prerogative, became in fact a conservative
defence of the new constitution as defined by the lawyers who
framed it. For this reason, says Dr. Trevelyan,

> "the period of Walpole and the Pitts was the heyday of un-
> challenged abuses in all forms of corporate life. Holders of
> ecclesiastical, academic, charitable, and scholastic endowments
> had no fear of enquiry or reform. Schoolmasters could draw
> their salaries without keeping school. Universities could sell
> degrees without holding examinations or giving instruction.

Parliamentary boroughs and municipal oligarchies could be as
corrupt and ridiculous as they liked; it was enough that they
were old. 'Whatever is is right—if it can show a charter' seems
the watchword of the eighteenth century.''

The Revolution freed the country from political tyranny.
It did nothing to restrain the social tyranny of those who had
the mind to use it. The small farmer and agricultural labourer,
as well as the poorer type of clergyman, were still in bondage
to the landowner and the squire, and their lot, whether happy
or otherwise, depended upon the individual caprice of their
superiors. Though the cultural improvement begun by
Steele, Addison, and others was bearing some fruit, and while
actual societies for "the reformation of manners" had sprung
up, there was still no type of English gentleman. It was one
thing to work for a Sir Roger de Coverley, though even he
would have brooked no new-fangled democratic nonsense,
had there been any evidence of it in his day; it was quite
another thing to be at the mercy of a Squire Western. The
good- or ill-fortune of apprentice or artisan similarly turned
upon the character and generosity of his employer. There
was often a bond of respect or affection between master and
man that is pleasant to recall in these days of limited liability
companies, multiple stores, and office robots. There was
often also a callousness that lingered on until Dickens im-
personated it as Scrooge and prepared the public conscience
for the legislation of a later age.

The inevitable counterpart of the eighteenth-century
laissez-faire—it is wrong to call it a sequel, since the very
revolt was an integral element in the period—was the Wesleyan Revival. Yet the political stagnation of the first half
of the century served good, no less than evil, ends. It gave
an interval for old feuds to die and be forgotten. If it made
for corruption, it made also for toleration. If it allowed
individual abuses, it also allowed individual initiative. The
new freedom for initiative helped further, in its turn, the
cause of tolerance. The growth of interest in the expanding
trade of the country lessened the pre-occupation of the
Puritans with religion—or shall we say with militant theology? Even the latitudinarianism of the Establishment, though

we cannot on that account condone the apathy (or worse) of Christ's individual representatives, has, in historic perspective, its brighter side. Not merely was the policy of making latitudinarian appointments forced upon the Government by the fact that Jabobitism was still espoused by many of the "high-flying" clergy: an interlude of quiescence offered reason a hitherto denied opportunity to find its voice in religion. It was the time of Bishops Berkeley and Butler. And the temporary shifting of interest from heaven to earth gave to the Evangelical Revival, when it came, an ethical challenge and potency that were wholly new.

The religious background of Cowper's life will later need detailed examination. It is enough at the moment to suggest that the temper of the time turned men's thoughts from persecution to philanthropy. The eighteenth century was the period of John Howard, Robert Raikes, Mary Wollstonecraft, and many other pioneers of modern social reform; and there is fitness in the fact that the aged Wesley's last letter, written in 1791, was addressed to young William Wilberforce. Reform was long overdue. The common people depicted by Gay and Hogarth, earlier in the century, were poor, ignorant, and coarse beyond description. The torture of animals was a favourite pastime; crimes of violence, in the absence of any effective police force, were rampant; and even for trivial offences "the law," as Mr. Vulliamy says, "treated men, women, and children with fierce impartiality, and strung them up on hundreds of gibbets." Insobriety was vastly increased by the new taste for gin, which was not seriously taxed till 1735. (Tea was then only beginning to be imported in any large quantities.) The state of the hospitals and prisons hardly bears contemplation. The gaols were farmed out by the State to private contractors, who recouped themselves by extorting money from their charges. Rich prisoners could make prison "a home from home"; the very poor ones sometimes died of starvation in filthy cellars.

While the two universities were semi-decaying, partly through the exclusion of dissenters, partly through the reservation of many chief posts to the clergy, and partly through internal friction, the schools were in equally parlous condition. The public schools suffered from indiscipline, bullying, and lack of organisation. The Elizabethan and Stuart grammar schools had fallen into decline, though new ones, less uniformly fine in spirit, were springing up. The middle and lower classes, when their members received any tuition at all, had to take the best (or worst) that regional private enterprise could offer. The Society for the Promotion of Christian Knowledge, which had been founded by a few private gentlemen in 1696, was fostering the growth of charity schools, in addition to the main work of circulating cheap Bibles and tracts; while the dissenters and Quakers were beginning to provide their own establishments. Broadly speaking, however, education in the eighteenth century was, like most other things, a matter of chance. The boy Wordsworth was fortunate in attending the school for farmers' sons at Hawkshead. The six-year-old Cowper was tragically unlucky in being entrusted to Dr. Pitman's care.

What has been said about the common people in Cowper's century is true enough of the lower strata; but generalisation must again be avoided. The ignorance and brutality of the submerged classes in the great cities—particularly London and other seaports—defy exaggeration. Nevertheless, while the larger cities were developing, the bulk of the population still resided in country towns or villages. Parochialism may have limited the mind, but at least it provided the focus and stimulus of a corporate life, to which many different crafts contributed variety in unity. Moreover, while most people were illiterate, oral tradition was still alive. Ballads and Bible tales were familiar to the better class of the poor, and popular belief survived in fairies, magic, and the like. The rationalistic and academic literature of the eighteenth century, which was read only by the aristocracy, must not colour for us the period as a whole. "It is even arguable," says Dr. Trevelyan, "that the eighteenth century, which produced William Blake and Burns and Wordsworth, was in its true nature more 'romantic' than the following century with its efforts to escape by feats of imagination from the drabness of its real surroundings."

VI

Marlborough had died in 1722. Addison had gone to his rest in 1719, and Steele had followed him ten years later. In 1730 there appeared Thomson's *Autumn* and Gay's *Beggar's Opera*. In 1731, when Cowper was born, Sir Robert Walpole had recently quarrelled with Townshend. He still basked in the favour of Queen Caroline, who had six more years to live: but popular opinion was already turning against him. Horace Walpole, who disputes with Cowper the title of his century's best letter-writer, was at Eton with his friend Thomas Gray, another future master of "the gentlest art." Lord Chesterfield was negotiating the second Treaty of Vienna; his natural son, Philip Stanhope, to whom other famous letters were to be addressed, was born in the following year. The future Lord Chatham, having left Oxford because of "the gout," was "a young Cornet of Horse" in Lord Cobham's regiment. Samuel Johnson, whose shabby shoes had evoked the cruel mirth of his fellow undergraduates, had just left Pembroke College without taking his degree. He was soon to become an usher in Leicestershire and later to open a school near Lichfield, where David Garrick was among his three pupils. "Little Davy" at the moment was fourteen, and was writing precocious letters to his father, Captain Garrick, at Gibraltar.

John Wesley, aged twenty-eight, had recently been elected a Fellow of Lincoln College. As leader of the Holy Club, founded by "Brother Charles," he was "laying a deeper foundation of repentance," but seeing "little fruit." He was still the High Church ecclesiastic; the vision of Aldersgate Street was not yet. Meanwhile, George Whitefield, between irregular periods of schooling, was helping his mother to draw ale for her customers at the Bell Inn, Gloucester. "*Analogy* Butler," in his wealthy rectory at Stanhope, was writing his best-known work. Dean—the embryo Bishop—Berkeley was returning to England after three years of retirement and study in Rhode Island, whither he had gone for the purpose of founding a college in the Bermudas and of extending its benefits to the Americans: a scheme that never materialised, as the Government's promised grant was not forthcoming.

Pope, having finished the earlier drafts of *The Dunciad*, was composing his *Epistles*. Samuel Richardson, with his town house and "country-box," was already the prosperous Government printer, but had not yet written *Pamela*. Swift had made his last visit to England. He was still a popular idol in Dublin, though the shadows of misanthropy and madness were deepening. Henry Fielding was achieving success with his early comedies at the newly opened theatre in Goodman's Fields. Hogarth had completed, and was beginning to engrave, *The Harlot's Progress*. Beau Nash was Master of the Ceremonies at Bath, and, while discouraging the duel and insisting that gentlemen should dance in shoes instead of boots, was co-operating with John Wood in rebuilding the city on classic lines. Handel, who had five years earlier become a naturalised Englishman, was ending his career as composer and conductor of Italian Opera for the Haymarket Theatre. He had yet to assert his true greatness as a choral writer.

David Hume, aged twenty, was fretting out his heart in a Bristol counting-house. Tobias Smollett was studying at Glasgow University before being apprenticed to a surgeon in that city. Gilbert White, a boy of eleven, was being educated at Basingstoke under Thomas Warton, father of the poet. He was already, no doubt, roaming the countryside, with every sense alert. It is questionable if Adam Smith, at Kirkcaldy, had begun to reflect upon the wealth of nations. He was only eight, but, through being kidnapped by gipsies, had already had his "only adventure." Joshua Reynolds, also eight, was attending his father's free grammar school at Plympton Earl. Gainsborough was only four—the youngest of nine children frisking upon the banks of the Suffolk Stour. William Collins was pursuing his juvenile studies at Chichester, where his father, a wealthy hatter, was mayor. Robert Clive, on his ancestral acres in Shropshire, was manifesting his love for perilous adventure, and was already, at six, the despair of his teachers. The future Captain Cook was a child of three, whose father was a Yorkshire bailiff. Oliver Goldsmith, the son of an Irish clergyman-farmer whose sordid fortunes had recently taken a better turn, was of similar age. John Howard, in Bedfordshire, was five; Edmund Burke, in Dublin, was two. In the following year Warren Hastings was born at Churchill, in Oxfordshire. A decade later, a small boy in Greenock was, we may surmise, watching the steam escape from the domestic saucepans.

The list, which might be extended, will suffice both as a rough "map" of Cowper's age and as an indication of its wealth and variety of genius. The eighteenth century reared greater men than Cowper. It produced few in whom its diverse aspects are more interestingly focussed.

Chapter Three

CHILDHOOD AND YOUTH

I

THE EIGHTEENTH-CENTURY improvement in manners was but relative to the crudity and coarseness that had hitherto characterised even the nobility. While every age has its shining exceptions, it is a fair generalisation that society in the eighteenth century had reached, as it were, the stage of a youth who, emerging out of lusty and thoughtless boyhood, becomes suddenly aware of his gaucherie. The youth's idea of good form is apt to be superficial: his one aim is to avoid calling attention to himself by making a *faux pas*. Not until later, as a rule, does he realise that surface manners do not make a gentleman, and that even surface manners, if they are to be truly well bred, must spring from gentility of heart.

Commenting on the famous encounter between Wesley and Beau Nash, Mr. Laver [1] says that those who have told the story have been, with one exception, a little hard on Nash. "The exception is Miss Sitwell, who, in her book on *Bath*, is a little hard on Wesley." It is possible, Mr. Laver suggests, to be just to both men. "If Wesley were the great civiliser of the lower classes, Nash was the great civiliser of the aristocracy, and, if we forget religious questions for a moment, both were working for the same end: the reformation of manners, and both, in their different ways, were equally successful." The claim is exaggerated, as any claim that ignores religious questions, even "for a moment," must be. It holds, nevertheless, a grain of truth. Nash, and his contemporary reformers in the same field, did a salutary work. They were, within the limits of their circumstances and vision, apostles of light. It is easy to smile now at their stilted code of decorum. For average society at the time such a code was necessary.

The fact remains that the eighteenth-century notion of

---

[1] *Wesley.* By James Laver. 1932.

gentility was concerned with manners rather than with morals,[1] save in so far as it encouraged fair play among gamesters. It assumed, too, an impassable gulf between the aristocracy and the "lower orders." Everybody is familiar with the reply made by the Duchess of Buckingham to Lady Huntingdon, who had invited her to hear Whitefield preach:

"I thank Your Ladyship for the information concerning the *Methodist* preachers: their doctrines are most repulsive, strongly tinctured with Impertinence and Disrespect towards their Superiors, in perpetually endeavouring to level all Ranks, and do away with all Distinctions. It is monstrous to be told that you have a heart as *sinful* as the Common Wretches that crawl the Earth. This is highly *offensive* and *insulting*; and I cannot but wonder that your Ladyship should relish any Sentiment so much at variance with High Rank and Good Breeding."

In these words, extraordinary as they sound to modern ears, the Duchess merely voiced the normal opinion of her time and class.

Even Cowper never forgot that he was, in the contemporary sense, a gentleman. The poor people of Olney called him "Sir Cowper" or "The Squire," and he took their respect as being, socially, his due. But he valued far more highly their affection, which he reciprocated, in a manner very uncommon in his day, without patronage. He accepted social inequalities as part of the wise, if inscrutable, plan of Providence. Yet he regarded all men as brothers because he saw them as equal in the sight of God and the perspective of eternity. In practice, of course, that faith, which inspired the Evangelical movement at its best, had the effect of breaking down the class barriers which it theoretically supported. It is amazing that many critics have searched Cowper's work with a microscope for the few evidences of real Calvinistic doctrine which it contains, and have ignored the incomparably greater number of passages in which "love to God" and "love to man" are not merely named, but defined in a way that still bears scrutiny, as being inseparable elements in religion "pure and undefiled."

---

[1] " New-fangled sentiment, the boasted grace
Of those who never feel in the right place."—*Tirocinium*.

Cowper, insisting on a Christianity that could be judged by its fruits, was not only ahead of his time in bringing religion into vital relation with humanity: in the process, he greatly extended and deepened the idea of "refinement." He had, of course, the limitations of contemporary Evangelical piety: he regarded some normal activities and amusements as dangerous, if not sinful. But every form of religion in every age has its own eccentricities, and must be judged by its wheat, not by its tares. There is still little, essentially, to be learned about the true character of a "gentleman" that cannot be found in Cowper's poetry, pedestrian as is sometimes the verse itself. Nor did Cowper merely exhort. He seldom failed in exquisite courtesy towards all, high born or low, with whom he had dealings. That is one of his most important and engaging aspects, and one for which Evangelicalism has probably received too little credit. Indeed, if we bear in mind his period, and also the innate fastidiousness that might almost excusably have made him, as we now say, a snob, is it too paradoxical to suggest that he was a "gentleman" in spite of his birth?

II

Sir William Cowper, Bart., of Ratling Court, Kent, died, aged eighty-two, in 1664. He is remembered for his loyalty to Charles I, and for having erected a monument to Hooker, with an epitaph in verse. His grandson and successor was the second Sir William. The third William, born in 1665, became in 1718 the first Earl Cowper. He had declared for the Prince of Orange in 1688, and, having successively been Recorder of Colchester, Public Prosecutor, Lord Keeper, and Commissioner for the Union with Scotland, became the first Lord Chancellor of England in 1702. He held this position until 1710, when he presided at the Sacheverell trial. He was again Lord Chancellor from 1714 to 1718, and during this term of office wrote a description of English politics and parties for the guidance of that ill-informed alien, George I. He died in 1723. Spencer Cowper, a younger brother, was born in 1669 and died in 1727. After a period on the Home Circuit, he became a judge in the Court of Common Pleas. One oft-described episode, which throws its own light upon the period, marked his earlier career. When attending the Assizes at Hertford, he stayed with a Quaker family named Stout. Sarah Stout, though already married, became so attached to him that she pined in his absence, and eventually drowned herself. Spencer Cowper was charged with her murder, tried, and acquitted. The best authorities assert that he was "innocent beyond a doubt," and that the accusation arose because the Tories of Hertford wanted to hang a member of an eminent Whig family, and because the Quakers wished to remove the odium of suicide from one of their members. Spencer helped his more distinguished brother in managing the Sacheverell trial. The Tory reaction cost him his seat in Parliament as member for Bere Alston. He subsequently represented Truro.

The Rev. John Cowper, D.D., was Spencer's son, and the poet's father. He was Rector of Great Berkhampstead and a chaplain to George II. In 1728 he married Ann Donne, who traced her descent through several noble families to Henry III, and numbered the poet Donne among her ancestors. To Dr. John Cowper and herself were born three children who died in infancy. William, the fourth child, was born on November 15, 1731.[1] Two later children died young. Besides William, only the seventh child, John, born in 1737, lived to maturity. His mother died a few days after his birth. It is a record pathetically typical of the times.

III

Berkhampstead, now an outpost of London, then consisted of some three hundred houses, and had a population of about fifteen hundred people. Its High Street extended for half a mile along the line of the old Akeman Street, the Roman road which connected Verulam with Bicester and beyond. The street next in importance led to the ruins of what had once been a royal castle. Ravens Lane, Grubbs Lane, Barn Lane, and Water Lane almost completed the map of this little country town, whose main thoroughfare ran parallel

[1] Or November 26, New Style.

with a small stream called the Bulborne, from which it was separated by swampy ground and watercress beds. Beyond the Bulborne the earthworks and moats of the castle remained intact, though most of its masonry had been used, a century and a half earlier, to build Berkhampstead Place.

The town was an agricultural centre, with a weekly market. It also had its industries, of which malting and woodturning were the chief. It was so famous for the latter craft that it was said that a Berkhampstead man could make a bowl of beechwood thin enough to be turned inside out. The women made lace and plaited straw, and every poor child was put to work at a very early age. Most of the cottages were probably constructed of wattle and daub, but some of the substantial houses of the period still survive.

St. Peter's Church,[1] an early foundation built in many mixed styles, dominated the town. Much care was taken of its great yew tree that overshadowed the High Street, and the Churchwarden's Accounts show how regularly it was clipped and otherwise tended. Apart from the church, the principal building was the fine grammar school in Castle Street. It was among the schools that maintained their reputation throughout the eighteenth century, though it later declined before achieving its present fame. Near to the church were Sayer's Almshouses, a beautiful row of stone cottages, built fifty years before the birth of Cowper through money provided by the Will of John Sayer, the owner of Berkhampstead Place and chief cook to Charles II. Close by the workhouse stood a number of dilapidated hovels known as Ragged Row, which belonged to the Overseers of the Poor. The Bridewell, which occupied the site of the modern police station, was too derelict a structure to prevent the escape of determined criminals, especially as there was only one gaoler, and that sometimes a woman. The High Street was usually in bad condition, and complaints were often made to Quarter Sessions by the principal inhabitants, such as that "it is out of repair and so dirty that they cannot walk without great

---

[1] Thanks to the initiative of the Rev. J. W. Cobb, a rector of recent times, a glass in the east window now commemorates Cowper in a series of Biblical and other scenes, including a representation of the poet praying at his desk, with his tame hares around him. There are also quotations from the Olney hymns.

D

inconvenience." A scavenger was then appointed again for a time, and a rate made to defray the expense.

The surrounding landscape must have resembled "the small green Hertfordshire" of to-day, with its "flattish fields and leafy coppices," save that Enclosure may not have been complete and that the canals which are now so pleasant a feature of the scene were not yet built.

IV

Several writers have shown how gracefully, in the manner of fiction, the meagre facts about William's childhood may be embroidered. When all is said, however, only two things still clearly emerge: his love for his mother, and the devastating shock which he sustained through her death. And nothing can add either colour or poignancy to the poet's own record:

> " *My mother! when I learn'd that thou wast dead,*
> *Say, wast thou conscious of the tears I shed?*
> *Hover'd thy spirit o'er thy sorrowing son,*
> *Wretch even then, life's journey just begun?*
> *Perhaps thou gav'st me, though unseen, a kiss;*
> *Perhaps a tear, if souls can weep in bliss . . .*
> *Ah that maternal smile! it answers—Yes.*
> *I heard the bell toll'd on thy burial day,*
> *I saw the hearse that bore thee slow away,*
> *And, turning from my nurs'ry window, drew*
> *A long, long sigh, and wept a last adieu. . . .*
> *Thy maidens, griev'd themselves at my concern,*
> *Oft gave me promise of a quick return.*
> *What ardently I wish'd, I long believ'd,*
> *And, disappointed still, was still deceived;*
> *By disappointment every day beguil'd,*
> *Dupe of* to-morrow *even from a child.*
> *Thus many a sad to-morrow came and went,*
> *Till, all my stock of infant sorrow spent,*
> *I learn'd at last submission to my lot;*
> *But, though I less deplor'd thee, ne'er forgot."*

So, at the age of fifty-nine, he wrote in his immortal lines "On the Receipt of my Mother's Picture out of Norfolk."[1]

[1] The picture in question was a miniature in oils by Heines, and was sent to Cowper by his cousin Ann (Rose), wife of Thomas Bodham, Rector of Mattishall.

The poem supplies the only reliable background for his early years:

> "*Where once we dwelt our name is heard no more,*
> *Children not thine have trod my nurs'ry floor;*
> *And where the gard'ner Robin, day by day,*
> *Drew me to school along the public way,*
> *Delighted with my bauble coach, and wrapt*
> *In scarlet mantle warm, and velvet capt,*
> *'Tis now become a history little known*
> *That once we call'd the pastoral house our own.*
> *Short-lived possession! but the record fair*
> *That mem'ry keeps of all thy kindness there,*
> *Still outlives many a storm that has effac'd*
> *A thousand other themes less deeply trac'd.*
> *Thy nightly visits to my chamber made,*
> *That thou might'st know me safe and warmly laid;*
> *Thy morning bounties ere I left my home,*
> *The biscuit, or confectionary plum;*
> *The fragrant waters on my cheeks bestow'd*
> *By thy own hand, till fresh they shone and glow'd;*
> *All this, and more endearing still than all,*
> *Thy constant flow of love, that knew no fall,*
> *Ne'er roughened by those cataracts and brakes*
> *That humour interpos'd too often makes;*
> *All this still legible in mem'ry's page,*
> *And still to be so, to my latest age,*
> *Adds joy to duty, makes me glad to pay*
> *Such honour to thee as my numbers may.*"

It might be argued that Cowper, writing so many years afterwards, idealised his early childhood. He himself recognised the danger. "There are few people in the world," he wrote in 1790 [1] to his cousin Ann, "who have not cause to look back with regret on the days of infancy; yet, to say the truth, I suspect some deception in this. For infancy itself has its cares; and though we cannot now conceive how trifles could affect us much, it is certain that they did. Trifles they appear now, but such they were not then." Four years later, however, when he was sixty-three, he wrote of his mother to Joseph Hill: "I can truly say that not a week passes (perhaps I might with equal veracity say a day), in which I do not think of her. Such was the impression her tenderness

---

[1] The same year in which he composed the poem on his mother's portrait.

made upon me, though the opportunity she had for showing
it was so short." Apart from this evidence and from the fact
that Cowper was obviously forearmed against sentimentality,
it seems to me that the poem bears its own inward guarantee
of truth. Such lines as

> " Ne'er roughened by those cataracts and brakes
> That humour interpos'd too often makes "

could be the fruit only of adult reflection; but the reflection
itself would hardly have risen save in one who genuinely
recalled a devotion between mother and child that may have
been hypersensitive on both sides, but was none the less
idyllic in harmony and repose.

It is usually said that Cowper inherited his delicate nervous
constitution from his mother, and his "masculine temper"
from his father. The first part of the assumption is probably
valid enough; but there seems no ground for concluding that
all his robuster qualities came from the paternal side. Sensitiveness has its own special dangers; but it is compatible, and
often co-existent, with the truest "good sense." If the
equipoise then be precarious, it is, as I have suggested,
because the sanity is inspired. I would hazard the guess that
Cowper derived his large fund of "common sense" from his
father, but that the higher faculty of reason was a legacy
from his mother. Actually, of course, we know very little
about Mrs. Cowper, and still less about her husband. Through
Cowper's poem on his mother's portrait we have at least a
vital impression of a woman not only sensitive, but of very
fine character. There is no such material for forming an
image of his father.

Dr. Cowper, whose second wife survived him by six years
and was buried in Bath Abbey, died in 1756, aged sixty-one.
The poet hastened to Berkhampstead on hearing that his
father was ill, but reached it too late to see him alive. "Then,
and not till then," he wrote later, "I felt for the first time
that I and my native place were disunited for ever. I sighed
a long adieu to fields and woods, from which I once thought
I should never be parted, and was at no time so sensible of
their beauties as just when I left them all behind me, to

return no more." Some have imagined that Cowper was little affected by his father's death. But we have none of his letters written about the time of that event; nor need we too seriously interpret his reticence in the *Memoir*. When, in 1765, Cowper wrote that brief autobiography of his early life—it was not published until after his death—he was in the first flush of his Evangelical fervour, and would then have been most intolerant of other religious forms. One fact alone may safely be deduced. Dr. Cowper was not "enthusiastic."

In one of several stray references in the letters Cowper says that his father was fond of poetry and "succeeded well in ballad writing." Elsewhere he describes him as having been "most indulgent." It is a vague term! "Indulgence" towards a child may imply anything from parental indifference that takes the line of least resistance to the positive spoiling that is hardly less dangerous than repression. There is no hint that Dr. Cowper spoiled his son, who was in fact seldom at home. It is possible to assume a certain sympathy and some affinity of interest between father and child; but there seems to have been no really deep bond of union. The chances are that Dr. Cowper was good-natured, well-meaning, and easy-going. He was probably a decent latitudinarian of his time: preaching innocuous sermons, and decorously performing baptisms and funeral rites: not consciously lax in the service of his Master; accepting bereavements, perhaps, as His will; yet content, on the whole, with a good living and a position of social importance. So, at least, I picture him. The portrait may be flattering. May his shade forgive me if, on the contrary, I fail in justice!

It would certainly be unfair to judge Dr. Cowper by the one allusion to him in his son's *Memoir*. Chance may have played unkindly with his memory. "I well recollect," says the poet,

"when I was about eleven years of age, my father desired me to read a vindication of self-murder, and give him my sentiments upon the question: I did so, and argued against it. My father heard my reasons, and was silent, neither approving nor disapproving; from whence I inferred that he sided with the author against me; though all the time I believe the true motive for his conduct was that he wanted, if he could, to think favourably of the state of a departed friend, who had some years before destroyed himself, and whose death had struck him with the deepest affliction."

In 1763, when Cowper himself was prompted by melancholy to attempt his own life, this incident of his boyhood recurred to his mind and "weighed mightily" with him. His subsequent explanation of it may have been correct. There is no other evidence for suspecting the father of anything more than indiscretion. There may, nevertheless, have been a latent morbidity in him. This possibility will be considered when we come to analyse, so far as is possible, the nature of Cowper's own madness.

It is hard to forgive the father—though again we must remember his period—for having sent the infant William, soon after his mother's death, to "a considerable school in Bedfordshire." This was Dr. Pitman's boarding establishment at Market Street. "Here," wrote Cowper, "I had hardships of different kinds to conflict with, which I felt more sensibly, in proportion to the tenderness with which I had been treated at home":

"But my chief affliction consisted in my being singled out from all the other boys, by a lad about fifteen years of age, as a proper object upon which he might let loose the cruelty of his temper. I choose to forbear a particular recital of the many acts of barbarity, with which he made it his business continually to persecute me: it will be sufficient to say, that he had, by his savage treatment of me, impressed such a dread of his figure upon my mind, that I well remember being afraid to lift up my eyes upon him, higher than his knees; and that I knew him by his shoe-buckles, better than any other part of his dress. May the Lord pardon him, and may we meet in glory!"

The boy was at length expelled. We may infer either that Dr. Pitman was not so bad, after all, or that the bullying was indeed so brutal that not even an eighteenth-century headmaster could wink at it.

The *Memoir* has another allusion to that time:

"One day as I was sitting alone on a bench in the school, melancholy, and almost ready to weep at the recollection of what I had already suffered, and expecting at the same time my tormentor every moment, these words of the Psalmist came into my mind, 'I will not be afraid of what man can do unto me.' I applied this to my own case, with a degree of trust and confidence in God, that would have been no disgrace to a much more experienced Christian. Instantly, I perceived in myself a brisk-ness of spirits, and a cheerfulness, which I had never before experienced; and took several paces up and down the room with joyful alacrity—*his* gift in whom I trusted. Happy had it been for me, if this early effort towards a dependence on the blessed God had been frequently repeated by me. But, alas! it was the first and last instance of the kind, between infancy and man-hood."

Those who have taken these last two sentences (and similar utterances throughout his work) as self-evident proof of Cowper's adult morbidity fail, again, to penetrate behind the formal exterior of eighteenth-century Evangelicalism. The anecdote, despite the writer's use of it in the contrary sense, suggests that Cowper had as a child a precocious religious sensibility. The incident is hardly of the kind that he would have invented thirty years afterwards; and his memory of it proves that its influence must have been genuine and deep at the time.

We may allow for the conventionally puritanical style in which in the *Memoir*, like Bunyan in *Grace Abounding*, Cowper writes about his childhood, with its apathy and sin-fulness. We cannot ignore the underlying fact. From his earliest years he had a nature that craved for more than mundane satisfactions. He had a thirst for the inner life and joys of the spirit, and there was nothing in the circum-stances of his earlier career that met his need. Had his nervous constitution been less delicate, or had he been temperamentally independent and solitary, his inner life might have flourished even in neglect. But, while spiritual impulses were strong in him, he was no ascetic, completely renouncing the world or able to dispense with the stimulus of human affection. How different his history might have been had his mother lived, or even if in youth he had come within the orbit of a vital religious movement!

And here we must return for a moment to his father. It would be unjust to blame Dr. John Cowper for not having been—as his son William became—a pioneer. The day of the emancipated father, which the poet Cowper foresaw in his *Tirocinium*,[1] is even now only dawning, and there is still much fundamental truth in his indictment:

> "Hark! how the sire of chits, whose future share
> Of classic food begins to be his care,
> With either likeness plac'd on either knee,
> Indulges all a father's heart-felt glee;
> And tells them, as he strokes their silver locks,
> That they must soon learn Latin, and to box;
> Then, turning, he regales his list'ning wife
> With all th' adventures of his early life;
> His skill in coachmanship, or driving chaise,
> In bilking tavern bills, and spouting plays;
> What shifts he used, detected in a scrape,
> How he was flogg'd, or had the luck t' escape;
> What sums he lost at play, and how he sold
> Watch, seals, and all—till all his pranks are told.
> Retracing thus his frolics ('tis a name
> That palliates deeds of folly and of shame),
> He gives the local bias all its sway;
> Resolves that where he play'd his sons shall play,
> And destines their bright genius to be shown
> Just in the scene where he display'd his own."

Had Cowper possessed a father of the best modern kind—one who regards his child's welfare and training as being hardly less intimately his concern than it is a mother's—how different, again, might have been the course of his life!

In the closing pages of *Tirocinium*, he calls upon fathers to realise their responsibilities. The appeal, though earnest, is unsentimentalised; and, while the poetry itself is often turgid, there are several unforgettable little pictures, like that of the awkwardness between parents and the boy returning from boarding-school: an awkwardness still felt in many homes, and one from which

> "begins with most that long complaint
> Of filial frankness lost, and love grown faint,
> Which, oft neglected, in life's waning years
> A parent pours into regardless ears."

[1] *Tirocinium: or a Review of Schools*, published in 1785.

I would like to quote the last few hundred lines of *Tirocinium*, not only for the confutation of readers who either regard Cowper as a mere versifier of mild Nature or join with Swinburne in sneering at his "tea-pot pieties," but because the poem is vital to an understanding both of the writer and of the tragic interludes in his career. I have said that *Tirocinium* is not sentimentalised. It is, on the contrary, compact of close argument and inspired reason: I fear contradiction from none who will study it for himself. Nevertheless, it is a most poignant poem if we read, as we surely may, between the lines.

Cowper describes what, in his opinion, a true father should be. Had his own father passed the test—an exacting one for the eighteenth century, but rather less so for our day—he would certainly have stated, and lovingly embroidered, the fact. He lost no opportunity of paying tribute in verse or letters to those whose friendship or memories he prized: was any occupation more congenial to him? His silence about his father in the *Memoir* necessarily implies, as I have said, nothing more than Dr. John Cowper's want of religious "enthusiasm." Nor need we surmise from *Tirocinium* that Dr. Cowper was not a relatively good father of the period. But we *can* safely infer that he lacked those finer qualities of paternity which the poem defines and praises. *Tirocinium* is clearly inspired by Cowper's meditation upon his own childhood, though he obliquely reflects his experience in the mirror of an ideal. While eschewing autobiography, he pleads in effect that other fathers may be to their children what his own father was not to him. Cowper was no milksop. He believed in discipline.[1] But he knew that discipline had salutary force only "when back'd by love." All boys need love no less than discipline; each, if it be a true influence, implies the other. Cowper, supersensitive and eminently sociable by nature, needed deep and enlightened affection even more than do most boys.

Unbroken gloom is fortunately alien to childhood in the least favourable circumstances; and the young Cowper,

---

[1] For a characteristic passage on discipline, with the poet's conception of it in its truest form, see *The Task*, Book II, 699-724.

"slender in build, fresh coloured, and with refined features,"
had in fact some natural joys. He was fond of reading, and
liked especially the fables of Gay, which he used to recite for
the amusement of company. He had a pleasant countryside
around him, and took a deep delight in exploration:

> " *My very dreams were rural, rural too*
> *The first-born efforts of my youthful muse,*
> *Sporting, and jingling her poetic bells*
> *Ere yet her ear was mistress of their powers.*
> *No bard could please me but whose lyre was tuned*
> *To Nature's praises.*"

In later life, again, he pleasurably recalled his visits, during
school holidays, to his Norfolk cousins,[1] who, in their turn,
came sometimes to Berkhampstead. Yet, surveying his childhood as a whole, we may conclude that it was abnormally
lonely. And he was the type of boy who most needs not only
a settled environment, but, with scope for solitude, a sympathetic and vital companionship. He lost his mother when
he was six; and it seems there was no one, however inadequately, to take her place.

V

In 1739, after he had been two years at Market Street,
Cowper showed symptoms of eye trouble. He was removed
from the school, and lived for the next year or more with an
"eminent surgeon and oculist," Mr. Disney, whose wife also
followed her husband's profession. We may again discount
the *Memoir*, which states that "religion was neither known
nor practised in their home"; but there are no references in
the poems or the letters to suggest that this period of Cowper's
childhood was happy. "Hardly indeed," said Bagehot, "can
the boldest mind, in the toughest hour of manly fortitude,
endure to be domesticated with an operation chair." The eye
trouble was not cured until an attack of smallpox in 1745 did

---

[1] Cowper's uncle, the Rev. Roger Donne, Vicar of Catfield, had four children.
Harriet afterwards became Mrs. Balls. Ann—whom Cowper called " the Rose
that used to sit smiling on my knee "—became, as we have seen, Mrs. Bodham.
Elizabeth married a Mr. Hewitt. The poet remembered Castres as " an amiable
boy," of whom he was " very fond."

what Dr. and Mrs. Disney only partially achieved. But in 1741, at the age of ten, Cowper was well enough to go to Westminster, where he remained until 1748.

Dr. Nicholls was the Headmaster. The entire school was then—as until 1884—taught in the Great Hall, formerly the dormitory of the monks. In the foreground still stands the seventeenth-century Rod Table, from the drawer of which two birches protrude during school hours. Behind it are the Masters' chairs, dating from the time of Henry VIII. In the background is the bust of Dr. Busby, whose reign extended from 1638 to 1695. In front of it is the Headmaster's chair, given by Charles II. On the wall behind are the coats of arms of famous old Westminsters, including Warren Hastings, who was Cowper's contemporary. Among Cowper's other school-fellows were Robert Lloyd, author of *The Actor*; Charles Churchill; Colman the elder, who wrote *The Jealous Wife*; Bonnell Thornton, the translator of Plautus; and, most intimate of all, Sir William Russell, whose early death in 1757 moved Cowper to a grief which helped to precipitate his second attack of insanity.

The usher of the fifth form was Vincent Bourne. Cowper, when rendering some of his old master's Latin verses into English many years later, wrote to William Unwin:

"I love the memory of Vinny Bourne. He was so good natured, and so indolent, that I lost more than I got by him; for he made me as idle as himself. He was such a sloven, as if he had trusted to his genius as a cloak for everything that could disgust you in his person; and indeed in his writings he almost made amends for all. His humour is entirely original; he can speak of a magpie or a cat in terms so exquisitely appropriated to the character he draws, that one would suppose him animated by the spirit of the creature he describes. And with all this drollery there is a mixture of rational, and even religious, reflection at times: and always an air of pleasantry, good nature, and humanity. . . . It is not common to meet with an author who can make you smile, and yet at nobody's expense; who is always entertaining, and yet always harmless . . . yet such was poor Vinny."

And such in large measure, except for the slovenliness of

person, was Cowper himself. Here, truly, were kindred spirits.

Tirocinium contains one incidental passage which shows that Cowper's mature objection to public schools had no basis in any memory of personal suffering at Westminster:

> "*Be it a weakness, it deserves some praise;*
> *We love the play-place of our early days—*
> *The scene is touching, and the heart is stone*
> *That feels not at that sight, and feels at none.*
> *The wall on which we tried our graving skill,*
> *The very name we carv'd, subsisting still;*
> *The bench on which we sat while deep employ'd;*
> *Tho' mangled, hack'd, and hew'd, not yet destroy'd;*
> *The little ones, unbuttoned, glowing hot,*
> *Playing our games, and on the very spot;*
> *As happy as we once, to kneel and draw*
> *The chalky ring, and knuckle down at taw;*
> *To pitch the ball into the grounded hat,*
> *Or drive it devious with a dext'rous pat—*
> *The pleasing spectacle at once excites*
> *Such recollection of our own delights,*
> *That, viewing it, we seem almost t' obtain*
> *Our innocent sweet simple years again.*"

The letters add their testimony. The *Memoir*, of course, strikes its own different note. Cowper there says that whatever seeds of religion he carried to Westminster were all marred and corrupted; "the duty of the schoolboy swallowed up every other; and I acquired Latin and Greek at the expense of a knowledge much more important." He adds, however, a tribute to Dr. Nicholls, who took genuine pains in preparing the boys for confirmation:

> "The old man acquitted himself of this duty, like one who had a deep sense of its importance. . . . For my own part, I then, for the first time, attempted prayer in secret; but being little accustomed to that exercise of the heart, and having very childish notions of religion, I found it a difficult and painful task. . . . This difficulty, though it did not subdue my good purposes, till the ceremony of confirmation was past, soon after entirely conquered them; I relapsed into a total forgetfulness of God, with the usual disadvantage of being more hardened, for having been softened to no purpose."

There spoke the adult Calvinist, and we may read into the passage a very different conclusion from his own. It is clear that Cowper as a boy responded to any sincere spiritual influence, however conventional its form might be. But while his religious sensibility was probably uncommon, as it had been in childhood, there is no sign that it was developed to an unhealthy degree. We may welcome the *Memoir's* statement that he was "an adept in the infernal art of lying." There is something wrong with the schoolboy who never tells an innocent fib.

He had, of course, his morbid moments. One evening, as he was crossing St. Margaret's Churchyard, a gravedigger, working by the light of a lantern, threw up a skull which struck his leg. This incident was for a time "an alarm" to his conscience, and is numbered in the *Memoir* "among the best religious documents" which he received at Westminster. The impression, however, soon faded, and even left him— surveying his "activity and strength," and observing the "evenness" of his pulse—with the feeling that he would never die. But there came a sudden fear of consumption, which—"a messenger from the Lord"—persisted long enough to do its "errand" and convince him that he was mortal. Again we must not take the *Memoir* too solemnly. Even the least imaginative schoolboy dislikes peremptory reminders of death and may suffer occasional delusions about his health.

Cowper was no ordinary boy, and we may be sure that he suffered hours of more than average darkness—as also, perhaps, of delight. But the aggregate witness of his poems and letters proves beyond doubt that he was not abnormal enough —a fairly exacting test—to be a "misfit" at Westminster. The modern public school is no haven for a sensitive boy. That Westminster in Cowper's day must have been "a scene not merely of hardship, but of cruel suffering and degradation to the younger and weaker boys, has been proved," said Goldwin Smith, "by the researches of the Public Schools Commission." Yet, strange as it may seem to those who still imagine him to have been "effeminate," Cowper was reasonably happy there.

The education, being wholly classical, suited his temperament. His social instinct responded to opportunities of friendship, and he found congenial tastes among some of his companions. His earliest literary composition, written when he was fourteen, was a translation from Tibullus.[1] At Westminster, too, he began his lifelong hobby of keeping pets, though his first experiment—with a mouse that devoured her young—was not encouraging. Nor did he lack more strenuous pursuits. We have it on his own authority, and the fact should carefully be noted, that he "excelled at cricket and football." His love of nature, already intense, prompted him to play truant sometimes,

> "*T'enjoy a ramble on the banks of Thames*";

and the boy in Cowper was father also of the man who wrote *John Gilpin*. The whimsical eye, which later gazed upon human foibles from a window overlooking Olney market-place, was alert for amusement, and keenly enjoyed the fun when young Lord Higham Ferrars visited the school dressed as a titled lady, and was carried up into the Hall in a sedan-chair, preceded by the Headmaster, or when the little Duke of Richmond set fire to "Vinny" Bourne's wig and then boxed his ears in order to extinguish the flames. On holidays he visited the Tower and other resorts to which Londoners flocked for amusement. Among them was Bedlam,[2] which in those days was open to "the cruel curiosity" of sightseers. "Though a boy," wrote Cowper to Newton in 1784, "I was not altogether insensible of the misery of the poor captives, nor destitute of feeling for them. But the madness of some of them had such a humorous air, and displayed itself in so many whimsical freaks, that it was impossible not to be entertained, at the same time that I was angry with myself for being so." Cowper, as a schoolboy, was already capable of pity: but he was no weakling and no prig.

[1] " At Westminster, where little poets strive
      To set a distich upon six and five,
      Where discipline helps op'ning buds of sense,
      And makes his pupils proud with silver pence,
      I was a poet too."—*Table Talk*.

[2] The Bethlehem Hospital, originally founded in 1247 as a priory, became in 1547 the first lunatic asylum in England, and, except for a similar institution in Granada, Spain, the first in Europe. It was famous and then infamous for its treatment of the feeble-minded. In Cowper's time it was situated in Moorfields.

VI

The fact that the poet was not unhappy at Westminster lends added weight to his criticism of public schools in *Tirocinium*. Public-school boys no longer habitually frequent taverns or consort with loose women, though secret vice may sometimes be practised. If, however, we make allowance for changes of fashion in morals, manners, and literary style, Cowper's protest might have been written to-day. It is, in substance, amazingly up-to-date. Cowper sees not only moral dangers in a public-school education; he blames it for breeding "slaves of custom and established mode," and for fostering the competitive spirit that lies at the root of many social evils. He touches upon another important point—even now too much ignored—when he ironically depicts the men who climb into responsible positions not through their own merits, but through the friendships formed at school. Cowper, though a gentleman by birth and an old Westminster, was, before his time, in the best sense of the word, a democrat. He believed, so far as it might be practicable, in equality of opportunity: the only aristocracy he reverenced was that of intrinsic virtue. He had, however, no easy illusions. He saw that the public-school system was too deeply entrenched to be changed in a moment, and he condemned less the system itself than the parents—especially the fathers—who delegated to it their own responsibilities.

He was thinking, again, of his own boyhood, and reflecting that, notwithstanding his comparative happiness there, Westminster had failed, after all, to meet the truest needs of his nature during a most impressionable, if superficially resilient, period. It had offered him an environment pleasant by contrast with any he had known in the years that had intervened since his mother's death. It had brought him companionship; his studies and games had been congenial; he had been fully occupied, with little leisure for introspection; and he had been spared more rude shocks like those he had previously experienced. Yes; it had been, on the whole, a happy time. But what, in his retrospect, had it done to fortify him against the further difficulties and catastrophes that followed? It had given him neither sustaining affection nor a vital faith.

His Westminster record shows that Cowper possessed essential hardihood. But his hypersensitiveness, while less adversely stimulated than it previously had been, was not there directed to really constructive purpose. Though dormant for a while, a predisposition to hypochondria remained. There may have been an inherited taint; at all events, the disaster and the loneliness of his childhood had been enough to create a morbid tendency in one of his temperament. Westminster provided an anodyne; it did not supply a solvent. The demon of melancholia lurked in the background, awaiting fresh opportunities to pounce into the open. Those opportunities were now to come.

Chapter Four

THE LAW STUDENT

I

COWPER, THROUGHOUT LIFE, lacked personal initiative. He moved only in response to pressure from outside. This applies even to his literary activity. Such dependence upon external influence bespeaks a real vein of weakness. In Cowper it was mainly due, perhaps, to excessive humility. But sensitiveness and self-distrust, though they need wise treatment in youth, do not necessarily imply a fundamental lack of courage. Cowper's Westminster phase alone disproves the superficial charge that he was constitutionally "effeminate." Nor was he a lotus-eater. Bagehot,[1] viewing literature through the eyes of a prosperous Victorian man of affairs, ascribed his affliction in large measure to laziness. I doubt, however, if even in early manhood Cowper was quite so indolent as he himself suggests in the *Memoir*; he had, in any case, the kind of temperament to which leisure for meditation is a sheer necessity. Such a temperament develops more slowly than one in which an active or lyrical impulse is strong; and the reflective nature often subconsciously resists the forces that would galvanise it into premature or alien growth. Cowper had much of this negative strength. If he had received the right stimuli in his formative years, he might never have succumbed to melancholy.

It is unlikely that, on leaving Westminster, he had any sense of vocation. Like other young men, he sometimes wrote essays and verses. His earliest extant poem was written during a holiday at Bath, where he found the heel of a shoe and saw in it "hints worthy sage philosophy." Having pictured in fancy its owner hobbling, maimed, upon his journey, "the sport of vagrant boys," he compares with him the statesman who thus

---

[1]. *Literary Studies.* Volume II. By Walter Bagehot. 1879.

"Up the steep road, where proud ambition leads,
Aspiring first uninterrupted winds
His prosp'rous way; nor fears miscarriage foul,
While policy prevails, and friends prove true:
But that support soon failing, by him left
On whom he most depended, basely left,
Betray'd, deserted, from his airy height
Head-long he falls; and thro' the rest of life
Drags the dull load of disappointment on."

The poem shows Cowper's eye for little things, and his habit of transition from whimsicality to moralising, already at work. Yet the verses are such as any gifted boy could write. Many youths of eighteen have vague literary ambitions that are soon forgotten; and it is questionable whether young Cowper had much ambition at all. He must have been an unusually charming youth. He was also, we may guess, abnormally "awkward," and (save for his passive stubbornness) irresolute.

What, in the circumstances, was more natural than that Dr. Cowper, proud of the tradition of his family, and having influential legal connections, should apprentice his son to the law? It was, nevertheless, a tragic mistake. Not that William lacked the reasoning faculty. The difficulty was that he possessed it in sublimated form. He would never have been content with mere logic for lawyers' limited and sometimes biased ends; while his sensitiveness would have made equally irksome to him the physical conditions of a legal career.

II

The tragedy began. Cowper, wishing to "please" his father, made no demur at being articled to Mr. Chapman, a solicitor, of Ely Place, Holborn. His fellow-clerk was Edward Thurlow. It was an ironic chance which threw Cowper and Thurlow together in that office beneath the shadow of St. Ethelfreda's Church. There could be no greater contrast between two young men than there was between the future author of *The Task* and the future Lord Chancellor. Cowper seems early to have realised that Thurlow was born for success, and that, though capable of impulsive generosity, he would allow no scruples to bar his progress. Not only had Thurlow in conspicuous degree the self-confidence and driving force which Cowper lacked; his appearance was another asset. His "dark complexion, harsh but regular features, severe and dignified demeanour, piercing black eyes, and bushy eyebrows" provoked in later years the sarcasm of Fox that he *looked* wiser than any man ever *was*. Thurlow lived till 1806, and was prominent in public affairs until 1792. He was a vehement Tory, implacably opposed to reform, and, with his caustic and profane wit, exercising almost autocratic sway in the House of Lords. He was the patron of Johnson and of Crabbe; but he forgot or ignored the promise of his 'prentice days that he would help Cowper when he had gained the Woolsack. The only thing that Thurlow, as Chancellor, gave Cowper was his advice on translating Homer.

The considerable legal knowledge which Cowper evinced in later life proves that he was not entirely idle. Inclination, however, did not make him zealous; and compulsion was absent. Referring in the *Memoir* to Mr. Chapman's office, he says:

> "There I might have lived and died, without hearing or seeing anything that might remind me of a single Christian duty, had it not been that I was at liberty to spend my leisure time (which was well nigh all my time) at my uncle's in South-ampton Row. By this means I had the opportunity of seeing the inside of a church,[1] whither I went with the family on Sundays, which probably I should otherwise never have seen."

That is Cowper's only allusion in the *Memoir* to this period. But the letters and poems show that church attendance was not the only lure which drew him to the home of Ashley Cowper. This very little man with his white hat lined with yellow, of whom his nephew said that he would one day be mistaken for a mushroom, had three daughters: Harriet, Theodora, and Elizabeth.[2] Cowper had first met Harriet during his Westminster days. He had been dining one Sunday with Mr. De Grey (afterwards Lord Walsingham), and was just taking his leave when Mr. and Mrs. Ashley Cowper, with Harriet, arrived for tea. Harriet seems then to have made an ineradicable impression on him, and, as Lady

---

[1] St. George's, Queen Square. [2] Later the wife of Sir Archer Croft.

Hesketh, she was to be one of the companions of his later years. Her personality, sparkling and witty, yet full of practical good sense, is familiar enough to us in outline. Nevertheless, it was Theodora who soon became the "Delia" of his love poems.

Of Theodora, save by inference, we know little. Her sister said that she had the face and figure of a goddess; but her one recorded sentence, while it may have been oracular, is hardly enlightening. Asked by her father what she would do if she married Cowper, she replied: "Wash all day, and ride on the great dog all night." Few of us, however, would like posterity to judge us by one facetious utterance of youth; and happily Theodora's actions bear testimony to the depth and constancy of her nature. The lovers, after a period of courtship, were not allowed to marry. Ashley Cowper may have forbidden the union on grounds of consanguinity. He may have been sceptical about his nephew's prospects. He may even have detected hints of his latent morbidity. From the time when further meetings were prohibited, Cowper did not see Theodora again. But, though she outlived him, she never married. She treasured to the end his letters and poems; she watched his progress with the deepest interest; she privily sent him presents by her sister, Lady Hesketh; and when she heard that he was comparatively in want, she gave him, through the same agent, a regular allowance. Cowper, who probably guessed but never alluded to her identity, called her his "Dear Anonymous."

To what extent was Cowper, the law student, in love with Theodora? His nineteen poems to "Delia," published twenty-five years after his death, supply no certain answer. Love poems are always self-conscious, and those of Cowper, charming and elegant though they be, were written at a time when there was a definite convention in *affaires d'amour*.

> " *The sparkling eye, the mantling cheek,*
> *The polish'd front, the snowy neck,*
> *How seldom we behold in one!*
> *Glossy locks, and brow serene,*
> *Venus' smiles, Diana's mien,*
> *All meet in you and you alone.*"

Through such verses we may detect the literary influences
then working upon the writer; we see no recognisable human
portrait. Indeed, what lady's features and character could
ever be judged by the rhapsodies of her admiring swain? In
despair of being able to form a clear impression of Theodora,
we may turn to some verses which at least throw light on
Cowper's own development:

> "William was once a bashful youth,
>   His modesty was such,
> That one might say (to say the truth)
>   He rather had too much. . . . .
>
> Howe'er it happen'd, by degrees,
>   He mended and grew perter,
> In company was more at ease,
>   And dress'd a little smarter. . . . .
>
> The women said, who thought him rough,
>   But now no longer foolish,
> The creature may do well enough,
>   But wants a deal of polish.
>
> At length, improv'd from head to heel,
>   'Twere scarce too much to say,
> No dancing bear was so genteel,
>   Or half so dégagé.
>
> Now, that a miracle so strange
>   May not in vain be shown,
> Let the dear maid who wrought the change
>   E'er claim him for her own."

A deeper note inspires what is probably a slightly later poem:

> "Ah me! how long bewilder'd and astray,
>   Lost and benighted, did my footsteps rove,
> Till, sent by heav'n to cheer my pathless way,
>   A star arose—the radiant star of love. . . .
>
> Yet not the beaming eye, or placid brow,
>   Or golden tresses, hid the subtle dart;
> To charms superior far than these I bow,
>   And nobler worth enslaves my vanquish'd heart;
> The beauty, elegance, and grace combin'd
> With beam transcendant from that angel mind."

Was Cowper really in love with Theodora? There is wide disagreement on this point. One biographer suggests that in these stanzas he "approached as near ecstasy as his nature would allow," but that he was "deficient in animal energy." I know not upon what basis this assumption rests, unless it be an odd reference or two in the letters, in which, during later life, the poet speaks of having to guard his physical strength against mental excitement. At school he "excelled at cricket and football." He was in early manhood a fairly good swimmer, and he seems at one time even to have shot game. At Huntingdon he rode, and, though he said that nature did not design him for a horseman, and that if all men were of his mind "there would be an end of all jockeyship for ever," he sustained no disaster on his occasional journeys to and from Cambridge. He never lost his delight in walking, and his love of the open air in all weathers made him, like Wesley, a pioneer of hygiene in an age of closed windows. The facts contradict his own playful assertion that he was "universally disqualified for the common and customary occupations and amusements of mankind." One can no more safely judge Cowper by a single mood or utterance than one can build a theology upon an isolated Biblical text. Yet the very critics who condemn the latter practice fall too often into the former.

One writer suggests that such feeling as Cowper had for Theodora, "if less intense than that of passion, may be (within its own narrower limits) more sincere." We may agree with the essential point, however, without necessarily accepting his qualifying clauses. Cowper's conception of love was not that of the average sensual man. He thought of marriage in terms of a mutual companionship that—"By Virtue (sacred vestal) fed"—should wax more strongly

> "*While vulgar passions, meteors of a day,*
> *Expire before the chilling blasts of age.*"

But such a view may be held, if the spiritual impulse be vital in proportion, by one who is ardently passionate in the normal sense. Why should the "more sincere" kind of marital bond imply an absence of passion? May not passion, duly subservient and rightly handled, itself intensify the spiritual flame?

Other biographers assume that Theodora loved Cowper more truly than he loved her. Yet in each case the only reason adduced is that Cowper, after he was forbidden to marry her, never met and seldom spoke of Theodora again! As if that fact did not itself constitute an additional argument for believing that his love was of the deepest and truest kind! He was both supersensitive and, despite his love of the country, temperamentally urbane. He was the kind of man who delights in frank self-revelation within conventional limits, but who, not only because of an inward smart that lies "too deep for tears," but also in deference to good form, holds inviolable his ultimate secrets. I see no cause to underestimate either the genuineness or the intensity of his passion; and it is possible that marriage with Theodora might have healed the spiritual wound left open by his mother's death.

There remains, it is true, the eugenic difficulty. It is believed that Cowper wrote a thesis in Latin, attempting, with classical and Biblical allusion, to prove the lawfulness of marriage between cousins. If he did so, it was a further proof of his attachment to Theodora. But what may be lawful may not be expedient. "It is not thought," says Professor Stanford Read, "that inbreeding has any ill effects unless the stock is already tainted; then, of course, the chances of transmission are correspondingly increased." If Ashley Cowper had reason to suspect a morbid predisposition in his nephew, can we blame him for having wished to avoid the possible consequences of a union? Anyhow, the main points in question are not affected. It is tenable that Cowper was both passionately and spiritually in love with Theodora, and that disappointment in this connection was one more exciting cause of his malady.

Whatever may be said of his earlier poems to "Delia," the lines which he wrote after the final parting from her were certainly no literary gesture. Having likened himself to a mariner with "shatter'd vessel lost," who sees and even gains "the friendly coast" only to be borne back by "the refluent wave," he continues:

> "Had you, my love, forbade me to pursue
>   My fond attempt, disdainfully retired,
> And with proud scorn compell'd me to subdue
>   Th' ill-fated passion by yourself inspired;
>
> Then haply to some distant spot removed,
>   Hopeless to gain, unwilling to molest
> With fond entreaties whom I dearly loved,
>   Despair or absence had redeem'd my rest.
>
> But now, sole partner in my Delia's heart,
>   Yet doom'd far off in exile to complain,
> Eternal absence cannot ease my smart,
>   And hope subsists but to prolong my pain."

III

The poem just quoted was probably written in 1757. The parting from Theodora had taken place during the previous year. Cowper had first met her, as we have seen, in 1749, soon after he had been articled to Mr. Chapman. For a time all apparently went well with the lovers. "I did actually live three years with Mr. Chapman, the Solicitor, that is to say, I slept three years in his house; but I lived, that is to say, I spent my days, in Southampton Row, as you very well remember. There was I, and the future Lord Chancellor, employed from morning to night in giggling and making giggle, instead of studying the law. O fie, cousin! how could you do so?" The memory of happy days shines clearly enough through these lines, written to Lady Hesketh after three intervening decades. We may safely picture Cowper, as a gay and, within limits, even fashionable youth. All his natural fund of jollity, in no wise at variance with his and Theodora's underlying gravity, seems to have expanded under the genial influence of those years. We may guess that the giggling in Southampton Row was varied by excursions along the river to Vauxhall, with its "company gaily dressed, looking satisfaction, and the tables spread with various delicacies";

with "the lights everywhere glimmering through scarce-moving trees—the full-bodied concert bursting on the stillness of night—the natural concert of the birds in the more retired part of the grove, vying with that which was formed by art." [1] At nine o'clock in the evening a bell was rung, and we may fancy Cowper and his cousins hurrying with the company from all parts of the now illuminated gardens to witness the crowning wonder of the "cascade."

Sometimes, perhaps, they sought the more exclusive, if seemingly duller, attractions of Ranelagh, which, with its vast Rotunda, having an orchestra in the centre and tiers of boxes all round, in which refreshments were served, had been built at Chelsea in 1742. The entertainments there were restricted to breakfasts, concerts, and oratorios, with occasional balls and masquerades. The morning amusements were later prohibited because they tempted young men to neglect their business. Ranelagh became the favourite haunt of the aristocracy, though Horace Walpole remained faithful to Vauxhall; "for the Garden is pleasanter, and *one goes by water*." Dr. Johnson said that when he first entered Ranelagh, it gave him "an expansion and gay sensation" of mind. "But as Xerxes wept when he viewed his immense army, and considered that not one of that great multitude would be alive a hundred years afterwards," so it went to his heart "to consider that there was not one in all that brilliant circle that was not afraid to go home and think." Johnson, with his excessive fear of death, was himself a lifelong hypochondriac, often verging upon actual derangement. Had *he* been an "enthusiast," instead of a High Churchman, *his* melancholy, no doubt, would have been ascribed, like Cowper's, to Evangelicalism!

For the moment Cowper's own morbid thoughts were in abeyance. But clouds were soon to gather. In July 1752, he spent a holiday at Catfield, where he drove about in a *whiskum snivel* (as the old-fashioned gig was nicknamed) with his Donne cousins. He also visited Mundesley—little guessing in what different circumstances he would tread its sands again, nearly half a century later. During this holiday he wrote

[1] *The Citizen of the World.* By Oliver Goldsmith. 1751.

three of his love poems, including the one in which he begged
a lock of "Delia's" hair, that he might to that extent defraud
Time, the spoiler, of his prey. Another of the poems hints at a
lovers' misunderstanding and reconciliation. But only the
most solemn of German thesis-writers would care to base any
conclusion upon such slender evidence as that, for, as Cowper
himself wrote:

> *" The heart of a lover is never at rest,*
> *With joy overwhelm'd, or with sorrow oppress'd."*

It is possible, indeed, that the excitements of love were
straining his delicate nervous constitution. It is even possible
that he had already reason to wonder if his uncle would
sanction the marriage. Fears about his own mundane prospects may also have troubled him. Being nearly twenty-one,
he was, in any case, entering upon a difficult period of life;
and, on actually reaching his majority, he exchanged Ely
Place for chambers in the Middle Temple. Here, he says in
the *Memoir*, "I became, in a manner, complete master of
myself." The phrase is unintentionally ironic. Most young
men like to feel that they are at last set upon their own feet.
Had Cowper been surrounded by normal affections and safe-
guards in his earlier years, even he might have become hardy
enough to welcome liberty in adolescence. But the flower of
independence, if it is to grow strong, especially in supersensitive human soil, needs careful protection at first. Cowper
had lacked that protection, and had to pay the penalty now.
That he had no real liking for his profession made matters
worse.

To deny a man free-will is to make him less than a man;
and I have no wish to represent Cowper as having been an
automaton of inhibitions or complexes. While the charge of
indolence is far too crude, we cannot wholly exonerate Cowper
from culpability on that score. Yet it is equally impossible
to deny extenuating circumstances, or to attempt any nice
apportionment of blame. For of Cowper, as of few other
men, it may be said that he lacked the grosser human qualities,
and that his very faults were virtues run to seed. Few people
are in danger of carrying humility to excess; and Cowper's
weakness, as I have said, was an inverted kind of strength.

To what degree might he have exerted himself, and, by frankly facing his own nature and situation, have resolved, by positive means, to make the best of a bad job? We cannot say. He was no mere idler; he was too fond of his classical studies to be in sheer want of occupation, and subconsciously he must have felt that in that direction lay his true vocation. But he seems to have made no sustained effort either to establish a literary connection or thoroughly to master his nominal profession; and again compulsion was absent. The time was yet far distant when a student had to pass examinations before becoming a barrister; it was then necessary only to pay certain fees and eat a certain number of dinners. Of course, there were lectures for those who wished to hear them, and *mootings* or *moots*, at which students met to argue cases proposed by their "Reader." One wonders how many lectures or *moots* Cowper attended. To what extent, again, had he serious twinges of conscience when, in retrospect, he referred to "three years misspent in an attorney's office" and "twelve more equally misspent in the Temple"? He offers by no means the only example of a literary man whose apparent idleness in youth is now seen to have borne good later fruit. Whether youthful indolence can on that account be justified is a ticklish question in ethics. And it may have been young Cowper's seeming lassitude, rather than the fact of his close relationship to Theodora, that determined his uncle's opposition.

However much we try to penetrate the mists that surround it, we still move in a realm of conjecture when dealing with the poet's early manhood. The fact remains that he had not long been settled in the Middle Temple before he was struck, in his own words, "with such a dejection of spirits, as none but they who have felt the same, can have the least conception of. Day and night I was upon the rack, lying down in horror, and rising up in despair. I presently lost all relish for those studies, to which before I had been closely attached; the classics had no longer any charms for me; I had need of something more salutary than amusement, but I had no one to direct me where to find it." At length he met with Herbert's poems, and, though he found their style "gothic and uncouth," their "strain of piety" brought him such hope and relief that he pored over them "all day long." But "a very near and dear relative" [1] advised him to lay the poems aside, since he thought such an author more likely to nourish the disorder than to remove it. Whether Major Cowper was wise or unwise in offering this counsel has, again, been a point for lively dispute!

Anyhow, the dejected law student grew strong enough to take a holiday at Southampton with his cousin Harriet, then engaged to Thomas (afterwards Sir Thomas) Hesketh. There he spent several months. Writing to Newton in 1785, he said that he remembered the place well:

"But though I was young, and had no objection on the score of conscience either to dancing or card-playing, I never was in the assembly-room in my life. . . . A walk to Netley Abbey, or to Freemantle, or to Redbridge, or a book by the fireside, had always more charms for me. . . . I was also a sailor, and being one of Sir Thomas Hesketh's party, who was himself a born one, was often pressed into the service. But though I gave myself an air, and wore trousers, I had no genuine right to that honour, disliking much to be occupied in great waters, unless in the finest weather. How they contrive to elude the wearisomeness that attends a sea life, who take long voyages, you know better than I; but for my own part, I have seldom sailed so far as from Hampton river to Portsmouth, without feeling the confinement irksome. . . . Could I have stepped out of it into a cornfield or a garden, I should have liked it well enough; but being surrounded with water, I was as much confined in it as if I had been surrounded by fire, and did not find that it made me any adequate compensation for such an abridgement of my liberty. I make little doubt that Noah was glad when he was enlarged from the ark; and we are sure that Jonah was, when he came out of the fish; and so was I to escape from the good sloop the *Harriet*."

Cowper in his letters is always his own best interpreter. The *Memoir*, however, must again be read with caution. Cowper there describes the crowning incident of the holiday,

[1] William Cowper of Hertingfordbury—known as "Major Cowper" in the poet's letters—was a grandson of Spencer Cowper. His father—also William—was Spencer's eldest son. He died in 1740, and the younger William then became, in his stead, Clerk of the Parliament.

which occurred to him as he and his party sat upon an eminence overlooking the Solent:

"The morning was calm and clear; the sun shone bright upon the sea; and the country on the borders of it was the most beautiful I had ever seen. . . . Here it was, that on a sudden, as if another sun had been kindled that instant in the heavens, on purpose to dispel sorrow and vexation of spirit, I felt the weight of all my weariness taken off; my heart became light and joyful in a moment; I could have wept with transport had I been alone. . . . I think I remember something like a glow of gratitude to the Father of mercies, for this unexpected blessing, and that I ascribed it to his gracious acceptance of my prayers. But Satan, and my own wicked heart, quickly persuaded me that I was indebted, for my deliverance, to nothing but a change of scene. By this means he turned the blessing into a poison; teaching me to conclude, that nothing but a continued circle of diversion, and indulgence of appetite, could secure me from a relapse."

Mr. Fausset deduces from this passage that Cowper was divided in his loyalty between poetry and religion. Not that Mr. Fausset sees any final antagonism between the two. But he holds that true spirituality can only be attained through the full imaginative redemption of instinct. Such redemption, as in the case of George Herbert, may truly lead a creative artist into a position of religious orthodoxy; but conformity to a creed as such retards instinctive development and prevents a spiritual integration of the whole personality.

There is, of course, a profound element of truth here, though Mr. Fausset's conception of spiritual rebirth has its own difficulties and perils. Moreover, such a conception is comparatively new. The Romantic Revival paved the way for it, and modern psychology rides along the road thus made: and this road, like every other, may become a rut. The fact that Cowper was actually the forerunner of the Romantic Revival does not exonerate him in Mr. Fausset's eyes from having attempted to serve both poetry and a formal faith. At Southampton, Mr. Fausset contends, he should have submitted himself to the urge of poetry which was clearly awakened in him, and by the fulfilment of his own creative impulse have travelled towards the inevitable crisis that comes sooner or later to every man, when instinct may be transmuted into a spirituality freed from all egotism and acquisitiveness.

Mr. Fausset recalls William James's dictum:

"Ought all men to have the same religion? Ought they to approve the same fruits and follow the same leadings? Are they so alike in their inner needs that, for hard or soft, for proud and humble, for strenuous and lazy, for healthy-minded and despairing, exactly the same religious incentives are required? Or are different functions in the organism of humanity allotted to different types of man, so that some may really be better for a religion of consolation and reassurance, while others are better for one of terror and reproof?"

Mr. Fausset turns these words to his own purpose. He uses them as an additional argument against Evangelicalism. He fails to see in them a double-edged weapon. He is tempted to claim for his own spiritual panacea a general applicability that he rightly denies to that of John Newton. And while, of course, he is correct in saying that Cowper needed "a religion of consolation and reassurance," he errs, I think, in supposing that he could have found such a religion through reliance upon instinct. Instinct should be carefully fostered in every man —particularly in every child. But, even granted that instinct be the basis of all true spiritual development, the very attempt to safeguard it may become a preoccupation fraught with introspection and other dangers that threaten the very end desired. If instinct be allowed to atrophy, faith may become formality. But to keep one's finger on the pulse of instinct is no less perilous than surrender to dogma and ritual. Nor, indeed, has the average man much leisure for self-analysis.

The creative artist—and Mr. Fausset is himself one even in his criticism—stands somewhat apart. Mr. Fausset has applied his spiritual theory with a real measure of conviction to Wordsworth's case.[1] Wordsworth was a born poet, and the poet's distinctive function is to speak from intuition, as that of the scientist, antithetically opposed in method, is to deal only with demonstrable facts. That poetry and science

[1] *The Lost Leader.* By Hugh I'Anson Fausset. 1933.

may serve really complementary ends is here beside the point. The poet should be the champion of instinct, and, though he may seek allies in reason or revelation, he is false to his prime vocation if he let instinct be subservient. It is at least arguable that the later Wordsworth made a fatal compromise with convention. Becoming the mouthpiece of political reaction and ecclesiastical orthodoxy, he was false to himself because he was, to begin with, a poet in the full sense of being a *maker*. Cowper, I contend, was not.

I suggest that we miss the whole truth about the author of *The Task* if we think of him as inherently a creative artist, who, by timidly holding to a creed, denied in himself the possibilities alike of vital poetic and religious development. Cowper was essentially a critic, not a creator. But for other elements in him, he might have found his true *forte* as the observer of life and manners. He might have been an essayist in the tradition of Steele, Addison, and Goldsmith; or, with his more "intimate" style, he might have provided the link between them and Charles Lamb. His letters, though written with perfect spontaneity, are essays in miniature. They are sounder in their own literary form than is his poetry; for even in his poetry he remains an essayist. In this respect he holds a unique position among our singers. All attempts to estimate his poetry, merely as poetry, are futile; we cannot dissociate the poetry from the man.

Precision in psychology is, of course, unattainable. But every poet has his temperamental bias; and the difference between a Keats and a Pope is universally recognised. Cowper's position, however, has, it seems to me, been misunderstood by most writers except Bagehot, whose motive is to belittle Cowper, but whose verdict on this point is nevertheless sound. It may be, as Bagehot says, that the "critical" kind of poetry ranks lower in the artistic scale than the "creative." I shall not quarrel with that view. Even though I think that Cowper's poetry has of recent years been underrated, I have no wish to make excessive claims for it. The poet and the man are, in him, inseparable, and it is the man himself, the whole man, who interests me. I do not believe that he had the makings of a greater poet than he actually became. That instinct did not die in him will become apparent as we proceed. But I doubt if by abandonment to instinct he could have added one cubit to his poetic stature.

It was by accident rather than by design that Cowper started the reaction against the dominance of Pope. Like Pope, he was himself a born commentator, not a born maker. Where he differed from Pope, as from the essayists whom he might otherwise have outrivalled in prose, was in the substance and range of his interests, and in a more "enthusiastic" spirit. He was not only a whimsical and sometimes shrewd spectator. He was, for his time, exceptionally fond of Nature. He was also innately devout. He needed a warmer faith, and therefore a warmer expression of it, than did men like Steele, Addison, and Pope, who were moralists indeed, but of a more mundane order. Thus he sometimes became, though never for long sustained flights, "creative." Sometimes, moreover, his imagination outsoared his creed, and his verse then reflected, however imperfectly, a new conception of God's immanence in His creation. Yet he could not have gone beyond dogma unless he had first subdued himself to it. He was the type of man whose nature imperatively demands the help of reason as well as of instinct, and who, being a rationalist on the religious plane, must have a definite theology.

Mr. Fausset postulates a deep-seated dualism between Cowper's inborn love of Nature, together with his strong faculty of reason, and his acquired Evangelicalism. But I think it may be shown that Cowper's "enthusiasm" was *not* acquired. It was as fundamentally part of his temperament as was his love of Nature itself. The truth, as I see it, is that both factors, and even (as will later appear) his rationalism, *combined* inevitably to draw him *towards* Evangelicalism, and that but for Evangelicalism he would never have been a poet, as distinct from an amateur versifier. He regarded his poetry —and, as Leslie Stephen [1] says, "his entire sincerity lifts him above all suspicion of the affected self-depreciation of other writers"—as innocent trifling, save when it was devoted to his true purpose of sermonising. "His highest ambition,"

---

[1] *Hours in a Library*. Volume II. New Edition. 1892.

as Stephen puts it, "was to be a useful auxiliary to the prosaic exhortations of Doddridge, Watts, or his friend Newton." He was not a potentially creative poet whom Evangelicalism destroyed. He was a critic whom Evangelicalism moved to song and sometimes lifted above himself.

Chapter Five

"OF THE INNER TEMPLE, ESQ."

I

RECALLING THE DEJECTION which he suffered after moving into the Middle Temple, Cowper said that in this state of mind he "continued near a twelvemonth." If so, his depression must have been relative and spasmodic, for he wrote during this year several poems to "Delia," including one of his gayest. He was, nevertheless, in a perilously overwrought condition, and, though we may smile at his assertion that on returning from Hampshire he burnt his prayers and put away all thought of devotion, it would seem that the holiday had so far restored his animal spirits as to raise the hope that by seeking more diversion he could keep them equable. In January 1754, he was called to the Bar, and about this time he joined the Nonsense Club, the members of which included Thornton, Colman, Lloyd, Joseph Hill, and De Grey. Thornton and Colman, typical wits of the period, owned the *St. James's Chronicle* and wrote for the *Connoisseur*. Cowper contributed occasional essays to both journals. Several members of the Club were dissolute in habit and came to untimely ends. Only with Joseph Hill, a man of warm heart and practical sagacity, did Cowper retain any lasting friendship.

Unless it served to intensify his abstract hatred of vice—for towards individual delinquents he was always the Good Samaritan and not the Pharisee—the Nonsense Club seems to have left little permanent mark upon Cowper's life. It was inevitable, all the same, that his brief association with the Club should have provided a loophole for scandal. There is, as I have hinted, a vague rumour that in early manhood he was himself a rake. In an eighteenth-century equivalent of *Who's Who* [1] the entry about him states that "early in life

---

[1] *A Catalogue of 500 Celebrated Authors of Great Britain now Living.* London : R. Faulder, New Bond Street. 1788.

82

he was the intimate friend of Lord Thurlow, and lived in a sociable and somewhat dissipated manner." That is the only direct accusation that I have ever seen, and it does not carry much weight. Cowper lived at a time when the Chesterfield code was still widely accepted, and when it would almost naturally be assumed—as a compliment rather than a slur—that a young gentleman, who was known to have associated with gay companions, should himself have been dissolute. The facts that he went mad, and that madness is sometimes due to licentiousness, have provoked the further suggestion that his derangement was the result of venereal disease. In private conversation, I have even heard two well-known men of letters refer, in support of this theory, to his eye trouble: though the affliction of his eyes, from which he never quite recovered, started, as we have seen, in childhood!

Innuendo has taken additional specious colouring from the slightly less vague legend of his physical deformity. Whence, in turn, comes that legend, if such it be? In the *Greville Memoirs* [1] reference is made to some letters from Newton to Thornton, which were offered to Southey as material for his "Life" of the poet. These letters were said to reveal "one curious fact," which "accounts for much of Cowper's morbid state of mind and fits of depression, as well as for the circumstance of his running away from his place in the House of Lords. It relates to some defect in his physical conformation; somebody found out his secret, and probably threatened its exposure." We have not yet reached the House of Lords incident; but, since Cowper's connection with the Nonsense Club has helped to bring him under suspicion, the whole matter may conveniently be mentioned here.

"Some defect in his physical conformation" is translated by one biographer into "an intimate deformity." Thus do myths grow! There is no reason to conclude that Cowper's physical defect, if he had one, was of an "intimate" kind. Whatever be thought of Newton's theology, his genuine affection for Cowper is established beyond dispute; and, even if he had any knowledge of an "intimate" defect in his friend, his Puritanism would alone have made him withhold

---

[1] Volume III, pp. 134-135.

any information that might, in his opinion, be liable to mis-construction. Cowper may indeed have had some trivial physical peculiarity, which would be vastly magnified in his own sight. Need we surmise anything more?

And in fact, though they all mention it, none of Cowper's accredited biographers takes seriously this twin-tradition of his physical defect and his immorality. He certainly was not the kind of man who regards the sowing of wild oats as being either necessary or genteel; and there is no shred of proof that Cowper's "white flower of a blameless life" was ever thus blemished. Circumstantial "evidence," in its turn, has so to be selected as to put the severest strain upon credulity. Let us look, for example, at the "map." Though it was not until 1763 that Cowper first became actually insane, symptoms of the coming affliction were evident years earlier. Goldwin Smith is convincing when he says that "his virtuous love of Theodora," with whom there had been no break, "was hardly compatible with gross amours." I have already outlined the causes that may have awakened his latent morbidity in 1752, while he was still meeting his cousin and was (as his poems written during that year testify) deeply attached to her. If conceivably he did so at all, it would more likely have been after the parting from Theodora in 1756 that he contracted a casual alliance. But, in that case, licentiousness would not itself explain the breakdown of 1763, the obvious precursor of which was "the dejection of spirits" which he had experi-enced a decade previously, while yet in hope of marrying Theodora.

Medical science still cannot fully account for the causes of insanity or for the various forms which it takes when excited; and the clearest medical statement of the relation between madness and vice is so beset with qualifying clauses that a layman loses his way in the thicket. It seems probable to me that Cowper's insanity was of the manic-depressive kind, which, if it *may* sometimes be due to immorality, is char-acteristically constitutional in origin. In any case, the matter need be pursued little further. I have referred to it at some length merely because I have not wished to blind myself to any possibility. Having looked into the matter with an open mind, I see every reason to dismiss the possibility as the greatest of improbabilities. The actual data lend no support to it; and all that we positively know of Cowper gives the weightiest circumstantial denial.[1]

I have said, in reference to his love of Theodora, that Cowper was the type of man who holds inviolable his ultimate secrets. But it must be reiterated that the *Memoir* was written after a determining crisis in his life. Having just recovered from madness, and attributing the fact to Evangelicalism, he was moved to an uncommonly intimate recollection of his *spiritual* experience in the light of his newly acquired faith. Theodora is not mentioned in the *Memoir*, because his affection for her would, at the moment, have seemed irrelevant. But "sins" were not irrelevant, and he was in no mood to spare himself. The *Memoir* recalls twelve years spent in the Temple "in an uninterrupted course of sinful indulgence." But if we read this very frank document with due regard for conventional Puritan idiom and standard of values, it is clear that the "temptations" there recorded had in fact been nothing more than theological difficulties, and that "appetite" may be construed as a mere taste for harmless pastimes. Cowper's conscience was so sensitive that it would have been permanently seared by the memory of his having fallen into the sin which ranked above all other evils in Puritan eyes. That it was not so seared will become evident as we proceed.

During his melancholic interludes Cowper imagined himself to have forfeited the love of God. But it is significant that when he was first struck with the conviction of having committed the sin against the Holy Ghost, it was merely because he had neglected "to improve the mercies of God at Southampton, on the occasion above mentioned." The only definitely specified sins of *commission* were his having asked a kinsman to present him with a certain public office if the holder of it should happen to die—in the *Memoir* he accuses

---

[1] See also in this connection the obviously sincere letter written in August 1763 to Harriet in which Cowper says: "Oh my good cousin! if I was to open my heart to you, I could show you some strange sights; *nothing, I flatter myself, that would shock you*, but a great deal that would make you wonder." The italics are mine.

himself of having been guilty of "the spirit of a murderer"!
—and his having attempted, a little later, "the dark and
hellish purpose" of suicide. To these things we must presently turn. Here, finally, it may be said that Cowper's
longevity, and the fair measure of health which he enjoyed,
lend their own support to the belief that his life was one of
strictest virtue.

II

Cowper's association with the Nonsense Club is sufficiently
explained by the fact that most of its members had been his
contemporaries at Westminster. Small coteries of the sort
exist in every age, and bring together, for a brief time, young
men who may have certain ties or superficial tastes in common,
but whose later records—like those of the poets and artists of
the *Yellow Book* group—show how fundamentally different
they really are. The Club doubtless yielded Cowper a temporary diversion; but, inevitably, its excitement was followed
by reaction. As we know from his few surviving letters of
the period, the young law student did his best to acquire an
urban and a modish air; but his spirit of gay bravado cannot
long have deceived even himself. Having many affinities
with Lamb, he was not, like Elia, a Londoner. His chambers
looked into Pump Court, "in which," he wrote, "there are
lime trees, and where the sound of water, though passing into
pails and pitchers, is rather agreeable." Yet, for one whose
every dream was rural, the sound of water passing into pails
and pitchers must have been a poor substitute for running
brooks, and, though the Temple must then have been more
definitely *rus in urbe* than it is now, its environment was
relatively sordid. Alsatia was not yet utterly destroyed.

Dr. Johnson, walking up Fleet Street towards the Devil
Tavern or the Mitre, or making for Clifton's Eating House
amid the wretched hovels, with their projecting stories, in
Butcher Row, might swell with satisfaction at contemplating
the full tide of existence. Cowper, in this respect, had tend-
erer nerves. Though his whimsical eye watched, and inspired
him to commemorate in verse, the life-size figures of two

savages who struck the hours and quarters on bells suspended
between them on old St. Dunstan's Church:

> "*Beating alternately, in measured time,*
> *The clockwork tintinnabulum of rhyme*":

he would less pleasurably gaze at the heads, still affixed to
poles on Temple Bar, of some of the rebels executed after the
Jacobite rising of 1745; and the grim façade of the Fleet
prison, which he may have had in mind when many years
later he wrote his famous passage on the Bastille, would move
him to involuntary shudders of horror and compassion.

"God made the country, and man made the town."
Cowper has rightly been criticised for having contrasted the
virtue and happiness of rural folk with the vice and misery
of city-dwellers. Yet his love of the country had deeper than
aesthetic roots. Genius is often made the mouthpiece of
truths or sentiments beyond the range of its own conscious
understanding; and Cowper, to change the metaphor, was
among the sensitive human barometers that registered in his
day the oncoming of a wide disturbance of revolutionary ideas.
Sainte-Beuve called him the English Rousseau, and those
who wish to pursue the analogy may be directed to Leslie
Stephen's admirable essay.[1] In character the two men were
utterly dissimilar. Rousseau could be eloquent about the joys
of domesticity; but his own private life was as repulsive as
Cowper's was beautiful. Rousseau had the greater intellect,
but was nevertheless a sentimentalist. He could, according
to his moods, make a luxury of his own grief or see the world
through rose-tinted spectacles. "Cowper's tears," as Stephen
says, "are always wrung from him by intense anguish of soul,
and never, as is occasionally the case with Rousseau, suggest
that the weeper is proud of his excessive tenderness."

Cowper, again, though he never despaired of anyone but
himself, was not theoretically an optimist. Rousseau believed
that the millennium might be established if "the noble
savage" in man were freed from political restraints and
conventional distractions. Cowper had no faith—at least,
again, no formal faith—in an earthly paradise. He joined

---

[1] "Cowper and Rousseau." *Hours in a Library.* Volume II. 1876.

with Rousseau in condemning artificiality and luxury; with Rousseau he praised the peasant, not because he thought the peasant inherently more virtuous than the townsman, but because the peasant was spared the greater temptations of city life. But while Rousseau thought in terms of men's mundane happiness, Cowper had his eye to their spiritual welfare. He was, similarly, at one with Rousseau in his championship of liberty; but, while he denounced slavery and mused upon the misery of the prisoners in the Bastille, he always returned to devotional comment:

> "*He is the freeman whom the truth makes free,*
> *And all are slaves beside.*"

Cowper, then, with a certain identity of aim, but with an underlying difference of motive, agreed unconsciously with Rousseau in calling men back to Nature. He was, of course, illogical in thought—as Rousseau was in practice. Since man is part of Nature, and since man, according to Cowper's religion, was "naturally" evil, how could Nature itself be good? We look in vain, however, for strict logic in Cowper, as indeed in many greater thinkers; nor in the eighteenth century was there yet the necessary material for what would now be deemed a satisfactory philosophy embracing Nature, man, and God. Cowper was drawn to Nature not merely by his love of beauty and his constitutional need of peace, but because he saw in Nature the symbol of the simple life in which virtue and inward freedom could more easily flourish. His intuition overflowed the banks of dogma. Yet he was essentially a religious rationalist who needed a doctrinal system of belief. His love of Nature, therefore, was not an impulse stifled by allegiance to the faith of his adoption. His very love of Nature inevitably led him towards Evangelicalism, which might theoretically frown upon the unredeemed "natural" man, but which, alone among the religious forms of the time, dared to oppose the evils which Cowper, in passage after passage of his poems, condemned as being disruptive of spiritual life.

Nor was Cowper, in his predominating moods of sanity, an acrimonious kill-joy. Like all contemporary Evangelicals, he denounced certain amusements that even most Baptists and Quakers now deem innocent.[1] But he knew that there are inward satisfactions for which card-playing and the like form, after all, poor substitutes. He held that "true piety is cheerful as the day," and carried war into the enemy's camp by claiming that the "honour" to be called "gay" had long been

> "*The boast of mere pretenders to the name.*"

And there was cause for the protest. The countryman might not always be exemplary in virtue; but luxury, corruption, and vice openly flaunted themselves in the urban society of the period, and received merely formal rebuke, if rebuke at all, from latitudinarian, and even many dissenting, pulpits.

III

Some years were yet to pass, however, before Cowper embraced Evangelicalism, and many more before he wrote *The Task*. Yet, despite the formal denial of the *Memoir*, it is clear, even from its own pages, that, while he was still a briefless barrister in the Temple, he was much preoccupied with religion. His self-condemnation in retrospect points to the fact, not that he had forgotten religion, but merely that, like other young men, he had doubts and perplexities. It occurred to him, for example, to wonder "whether the gospel were true or false." That was hardly "sinful" for one in his twenties! And his fundamental faith is revealed by his confession that when he was "in the company of Deists, and heard the gospel blasphemed," he never "failed to assert the truth of it with much vehemence." "Thus," he adds, "have

---

[1] In 1693, much to the annoyance of Queen Mary, 175 out of the 700 hackney coaches in London were allowed to ply on Sunday. Even the utilitarian Defoe regarded it as " the worst blemish of the reign of William " that " all the coaches that please may work on the Sabbath Day." And in the eighteenth century Puritanism, as is well indicated by the prevailing attitude towards Sunday, remained very widespread among the community: its spirit was by no means *confined* to Evangelicalism. In the country Sabbath observance was still strictly enforced. Chancellor Harcourt was stopped by a constable for driving through Abingdon during the time of public worship. The travelling of wagons and stage-coaches on Sunday was almost, if not wholly, forbidden until about 1750. Public worship, however, became much neglected by the aristocracy, whose representatives, when they did attend church, were often vulgar in their levity.— See Lecky's *History of England in the Eighteenth Century*. Volume II. 1878.

I been employed, when half-intoxicated,[1] in vindicating the truth of scripture, while in the very act of rebellion against its dictates. Lamentable inconsistency of a convinced judgment with an unsanctified heart! An inconsistency, indeed, evident to others, as well as myself, inasmuch as a deistical friend of mine, with whom I was disputing on the subject, cut short the matter by alleging that if what I said were true, I was certainly damned by my own showing." There is a sinister note in this last sentence. Was it the taunt of that friend—probably playful though it were—which first awoke in Cowper the hallucination that was periodically to haunt him ever afterwards?

That he was at this time genuinely concerned with religion is further seen by his statement that he had been "an industrious and diligent inquirer into the evidences," and that he had once declared his willingness to have his right hand cut off, if he might thereby be enabled "to live according to the gospel." It is obvious, indeed, that, moved by subconscious influences and temperamental bias, he was already fumbling his way towards Evangelicalism. If he were on one side of his nature an eighteenth-century gentleman of "elegance," he was on another side a born religious "enthusiast."

Meanwhile, he was experiencing the religious growing pains of youth, though, because he was both more innately spiritual and sensitive than most young men, his sufferings were intensified. "I had need of something more salutary than amusement," he wrote when looking back on that time, "but I had no one to direct me where to find it." Did he ever discuss his religious difficulties with Theodora? He may have been too secretive and shy to mention them even to her. She, moreover, was young like himself, and though if she had married him she would doubtless have become an Evangelical in loyalty to her William, women in some matters are more practical than men, and, however patiently they may humour them, are apt to regard their metaphysical

---

[1] Here, perhaps, we have the clue to the real extent of Cowper's "sinful indulgence." He drank his wine with the other members of the Nonsense Club. But it will be noted that even here in the *Memoir*, with its puritanical excess of emphasis, he refers to having been only *half*-intoxicated.

propensities as being irrelevant to the plain duty of decent living. If women had their way, there would be more churches dedicated to St. James, and fewer to St. Peter or St. Paul.

It is possible, of course, that manifestations of "enthusiasm" in his nephew may further have stiffened Ashley Cowper's attitude. At all events, there came in 1756 the farewell to Theodora; and other events and circumstances were soon to accentuate Cowper's loneliness. In the same year his father died, and in 1757 he suffered a grievous loss through the death, while bathing in the Thames, of Sir William Russell, his favourite friend. It was, surely, a real measure of despair that prompted these lines, written soon after the last-mentioned calamity:

> "Doom'd as I am in solitude to waste
> The present moments, and regret the past;
> Depriv'd of ev'ry joy I valued most,
> My friend torn from me, and my mistress lost;
> Call not this gloom I wear, this anxious mien,
> The dull effect of humour, or of spleen!
> Still, still I mourn, with each returning day,
> Him snatch'd by fate, in early youth away,
> And her—through tedious years of doubt and pain,
> Fix'd in her choice, and faithful—but in vain."

During the years immediately before and after his parting from Theodora, he made repeated efforts to keep up his spirits by jesting,[1] and also by seeking recreation at Marylebone Gardens or elsewhere. In August 1758, he was at Gravesend, where he met an attractive girl. In a letter written in Latin, he described her as being "at that age, sixteen, at which every day brings with it some new beauty to her form. No one can be more modest, nor (what seems wonderful in woman) more silent; but when she speaks you might believe a muse was speaking. Woe is me that so bright a star looks to another, having risen in the West Indies." The few letters of this period which we possess are all written in this affectedly modish style, which does not hide the underlying despondency; and the fact that this particular letter is in Latin further stamps it as a mere literary diversion.

---

[1] See, for example, *An Epistle to Robert Lloyd, Esq.*, written in 1754.

However pathetically Cowper tried to delude himself or others by his pose of *bon viveur*, it is plain enough that his nerves were at snapping point. He was in London, which he detested. He had no prospects. He, who so sorely needed human affection, had lost his love, his father, and his most intimate friend. His mind, which was naturally devout, had found no satisfactory anchorage of faith. And now his means became straitened. His financial position was but slightly relieved when in 1759 he received the sinecure appointment of Commissioner of Bankrupts, at an annual salary of sixty pounds. When, in that year, he moved into the Inner Temple, his "patrimony" was "well-nigh spent," and, as he says in the *Memoir*, "there being no appearance that I should ever repair the damage, by a fortune of my own getting, I began to be a little apprehensive of approaching want."

A letter addressed about this time to Clotworthy Rowley, a friend and fellow-Templar, who later lived at Tendring Hall in Essex, seems to reveal, beneath its transparent braggadocio and incidental sound sense, a mind already verging upon disorder:

"Your letter has taken me just in the crisis; to-morrow I set off for Brighthelmstone, and there I stay till the winter brings us all to town again. This world is a shabby fellow, and uses us ill; but a few years hence there will be no difference between us and our fathers of the tenth generation upwards. I could be as splenetick as you, and with more reason, if I thought proper to indulge that humour; but my resolution is (and I advise you to adopt it), never to be melancholy while I have a hundred pounds in the world to keep up my spirits. God knows how long that will be; but in the meantime Io TRIUMPHE! If a great man struggling with misfortune is a noble object, a little man that despises them is no contemptible one; and this is all the philosophy I have in the world at present. It savours pretty much of the ancient Stoic; but till the Stoics became coxcombs they were, in my opinion, a very sensible sect. . . .

"If my resolution to be a great man were half as strong as it is to despise being a little one, I should not despair of a house in Lincoln's Inn Fields, with all its appurtenances; for there is nothing more certain, and I could prove it to you by a thousand instances, than that every man may be rich if he will. . . . Did you ever in your life know a man who was guided in the general course of his actions by anything but his natural temper? And yet we blame each other's conduct as freely as if that temper was the most tractable beast in the world. . . . There are some sensible folks, who having great estates have wisdom enough to know how to spend properly; there are others who are not less wise, perhaps, as knowing how to shift without 'em. Between these two degrees are they who spend their money dirtily, or get it so. If you ask me where they are to be placed who amass much wealth in an honest way, you must be as good as to find them first, and then I'll answer the question. Upon the whole, my dear Rowley, there is a degree of poverty that has no disgrace belonging to it; that degree of it, I mean, in which a man enjoys clean linen and good company; and if I never sink below this degree of it, I care not if I never rise above it. This is a strange epistle, nor can I imagine how the devil I came to write it: but here it is, such as it is, and much good may it do you. I have no estate, as it happens, so if it should fall into bad hands, I shall be in no danger of a commission of lunacy."

Cowper's financial situation was, indeed, becoming desperate; and, for once, under the spur of sheer necessity, he displayed some enterprise. But his nervous condition, aggravated by solitude and a series of sorrowful blows, was now too unstable to respond; and, ironically, it was his very initiative that proved the means at last of turning a nervous breakdown into positive madness. Major Cowper had in his patronage the office of Clerk of the Journals in the House of Lords. The young barrister asked his kinsman to give him the appointment if its present holder should die. As it happened, that individual did soon die. Moreover, the offices of Reading Clerk and Clerk of Committees, of which also Major Cowper held the patent, fell vacant simultaneously. The Major offered Cowper these last two positions, which were more profitable; but no sooner had Cowper eagerly accepted them than he shrank from the publicity which they would entail. He therefore persuaded the Major to give him instead the other office, whose duties could be performed in private. Then difficulties arose. The Major's right of presentation was suddenly questioned by a powerful party in the Lords, who wished to instal as Clerk an old enemy of the Cowper family. An order was accordingly issued that the Major's nominee should be examined at the bar of the House:

The *Memoir* shall take up the tale:

"All the horror of my fears and perplexities now returned. A thunderbolt would have been as welcome to me as this intelligence. I knew, to demonstration, that upon these terms the clerkship of the journals was no place for me. To require my attendance at the bar of the House, that I might there publicly entitle myself to this office, was, in effect, to exclude me from it. In the meantime, the interest of my friend, the honour of his choice, my own reputation and circumstances, all urged me forward; all pressed me to undertake that which I saw to be impracticable. Those whose spirits are formed like mine, to whom a public exhibition of themselves, on any occasion, is mortal poison, may have some idea of the horror of my situation; others can have none."

Continued misery brought on "a nervous fever." Quiet forsook the candidate by day, and peace by night. He attended regularly at the office, where the journals were thrown open to him. But he "read without perception," and every day, "for more than half a year together," his feelings were those "of a man when he arrives at the place of execution."

On August 9, 1763, he wrote to Harriet:

"My dear Cousin,—Having promised to write to you, I make haste to be as good as my word. I have a pleasure in writing to you at any time, but especially at the present, when my days are spent in reading the journals, and my nights in dreaming of them—an employment not very agreeable to a head that has long been habituated to the luxury of choosing its subject, and has been as little employed upon business as if it had grown upon the shoulders of a much wealthier gentleman. But the num-skull pays for it now, and will not presently forget the discipline it has undergone lately. If I succeed in this doubtful piece of promotion, I shall have at least this satisfaction to reflect upon, that the volumes I write will be treasured up with the utmost care for ages, and will last as long as the English constitution—a duration which ought to satisfy the vanity of any author who has a spark of love for his country. Oh my good cousin! if I was to open my heart to you, I could show you some strange sights; nothing, I flatter myself, that would shock you, but a great deal that would make you wonder. I am of a very singular temper, and very unlike all the men that I have ever conversed with. Certainly I am not an absolute fool; but I have more weakness than the greatest of all the fools I can recollect at present. In short, if I was as fit for the next world as I am unfit for this—and God forbid I should speak it in vanity!—I would not change conditions with any saints in Christendom.

"My destination is settled at last, and I have obtained a furlough. Margate is the word, and what do you think will ensue, cousin? I know what you expect, but ever since I was born I have been good at disappointing the most natural expectations. Many years ago, cousin, there was a possibility I might prove a very different thing from what I am at present. My character is now fixed, and riveted fast upon me; and between friends is not a very splendid one, or likely to be guilty of much fascination."

The visit to Margate brought temporary relief. Sea-bathing and seaside holidays had recently come into vogue.[1] Places like Weymouth, which had been described as being "but little" in 1733, were now growing; and, though it was not until the visit of the Prince Regent in 1783 and the building of the Pavilion in the following years that Brighton became fashionable, the fishing village of Brighthelmstone was waking from its ancient slumber. Cowper had already been there, and remembered it in after life as a "scene of idleness and luxury, music, dancing, cards, walking, riding, bathing, eating, drinking, coffee, tea, scandal, yawning, sleeping." His holiday of 1763 was recalled, sixteen years later, in a letter to William Unwin:

"When I was at Margate it was an excursion of pleasure to go to see Ramsgate. The pier, I remember, was accounted a most excellent piece of stonework, and such I found it. By this time, I suppose, it is finished; and surely it is no small advantage that you have an opportunity of observing how nicely those great stones are put together, as often as you please, without trouble or expense. But you think Margate more lively. So is a Cheshire cheese, full of mites, more lively than a sound one; but that very

[1] Dr. Johnson is said not to have seen the sea until he was fifty-six.

liveliness only proves its rottenness. I remember, too, that Margate, though full of company, was generally filled with such company as people who were nice in the choice of their company were rather fearful of keeping company with. The hoy went to London every week, loaded with mackerel and herrings, and returned loaded with company. The cheapness of the conveyance made it equally commodious for dead fish and lively company. So, perhaps, your solitude at Ramsgate may turn out another advantage, at least I should think it one.''

The happy effects of ''cheerful company'' and ''a new scene'' were short-lived. In October the prospective Clerk was back at the office to ''prepare for the push.'' So wretched he became that, though he had never hitherto thought of death ''without shuddering at the idea,'' he now recalled the treatise on self-murder which his father had given him to read as a boy, and his mind turned to suicide as the only means of escape from his approaching ordeal: though, indeed, there was just the chance that he might, in the meantime, go mad.

Twenty-five pages of the *Memoir* are filled with a minute description of the successive stages by which that desperate hope came to fulfilment. A week yet remained before the day of his examination. Every detail of that awful week, down to the moment when he was actually plunged into the merciful depths of insanity, was afterwards burnt into his recollection. He discussed the ethics of suicide with stray associates in taverns and chop-houses. He bought laudanum from an apothecary, who seemed, as well he might, to ''observe'' him ''narrowly.'' Determined to allow for any unforeseen possibility, he kept the poison secreted in his pocket. ''My mind, perhaps,'' he says, ''after this time, began to be disordered.'' Breakfasting at Richards's Coffee House on the morning preceding his trial, he fancied that a letter in the newspaper was a libel on himself by one who knew his purpose of self-destruction and wished to hasten it. He wondered, for a while, if he might not escape to France and enter a monastery. Then he decided in favour of drowning himself. He took a cab to Tower Wharf, but at Custom House Quay he found the water low and ''a porter seated upon some goods'' as if ''a message to prevent'' him. Returning to the Temple, he tried to take the laudanum, but found his fingers "closely contracted" and "entirely useless."

On the next morning, hearing the clock strike seven, and realising that there was no time to lose, as his chambers would soon be opened and his friend call to take him to Westminster, he arose. Having failed in his intention to bolt the door, he thrice attempted to hang himself with a garter. The third effort was nearly successful; he hung long enough to lose consciousness before the garter broke again. On regaining sensibility, he got into bed and soon heard "the laundress" lighting a fire in the dining-room. The laundress hastened to a friend, who summoned Major Cowper from a neighbouring coffee-house. On hearing explanations, the Major said: "My dear Mr. Cowper, you terrify me; to be sure you cannot hold the office at this rate—where is the deputation?" "I gave him," says Cowper, "the key of the drawers, where it was deposited; and his business requiring immediate attention, he took it away with him; and thus ended all my connection with the Parliament House."

Cowper tells us that hitherto he had felt "no concern of a spiritual kind." The *Memoir* cannot, again, be accepted as valid evidence on this point, which, as we have seen, even its own pages contradict. It was inevitable, however, that, in one of Cowper's delicate spiritual constitution, unutterable remorse should now set in:

"Conviction of sin took place, especially of that just committed; the meanness of it, as well as its atrocity, were exhibited to me in colours so inconceivably strong that I despised myself, with a contempt not to be imagined or expressed. . . . This sense of it secured me from the repetition of a crime, which I could not now reflect on without abhorrence. Before I rose from bed, it was suggested to me that there was nothing wanted but murder, to fill up the measures of my iniquities; and that, though I had failed in my design, yet I had all the guilt of that crime to answer for. A sense of God's wrath, and a deep despair of escaping it, instantly succeeded. The fear of death became much more prevalent in me than ever the desire of it had been."

At noon Major Cowper, his "dear friend and benefactor," called on him again. A doctor was summoned, who reassured

G

the patient about his physical condition, and suggested a change of air in the country. It was sound advice, if it were not already too late. Cowper, however, resolved to stay in his chambers, that he might have "full liberty" to consider his "spiritual state." Walking to and fro in his room, he decided that "*there never was so abandoned a wretch, so great a sinner.*" The italics are his own: but these following are mine: *he had not yet met John Newton.* He opened his Bible, and "the sword of the Spirit seemed to guard the tree of life" from his touch. He turned to Tillotson's sermons without happier result. He took up a volume of Beaumont and Fletcher, and when his eye immediately read, "The justice of the gods is in it," his heart replied, "It is a truth." He found something in every book to condemn him. "Everything," he says, "preached to me, and everything preached the curse of the law." If he went into the street, people, it seemed, stood and laughed at him; and when he dined alone, at tavern or chop-house, he slunk into the darkest corners. Sleep, when it could be wooed, brought him terrifying dreams, and when he awoke he "reeled and staggered like a drunken man."

It was about this time that he set down the strange sapphics which occupy less than one of the six hundred pages of the Oxford Edition of his poems, but which have sometimes been quoted as typical of his whole output, though in truth *The Castaway* is almost the only parallel.

"*Hatred and vengeance, my eternal portion,*
Scarce can endure delay of execution,
Wait, with impatient readiness, to seize my
　　　　　Soul in a moment.

Damn'd below Judas: more abhorr'd than he was,
Who for a few pence sold his holy Master.
Twice betrayed Jesus me, the last delinquent,
　　　　　Deems the profanest.

Man disavows, and Deity disowns me:
Hell might afford my miseries a shelter;
Therefore hell keeps her ever hungry mouths all
　　　　　Bolted against me.

> *Hard lot! encompass'd with a thousand dangers;*
> *Weary, faint, trembling with a thousand terrors;*
> *I'm called, if vanquish'd, to receive a sentence*
> > *Worse than Abiram's.*
>
> Him *the vindictive rod of angry justice*
> *Sent quick and howling to the centre headlong;*
> *I, fed with judgment, in a fleshly tomb, am*
> > *Buried above ground."*

Readers with a morbid taste may follow the story, if they wish, in the *Memoir*. There is no need to enlarge further upon it here.

> "*We are not ourselves when Nature, being oppressed,*
> *Commands the mind to suffer with the body*";

and no purpose can be served by dwelling upon the self-torture of one in the throes of coming lunacy. Suffice it to say that his brother, whom he had informed of his plight, came to see him. The Rev. John Cowper, a man of considerable learning and gentle disposition, had three years previously been elected Fellow of Benet (now Corpus Christi) College, Cambridge. His sweet reasonableness proved unavailing. Then it was that William thought of his cousin Martin Madan, a prominent leader of the Calvinist section of Evangelicalism, who was also chaplain to the Lock Hospital, near Hyde Park. "I used," says Cowper,

> "to think him an enthusiast, but now seemed convinced that if there were any balm in Gilead, he must administer it to me. On former occasions, when my spiritual concerns had at any time occurred to me, I thought likewise on the necessity of repentance. I knew that many persons had spoken of shedding tears for sin; but when I asked myself whether that time would ever come, when I should weep for mine, it seemed to me that a stone might sooner do it."

Madan arrived at the Temple; and we come at this point to Cowper's first *recorded* association with Evangelicalism. I do not suggest—there is no warrant for suggesting—that to Madan can be imputed any charge of originally turning Cowper's mind inward upon itself: at all events, it is manifestly absurd to make Newton the scapegoat! Not only had

Cowper not yet encountered Newton; he must have had many previous talks with Madan. It was not for a stranger that he sent in his extremity. Was not Madan, indeed, his cousin? And in a letter written years afterwards by the poet to Lady Hesketh is there not a reference to the days of their youth, when he and she walked "often" up and down Chancery Lane "in quest of the Madans"? I have already suggested, and shall further show, that Cowper's inevitable leaning was towards "enthusiasm." But, while at this juncture there is no reason to suspect Madan's good intentions, it seems probable, and must be regretted, that Cowper had early come under the influence of a Calvinist, and one whose character, in the light of his subsequent history, has evoked very diverse opinions.

Madan was a man of robust constitution, imposing manners, and commanding voice. Without blaming him, however, for having a vigorous personality, we may well doubt whether his particular "balm" was of the kind most needed at the moment, even though when he "spoke of original sin, and the corruption of every man born into the world, whereby every one is a child of wrath," Cowper immediately felt "something like hope," since "this document" set him "more on a level with the rest of mankind" and made his condition "appear less desperate." When the Scriptures were expounded on the divine atonement for sin, Cowper's heart "began to burn." But when Madan finally urged the necessity of a lively faith in Jesus Christ—"not an assent only of the understanding, but a faith of application, an actually laying hold of it, and embracing it as a salvation wrought out" for him personally—Cowper could only deplore his "want of such a faith." Madan told him that it was the gift of God, which he trusted He would bestow upon him. Cowper replied: "I wish He would"—"a very irreverent petition," as he adds in the *Memoir*, "but a very sincere one, and such as the blessed God, in His due time, was pleased to answer."

Cowper was temporarily so much "easier" that his brother, though himself disliking "enthusiasm," sent for Madan again. It is just conceivable that some representative of Evangelicalism in its mellower form might, even at this eleventh hour, have ministered efficaciously to a mind diseased. The probability is, however, that Cowper, for the present, was beyond the restorative power of the best ghostly counsellor. At any rate, after Madan's second departure, his condition became demonstrably worse. His brother and friends agreed that there was nothing for it but an asylum. He was therefore taken to Dr. Cotton's "Collegium Insanorum" at St. Albans. Shortly before he left the Temple, Harriet, now Lady Hesketh, and her husband called on him. He was almost insensible, but said, as they were going: "Farewell! there will be no more intercourse between us for ever"—a prophecy that was happily to be disproved. His last thought was for his cat, which he entrusted to the care of kindly Joseph Hill.

IV

"The mind," says Dr. Stanford Read,[1]

"is the mechanism by means of which we adapt [ourselves] to our environment, and when, through its derangement, conduct is exhibited which the community looks upon as evidence of disease and as implying irresponsibility, the individual concerned is said to be insane and the law steps in to certify him as such. Strictly speaking, then, insanity is really a social and legal term and not medical. Mental illness is a broad concept which may include very efficient members of society. No satisfactory definition can therefore be arrived at, since it would be necessary to define what we mean by sanity, which would involve us in equal difficulties."

It was only towards the close of the eighteenth century that mental ailments, about which the mediaeval mystical conceptions had survived, were first scientifically studied; and, as this was a period in which materialism flourished and much research was devoted to anatomy, madness came to be identified almost exclusively with organic change in the brain—a conception that left little room for distinctions between "feeble-mindedness" and merely functional disorders. Under the influence of Freud, Jung, Adler, and Adolf Meyer, there

[1] "Insanity." By C. Stanford Read, M.D. *Encyclopaedia Britannica.* Fourteenth Edition.

is a tendency to-day to ignore the possible physical element in favour of the psychological. The materialistic school still holds, says Dr. Read, "that though in many states of insanity no structural changes are observable, they exist all the same"; they are such that our imperfect methods cannot yet detect them. The psychogenic school, on the other hand, argues that

"though mental disease may arise secondarily to physical disorder, the symptoms are psychological reverberations of that disorder, and the body of an individual must be regarded as environmental to the ego. In an integrated organism, though the basis of the wrong functioning lies in the physical sphere, some of the effects are manifested at the psychological level. The symptoms, then, are expressions of the personality, and, however much we stress the bodily aspect, that can in no way explain the content of a delusion or an hallucination."

Dr. Read recognises, of course, that the older materialistic view was superficial and inadequate. He equally admits that Freud and other psychologists have added much to our enlightenment. But he warns us that knowledge is still in such an empirical phase that we must avoid both of the opposing camps, and that, when we consider insanity, we must "take a very wide vista which will embrace the study of the individual, his personal and racial history, his environment, and his physical and mental structure." It is, unfortunately, impossible to take such a comprehensive survey of Cowper's case. While his physical constitution must have been fairly robust, we know nothing of it in detail; and there is the legend of some "defect." Of his heredity, so far as any morbid tendency is concerned, we are likewise ignorant. His father has incurred suspicion through having given his boy a treatise on suicide to read; but no safe deduction can be made from that isolated fact. There are suggestions that the poet's brother John, if in less degree than William himself, was nervously hypersensitive; [1] but, once more, we have small actual record of the brother.

It does not follow, however, because we lack direct evidence, that there was no morbid taint in the Cowper or Donne

[1] See, for example, the description of John Cowper's encounters with a gipsy. *William Cowper*. By Thomas Wright. Pp. 46 and 188.

stock. "It has to be admitted," says Dr. Read again, "that few scentific data are before us to establish on any firm basis our knowledge of the inheritance of mental instability." One fact, however, clearly emerges. An "hereditary taint is far commoner in normal people than is usually supposed," though the "exciting causes" may often not occur to waken the pre-disposition. While, therefore, I am less concerned to explain Cowper's madness than to point out the difficulties involved in any such attempt, I think it is at least possible to argue, by induction, that there may indeed have been a melancholic strain in his ancestry.

The various modern classifications of insanity represent merely working hypotheses. But, assuming their validity, I submit that Cowper's mental malady was probably of the "manic-depressive" type. "The *manic-phase*," says Dr. Read, "manifests itself by three main symptoms—elation, flight of ideas, and general hyperactivity of mind and body":

"In the *depressive phase* we note exactly the opposite symptoms of great depression, difficulty in thinking and under-activity of mind and body. Here again we may speak of three grades of severity. In the mildest the individual often realises his invalid-ism. He moves and speaks slowly, seems incapable of effort, and sees everything as through a glass darkly. In *acute melancholia* the symptoms are much more pronounced. The depression is profound and delusions of self-accusation referring to sin, poverty, and being 'lost' are in evidence. Hypochondriacal ideas, such as their bowels being stopped up or their brains decayed, are frequent. The personality may seem to the patient to be transformed, and hallucinations consonant with their delusions also occur. In the severest type there is stupor, and the patient lies in bed inert, with much clouding of consciousness, the victim of horrible delusions and hallucinations. Manic-depressive insanity may last a variable period, but, though recovery is usually the rule, a recurrence of attacks is highly likely. The interval between such attacks may progressively lessen. Certain cases may remain chronic. Any patient with any state of melancholia must be regarded as a potential suicide, and cared for accordingly."

Dr. Read adds that "the attacks are frequently noted for their apparent lack of cause. Usually, however, some difficulty in the individual's life is found as a precipitating factor."

There is no need to stress the similarity between the symptoms here described and those exhibited by Cowper. What I *would* emphasise is the fact that manic-depressive insanity is "constitutional, and can best be understood from a psycho-pathological standpoint. The deep-seated constitutional origin is marked by its hereditary taint." I think it not unlikely, therefore, that, if we knew more of Cowper's heredity, we should find there a melancholic predisposition. And even if it were not to be *found* there, it may nevertheless have existed. There may have been in the lives of his immediate ancestors an absence of those "exciting causes" which so plentifully and tragically mark Cowper's own earlier career.

I doubt if Cowper's madness can adequately be explained in psychogenic terms. I question whether any interpretation that fails to allow for a physical element in his successive derangements can be tenable. Even granted a physical origin, of course, morbidity may react favourably to wise psychological treatment or suggestion: but it is going far beyond our present understanding of mental disorders to suggest that psychological methods might, in a case like Cowper's, be fully restorative. The latent morbidity which the poet may have inherited had, during his childhood, youth, and early manhood, almost every conceivable disturbance to fight against; and, as he lived in an age when diagnosis and remedial measures were at the best very crude, the marvel is not that he failed to make a complete and permanent recovery, but that he rallied to the degree attested by his later history and work. Only one in whom there was essential vigour and sanity could so have won back from the abyss.

Chapter Six

AT ST. ALBANS AND HUNTINGDON

I

IF LUNACY STILL partially baffles doctors and psychologists, it was hardly understood at all in the eighteenth century. Until towards the close of that period, little attempt was made at diagnosis, and there was no regularised treatment. The Bethlehem Hospital, an official institution, received patients whose madness was legally certified by the local authorities of the areas in which they lived. Much depended, of course, upon the wisdom or caprice of the authorities concerned; and there were private asylums throughout the country to which persons rightly or wrongly said to be insane could be consigned, without official interference, by their friends—or enemies! Readers of the Life of Cruden,[1] of *Concordance* fame, will recall the story of how he was smuggled, apparently by a jealous rival in love, into such an establishment at Bethnal Green, where he suffered bitter humiliations before he managed to escape, carrying with him along the semi-rural road to Aldgate the post of the bed to which he had been chained.

Many of the asylums, like the prisons, were run with a sole view to private profit. Happily there were exceptions. We should like to have more details about the methods used by Dr. Cotton in his large E-shaped Elizabethan house at St. Albans, which Cowper entered in December 1763, and from which he emerged—a renewed, if not a new, man—eighteen months later. We may at least judge favourably of the "Collegium Insanorum" from what we know of Nathaniel Cotton himself, and from the fact that Cowper, in retrospect, called it the Place of his Second Nativity.

Modest Dr. Cotton, who never signed his writings in prose or verse, and whose tombstone gives neither dates nor description, was born in 1705. From the memoir by his son, we

---

[1] *The Eccentric Life of Alexander Cruden.* By Edith Olivier. 1934.

learn that he studied medicine at Leyden and settled at St. Albans in 1740, where, in addition to superintending his asylum, he carried on a general practice until his death in 1788. He wrote, in 1749, a treatise entitled "Observations on a Particular Kind of Scarlet Fever that Lately Prevailed in and about St. Albans." But he is best remembered as a poet. His "Visions in Verse, for the Entertainment and Instruction of Younger Minds"—an attempt to moralise the fables of Gay —was very popular for a time, and certain poems like "The Fireside" and "To a Child of Five Years Old" long kept his memory green. He contributed to Dodsley's "Collection," and was an intimate friend of Edward Young, the author of "Night Thoughts," whom he attended during his last illness. His posthumously collected works include sermons and letters, in which latter he is seen as a sound adviser and cheerful consoler of his correspondents. He was a religious enthusiast without fanaticism. Cowper contrasted him,

> *"whose humanity sheds rays*
> *That make superior skill his second praise"*

with the not rare type of

> *"grave physician, gath'ring fees,*
> *Punctu'lly paid for length'ning out disease."*

Wise, mellow, "human," and, in the truest sense, well balanced, Cotton would seem to belong to a later age rather than to his own.[1]

Cowper tells us comparatively little about his "bondage." During his first five and a half months under Dr. Cotton's roof, "a conviction of sin, and expectation of judgment" never left him. He then became "so familiar with despair" that he "contracted a sort of hardness or indifference" to the awaited event of "divine vengeance." He said to himself: "Eat and drink, for to-morrow thou shalt be in hell." While still convinced of his "irrevocable doom," he began to laugh at Cotton's stories, and to cap them with others of his own, though his smiles "were, in reality, very like the green surface

---

[1] Dr. Cotton was twice married. One of his sons, Joseph, became a well-known mariner and merchant. His grandson, William, who died in 1866, was Governor of the Bank of England and a celebrated philanthropist.

of a morass, pleasant to the eye, but a cover for nothing but rottenness and filth." The one thing needful for a cure—"an experimental knowledge of the redemption which is in Christ Jesus"—was yet wanting; and, indeed, at this time he harboured "a diabolical species of regret." He lamented that he had not seized every chance of indulging his "wicked appetites," so that he might now have had the consolation of knowing his miserable fate well earned. (How many school-boys, smarting from the cane or pining in "detention," have similarly felt this "diabolical" emotion!)

Three months later, Cowper's brother from Cambridge visited him. John was at first disappointed to find William less cheerful than Dr. Cotton's report had suggested. Here is William's own account of the meeting:

"As soon as we were left alone, he asked me how I found myself; I answered, 'As much better as despair can make me.' We went together into the garden. Here on [my] expressing a settled assurance of sudden judgment, he protested to me that it was all a delusion; and protested so strongly, that I could not help giving some attention to him. I burst into tears, and cried out, 'If it be a delusion, then am I the happiest of beings.' Something like a ray of hope was shot into my heart; but still I was afraid to indulge it. We dined together, and I spent the afternoon in a more cheerful manner. Something seemed to whisper to me, 'Still there is mercy.'"

Clouds gathered again, but there gleamed repeatedly "a vague presage of better things at hand." One morning, after sound sleep, Cowper dreamed that the sweetest boy he ever saw came dancing to his bedside: "he seemed to be just out of leading-strings," yet his tread was firm and steady. The vision greatly encouraged Cowper, even though he knew not yet "where to look for the establishment of the comfort" vouchsafed. Then, suddenly, a fuller light dawned:

"Having found a Bible on the bench in the garden, I opened upon the 11th of St. John, where Lazarus is raised from the dead; and saw so much benevolence, mercy, goodness, and sympathy with miserable men, in our Saviour's conduct, that I almost shed tears upon the relation; little thinking that it was an exact type of the mercy which Jesus was on the point of extending towards myself. I sighed, and said, 'Oh, that I had not rejected so good a Redeemer, that I had not forfeited all his favours.' Thus was my heart softened, though not yet enlightened."

Cowper realised that, while the terror of the Lord may make a Pharisee, "only the sweet voice of mercy in the gospel can make a Christian." Hope continued. Increasingly he felt that he was "not utterly doomed to destruction," and presently there came another revelation. He turned again to the Bible, and the first verse he saw was "Whom God hath set forth to be a propitiation through faith in His blood, to declare His righteousness for the remission of sins that are past, through the forbearance of God":

"Immediately I received the strength to believe it, and the full beams of the Sun of Righteousness shone upon me. I saw the sufficiency of the atonement He had made, my pardon sealed in His blood, and all the fulness and completeness of His justification. In a moment I believed, and received the gospel. Whatever my friend Madan had said to me, long before, revived in all its clearness, with demonstration of the Spirit and with power. Unless the Almighty arm had been under me, I think I should have died with gratitude and joy. My eyes filled with tears, and my voice choked with transport; I could only look up to heaven in silent fear, overwhelmed with love and wonder."

He now lost no opportunity of "repairing to the throne of grace." He "flew to it with an earnestness irresistible and never to be satisfied." He was so happy that he begrudged time for sleep, and joy welled up into song:

> " *All at once my chains were broken,*
>   *From my feet the fetters fell,*
>   *And that word in pity spoken*
>   *Snatch'd me from the jaws of Hell.*
>   *Sweet the sound of grace divine,*
>   *Sweet the grace that makes it mine.*"

The music is sustained through thirteen stanzas. The hymns written at St. Albans may sound unctuous to modern ears: they are at least patently spontaneous and sincere, and, contrasted with the sapphics of 1763, attest both Cowper's recuperative power and the wisdom of Dr. Cotton's regime.

"Oh, that the ardour of my first love had continued! But

I have known many a lifeless and unhallowed hour since;
long intervals of darkness, interrupted by short returns of
peace and joy in believing." Thus we read, a little later, in
the *Memoir*. We must remember, however, that this frag-
ment of autobiography, from which the foregoing extracts
have been taken, was written only a year or so after the time
of the events described. The reference to "long intervals of
darkness" does not apply to the whole later course of the poet's
life. Even in the *Memoir*, indeed, while lamenting the
decline of his enthusiasm, he added that since his conversion
he had met with no trial "but what might be expected in a
state of warfare." He was no longer prone to "sensual
gratification," though anger, to which his "easy, quiet disposition" had seldom previously been tempted, now occasioned
"the sharpest conflicts." "But Jesus being my strength, I
fight against it; and if I am not conqueror, yet I am not overcome." One tries, without much success, to picture an irate
Cowper. It is likely that sage old Dr. Cotton noticed a certain
irritability in his patient, and welcomed it as a sign of convalescence.

Spiritual ecstasy cannot last indefinitely: however abiding
its results may be, there comes, after the hour of transfigura-
tion, the inevitable descent from the mount. Because Cowper
soon mourned the seeming reaction, there is no cause to
doubt—there is, indeed, every reason to believe—that he had
undergone, if not a "conversion," at least a true spiritual
experience. We may smile a little, if we like, at the perfervid-
ness of "the first fine careless rapture." We may, to change
the metaphor, discard the shell of formal Evangelical language. The kernel remains.

II

Cowper was in no hurry to leave the asylum. It was to
him, after many lonely years, a veritable home. He remained
with his "little physician" nearly twelve months after his
recovery; "and much sweet communion," he says, "I had
with him, concerning the things of our salvation." He was
indebted to Dr. Cotton in more ways than one. He now owed

him a considerable sum of money; and his relatives, who had
to bear the brunt of the expense, thought the time had come
for him, if not to resume his profession, at least to seek cheaper
accommodation.   Disinclination and conscience alike forbade
his return to the Temple; and, feeling unable to take the
accustomed oath, he resigned his appointment as commissioner
of bankrupts. "By this means," he said, "I reduced myself
to an income scarcely sufficient for my maintenance; but I
would rather have starved in reality than deliberately offend
my Saviour."   These are brave words—or, as some may
think, glib ones. It is possible that had Cowper been actually
faced with the alternative of starvation or dishonour, he might
indeed have chosen the former.   As things were, he displayed
no excessive zeal for martyrdom.   Much as he disliked threatening to turn the "toad" out of his "hole," he allowed
Joseph Hill to bring pressure to bear upon the Welshman who
had for some time occupied his chambers in London without
paying the rent.   For the rest, he relied upon "the great
mercy of God, who has since raised me up such friends as have
enabled me to enjoy all the comforts and conveniences of life.
I am well assured, that while I live, 'bread shall be given me,
and water shall be sure' according to His gracious promise."

I have no wish to gloss over the foibles of Evangelicalism.
I know how irritating its terminology can be. It must sometimes have galled Cowper's relatives to hear him so airily
ascribe their own generosity to the Lord. They had even
truer cause for annoyance when, on leaving St. Albans, their
impecunious kinsman, aged thirty-four and having no prospects, not only took with him one of Dr. Cotton's servants to
whom he had become attached, but adopted the six-year-old
son of a drunken cobbler, whose hard case had aroused his
pity.   Roberts, the servant, was appropriately named Sam.
There seems to have been an immediate understanding
between him and Cowper, such as arose between Mr. Pick-
wick and the younger Weller.   Writing to Hill a few days
after he had settled in his new rooms at Huntingdon, Cowper
said:

"... I have a lodging that puts me continually in mind of our
summer excursions; we have had many worse, and, except the

size of it (which, however, is sufficient for a single man), but few better. I am not quite alone, having brought a servant with me from St. Albans, who is the very mirror of fidelity and affection for his master. And whereas the Turkish Spy says, he kept no servant, because he would not have an enemy in his house, I hired mine, because I would have a friend. Men do not usually bestow these encomiums on their lackeys, nor do they usually deserve them; but I have had experience of mine, both in sickness and in health, and never saw his fellow.''

The cost of maintaining the child "Dick" Coleman, whose father might have "poisoned him with gin" if "Providence" had not intervened, was for some years a constant cause of anxiety to the poet, who ultimately apprenticed the boy to a breeches-maker.

Cowper's munificence has its attractive side. Yet it was generosity at other people's expense. Cowper, at any rate in earlier life, was quite irresponsible in money matters, and his relatives seem, on the whole, to have been commendably long-suffering. There was—to anticipate events slightly—one storm. Ashley Cowper informed his nephew that "the family were not a little displeased at having learnt that he kept a servant; and that he maintained a boy also." Major Cowper went further, and recommended that his kinsfolk should not "give to one who knew so little how to make a right use of their bounty." He threatened, for his own part, to withdraw his subscription. It was then that Cowper received the letter, either from a stranger or in the disguised hand of a friend, in which, in "the kindest and most benevolent terms imaginable," he was exhorted not to distress himself, as the writer, who loved him tenderly and approved his conduct, would replace any deduction that others might make from his income. At first his thoughts turned to Lady Hesketh, then to her father. He must later have realised that his "Dear Anonymous" was Theodora. Nor was she his only benefactress. Mrs. Unwin, with whom he had at this time been living for some months, voluntarily reduced her fee, without diminishing her guest's accommodation, from eighty to forty guineas per annum. Even the Major was better than his word, and peace was restored.

If no full defence of Cowper's quixotry be possible, it may at least be urged that, while he was not indifferent to the good things of this life, such as soles and oysters, and while he was always fastidious about his attire, his tastes were essentially simple and innocent. While, again, he might often assign his good fortune to God, he was in fact very grateful to the human agents through whom it was forthcoming. There is an art of receiving as well as of giving, and few men have more charmingly or sincerely exemplified it. His letters of thanks, sometimes in verse, must have made the donors feel that their mercy was indeed twice blessed, rewarding the giver no less than the taker. Finally, it may be noted that when, in October 1767, on questioning Hill, his "Chancellor of the Exchequer," he found that his debts amounted to something like one hundred and forty pounds, he seems to have insisted, against Hill's advice, on selling some of his Consols in order to meet his obligations.

III

It was at four o'clock on a June morning in 1765 that Cowper bade farewell to Dr. Cotton, and set out from St. Albans for Cambridge. There he stayed with his brother for several days. John found William's proselytising zeal a little irksome; but there was a fraternal agreement to differ. As no suitable rooms could be found in Cambridge, Cowper settled at Huntingdon, fifteen miles away; and the brothers met every week, "by an alternate reciprocation of intercourse." William, despite his whimsical disclaimers, became a good enough horseman to manage the journey regularly without disaster, though he probably had his anxious moments, the memory of which served later to provide authoritative colour for *John Gilpin*.

He described Huntingdon as the "neatest" of towns. It had long since fallen from the days of its glory, when it possessed fifteen churches, a priory, and a castle. But it was a thriving agricultural centre, and was still famous, as in Cromwell's time, for its brewing. Its town hall had been built twenty years before the coming of Cowper, who noted, as something worthy of marvel, that "the roads, which are all turnpike, and strike out four or five different ways, are perfectly good in all weathers." The lumbering coaches and waggons passed through its mile-long High Street on their journeys between London and York, and several of its fine surviving inns were already scenes of lively activity. The Ouse, which here flows between some of the loveliest water-meadows in England, was navigable to small vessels from King's Lynn. The town was also a resort of huntsmen and anglers, and, like most other places of equal size in days when people had to find their amusements close at hand, it boasted its card and dancing assemblies, its racecourse, its club and bowling green. "I am well off, you perceive," wrote Cowper to Hill, "in point of diversions; especially as I shall go to 'em just as much as I should if I lived a thousand miles off. But no matter for that; the spectator at a play is more entertained than the actor; and in real life it is much the same."

At first Cowper found the surrounding country "flat and insipid." He came to like it better, and to acquire a special affection for the village of Hartford, where the church "is very prettily situated upon a rising ground, so close to the river that it washes the wall of the churchyard." He fell immediately in love with the Ouse, which, at Huntingdon and then at Olney, was to be his companion for twenty-one years. He spoke of the river as being "the most agreeable circumstance in this part of the world," and added: "It is a noble stream to bathe in, and I shall make that use of it three times a week, having introduced myself to it for the first time this morning." We may picture him, "having just emerged from the Ouse," returning to his lodging to grapple with problems of domestic economy.

"Whatever you may think of the matter" [he wrote to Hill] "it is no easy thing to keep house for two people. A man cannot always live upon sheep's heads and liver and lights, like the lions in the tower; and a joint of meat, in so small a family, is an endless encumbrance. My butcher's bill for last week amounted to four shillings and tenpence. I set off with a leg of lamb, and was forced to give part of it away to my washerwoman. Then I made an experiment upon a sheep's heart, and that was too

H

little. Next I put three pounds of beef into a pie, and this had
like to have been too much, for it lasted three days, though my
landlord was admitted to a share of it. Then as to small beer, I
am puzzled to pieces about it. I have bought as much for a
shilling as will serve us at least a month, and it is grown sour
already. In short, I never knew how to pity poor housekeepers
before; but now I cease to wonder at the politic cast which their
occupation usually gives to their countenance, for it is really a
matter full of perplexity."

Notwithstanding these anxieties, Cowper liked Huntingdon
"extremely." It was, in fact, admirably suited to his needs.
He was keenly susceptible to environment, and, while he
detested London, he enjoyed to some extent being in the
world, though not of it. The compact, busy little town on the
Great North Road, with its two thousand inhabitants, offered
him just that degree of mingled quietness and bustle which he
craved. The removal, in 1767, to Olney, a comparatively
isolated and dull place, and less healthy, was in some respects
unfortunate.

Despite his shyness, Cowper was a magnet that soon
attracted not only "two or three odd scrambling fellows" like
himself, but a number of solid friends. His first caller at
Huntingdon was a woollen-draper—"a very healthy, wealthy,
sensible, sponsible man, and extremely civil." The draper
possessed a cold bath, and promised Cowper the use of it in
winter. He also lent him the *St. James's Chronicle*, and took
him to see Hinchinbrook House, the great mansion of the
district, formerly the seat of the Cromwells. The next visitor
was Mr. Hodgson, the minister of the parish—"very sensible,
a good preacher, and conscientious in the discharge of his
duties." In September, Cowper wrote to Lady Hesketh:

"Another acquaintance I have lately made is with a Mr.
Nicholson, a north country divine, very poor, but very good and
very happy. He reads prayers here twice a day, all the year
round, and travels on foot to serve two churches every Sunday
through the year, his journey out and home again being sixteen
miles. I supped with him last night. He gave me bread and
cheese, and a black jug of ale of his own brewing, and, doubtless,
brewed by his own hands. Another of my acquaintance is

Mr. ——, a thin, tall, old man, and as good as he is thin. He drinks nothing but water, and eats no flesh; partly, I believe, from a religious scruple (for he is very religious), and partly in the spirit of a valetudinarian. He is to be met with every morning of his life, at about six o'clock, at a fountain of very fine water, about a mile from the town, which is reckoned extremely like the Bristol spring. Being both early risers, and the only walkers in the place, we soon became acquainted. His great piety can be equalled by nothing but his great regularity, for he is the most perfect timepiece in the world."

Evangelicalism had not dulled Cowper's eye for humour or his interest in the mundane scene. His religious fervour, in its turn, was unabated. In the *Memoir* he tells us that, on the day of his arrival in Huntingdon, he felt, after his brother had left him, "like a traveller in the midst of an inhospitable desert," and that, having found a sequestered spot in the fields near the town, he sought and found succour in prayer. On the following morning he attended church for the first time since his recovery, and had difficulty in restraining his rapture. His heart was "full of love to all the congregation," especially to "a grave and sober person" who sat beside him and sang the psalm in a manner befitting his holy employment:

"Though my own voice was silent, being stopt by the intenseness of what I felt, yet my soul sung within me, and even leapt for joy. And when the gospel for the day was read, the sound of it was more than I could well support. Oh, what a word is the word of God, when the Spirit quickens us to receive it, and gives the hearing ear, and the understanding heart! The harmony of heaven is in it, and discovers its author. The parable of the prodigal son was the portion. I saw myself in that glass so clearly, and the loving kindness of my slighted and forgotten Lord, that the whole scene was realised to me, and acted over in my heart."

After the service he returned to the place where he had prayed on the previous day, and found the relief which he had there received had been "but the earnest of a richer blessing." He now seemed to speak with his Saviour "face to face, as a man conversing with his friend," except that his speech "was only in tears of joy, and groanings which cannot be uttered."

He could but say "how lovely"—not, with Jacob, "how dreadful"—"is this place."

In his letters of this period, he passes naturally from playful comment on his outward life to glowing expressions of his inner joy. At first he made Lady Hesketh his closest confidante, and also tried to convert her to his own now definitely settled form of faith:

"You, my dear cousin, yourself will be apt to think that I carry the matter too far, and that in the present warmth of my heart I make too ample a concession in saying, that I am *only now* a convert. You think I always believed, and I thought so too; but you were deceived, and so was I. I called myself indeed a Christian; but He who knows my heart knows that I never did a right thing, nor abstained from a wrong one, because I was so; but if I did either, it was under the influence of some other motive. And it is such seeming Christians, such pretending believers, that do most mischief to the cause, and furnish the strongest arguments to support the infidelity of its enemies: unless profession and conduct go together, the man's life is a lie, and the validity of what he professes itself is called in question."

There are other letters in this vein, and it is possible for us, reading between the lines, to guess the nature of Lady Hesketh's replies:

"You say, you hope it is not necessary for salvation [he writes again] to undergo the same afflictions that I have undergone. No! my dear cousin. God deals with His children as a merciful Father; He does not, as He Himself tells us, afflict willingly the sons of men. Doubtless there are many, who, having been placed by His good providence out of reach of any great evil and the influence of bad example, have from their infancy been partakers of the grace of His Holy Spirit, in such a manner as never to have allowed themselves in any grievous offence against Him. May you love Him more and more day by day; as every day, while you think upon Him, you will find Him more worthy of your love; and may you be finally accepted with Him for His sake, whose intercession for all His faithful servants cannot but prevail!"

Here the sincerity and loving purpose are unmistakable. But Lady Hesketh was still comparatively young. She was not yet a widow, and neither her husband nor she, prosperous but moral folk of the world, quite understood what all the pother was about. It was not in Lady Hesketh, even at this period, to be resentful towards Cowper; but apparently she did not encourage him to send her more sermons. The correspondence lapsed, and was not renewed until twenty years later. The zealot now addressed himself mainly to two other first-cousins. These were Mrs. Martin Madan—whose husband, the eminent divine, we have already met and shall meet again—and her sister-in-law, Mrs. Cowper, the Major's wife, who, probably under Madan's influence, and perhaps to the disgust of the Major, had been recruited to "enthusiasm." Soon, however, an event was to happen which made letter-writing on religious topics less of an indispensable outlet.

IV

Cowper had not been long in Huntingdon before, as he was leaving the church one morning, he was stopped by a young man. In a small town a stranger in church attracts notice, and certain members of the settled congregation feel it their duty to speak to him. But this particular stranger was obviously unusual. There was an air of mystery about him. He was shy, refined, and distinguished looking: altogether somewhat aloof. He ought, of course, to be welcomed; but who was to break the ice? We may guess that this question agitated the Unwin family for some weeks before it was decided that William Unwin, the son, who had indeed been much attracted to the new-comer, should act. The plunge was taken, and the ice proved to be thinner than it had appeared. That same afternoon William Unwin drank tea with Cowper, and intimacy was at once established.

"To my inexpressible joy [runs the *Memoir*] I found him one whose notions of religion were spiritual and lively. . . . We opened our hearts to each other at the first interview, and when we parted, I immediately retired to my chamber, and prayed the Lord, who had been the author, to be the guardian of our friendship, and to grant to it fervency and perpetuity, even unto death."

On September 14 Cowper sent the good tidings to Lady Hesketh:

"The last acquaintance I made here is with the race of the Unwins, consisting of father and mother, son and daughter, the most comfortable social folks you ever knew. The son is about twenty-one years of age, one of the most unreserved and amiable young men I ever conversed with. He is not yet arrived at that time of life when suspicion recommends itself to us in the form of wisdom, and sets everything but our own dear selves at an immeasurable distance from our esteem and confidence. Consequently he is known almost as soon as seen, and having nothing in his heart that makes it necessary for him to keep it barred and bolted, opens it to the perusal even of a stranger. The father is a clergyman, and the son is designed for orders. The design, however, is quite his own, proceeding merely from his being and having always been sincere in his belief and love of the Gospel."

On the Sunday following his first conversation with the son, whose portrait, then recently painted by Gainsborough, certainly suggests a sincere and attractive personality, Cowper dined at the Unwins' gabled red-brick house in the High Street, with its long garden extending to a row of lime-trees, beyond which lay a common. Susanna, the daughter, received him on his arrival. Lady Hesketh, to whom again an account of the visit was despatched, may have drawn false conclusions from Cowper's eloquent reference to the young lady. Anyhow, she asked for fuller details, as is apparent from Cowper's next letter to her, which, ending with a characteristic homily, was, as we have seen, the last he wrote her for two decades:

"I am glad you think so favourably of my Huntingdon acquaintance; they are indeed a nice set of folks, and suit me exactly. I should have been more particular in my account of Miss Unwin, if I had had materials for a minute description. She is about eighteen years of age, rather handsome and genteel. In her mother's company she says little; not because her mother requires it of her, but because she seems glad of that excuse for not talking, being somewhat inclined to bashfulness. There is the most remarkable cordiality between all the parts of the family; and the mother and daughter seem to dote upon each other. The

first time I went to the house I was introduced to the daughter
alone; and sat with her near half an hour, before her brother
came in, who had appointed me to call upon him. Talking is
necessary in a *tête-à-tête*, to distinguish the persons of the drama
from the chairs they sit on: accordingly she talked a great deal,
and extremely well; and, like the rest of the family, behaved
with as much ease of address as if we had been old acquaintance."

But if, at this point, Lady Hesketh might still have entertained hopes or fears of an impending romance, the continua-
tion of the letter may have disappointed her—or set her mind
at rest:

"She [Susanna] resembles her mother in her great piety, who
is one of the most remarkable instances of it I have ever seen.
They are altogether the cheerfulest and most engaging family-
piece it is possible to conceive.

"Since I wrote the above, I met Mrs. Unwin in the street, and
went home with her. She and I walked together near two hours
in the garden, and had a conversation which did me more good
than I should have received from an audience of the first prince
of Europe. That woman is a blessing to me, and I never see
her without being the better for her company. I am treated
in the family as if I was a near relation, and have been repeatedly invited to call upon them at all times. You know what a
shy fellow I am; I cannot prevail with myself to make so much
use of this privilege as I am sure they intend I should; but
perhaps this awkwardness will wear off hereafter."

The awkwardness did wear off. Cowper's growing familiarity with the Unwins was soon communicated to Joseph Hill:

"They treat me more like a near relation than a stranger, and
their house is always open to me. The old gentleman carries
me to Cambridge in his chaise. He is a man of learning and
good sense, and as simple as parson Adams. His wife has a very
uncommon understanding, has read much to excellent purpose,
and is more polite than a duchess. The son, who belongs to
Cambridge, is a most amiable young man, and the daughter
quite of a piece with the rest of the family. They see but little
company, which suits me exactly; go when I will, I find a house
full of peace and cordiality in all its parts, and I am sure to hear
no scandal, but such discourse instead of it as we are all better
for. You remember Rousseau's description of an English

morning; such are the mornings I spend with these good
people; and the evenings differ from them in nothing, except
that they are still more snug, and quieter."

The date of this letter is October 25. Less than three weeks
later, Cowper entered the Unwin household as a paying guest.

The circumstances which led to this move are recorded in
the *Memoir*. After four months in lodgings at Huntingdon,
Cowper found himself "in a state of desertion." The communion which he had so long maintained with the Lord "was
suddenly interrupted." This, as Goldwin Smith says, "is his
theological version of the case; the rationalistic version
immediately follows: 'I began to dislike my solitary situation,
and to fear I should never be able to weather out the winter
in so lonely a dwelling.'" But, as Goldwin Smith recognised,
despite his touch of satire, the theological and the natural
man are in large degree interdependent. Cowper of all men
most needed a home; and, as things happened, he heard that
one of the Rev. Morley Unwin's pupils had just left for
Cambridge. Would it be possible, he wondered, for him to
fill the vacancy as a boarder in that "special good house" in
the High Street? No sooner had the thought struck him than
he was filled with remorse for such "want of submission to
the Lord's Will." Nevertheless, the hope persisted, until his
"mutinous and disobedient heart" cried: "Give me the
blessing, or else I die." He tried to concentrate his attention
on other matters; but one evening some words—"The Lord
God of truth will do this"—rang with such importunity
through his mind that he was convinced they were not of his
own production, and assumed them to be an "assurance of
success." He "immediately began to negotiate the affair,
and in a few days it was entirely concluded." He adds that
he found his new abode "a place of rest prepared for me by
God's own hand, where He has blessed me with a thousand
mercies—and communion with His dear disciples." The
Memoir ends with the supplication: "May nothing but
death interrupt our union." Death and marriage were early
to break up the family circle; but, so far as Cowper and Mrs.
Unwin were concerned, the prayer was abundantly answered.

Though his account of the father, on first acquaintance, was

complimentary, it is doubtful if Cowper's regard for Morley
Unwin deepened with greater intimacy. Unwin, who was
much older than his wife, had formerly been master of the
Free School, and lecturer to the two churches, in Huntingdon.
He left there, apparently in 1742, to become Rector of
Grimston, near King's Lynn, where he married Mary Cawthorne, the daughter of a draper at Ely, who already evinced
considerable culture and literary taste. Even while living at
Grimston, Unwin (after the manner of too many clergymen
of the period) delegated most of his work to a curate, and,
probably in 1748, he became non-resident. He came back to
Huntingdon, where he prepared a few pupils for the University. He was also re-appointed to the lectureship of St.
Mary's; but the parish books, says Canon Benham, "contain
several resolutions of censure upon him for neglect of duty,
and once he was nearly dismissed." The return to Huntingdon, it is only fair to add, was prompted by Mrs. Unwin, who
found both the situation and the people of Grimston too
"restricted" for her liking.

Mrs. Unwin was no born saint. She was, to the end, very
human. But she had obviously come under the influence of
the Evangelical Revival and her religion was already, by the
time when Cowper met her, more than a formality or—what
constituted one of the main perils of "enthusiasm"—an
emotional indulgence. It is equally clear that she steadily
"advanced in wisdom and stature." The phrase, applied to
her, is not rhetorical. In her later years, through the growing
fame of Cowper, her circle of acquaintances was considerably
widened, so that we have not only Cowper's own testimony
to the beauty of her character, but that of many and diverse
witnesses. Her essential sanctity is established beyond dispute, and it is no more necessary to emphasise the fact than
it is to enlarge upon the perfect mutual affection between
herself and the poet. The loss of a mother in childhood may
be, to a sensitive child, an irremediable disaster; but fate
made the best possible atonement to Cowper when it brought
Mrs. Unwin into his life. He had not long shared her home
before he said she "has almost a maternal affection for me,
and I have something very like a filial one for her, and her

son and I are brothers." A little later he wrote: "My future
expenses in the hosiery line will be small, for Mrs. Unwin
knits all my stockings, and would knit my hats too, if that
were possible." The gradual deepening of the bond—immortalised many years later in the "Sonnet to Mrs. Unwin"
and the lines "To Mary"—is one of the commonplaces of
literary history.

There is no need to gild Mrs. Unwin's halo. What does
perhaps need stressing is the fact that she was not only good,
but accomplished. "She was in truth," says Bagehot, "a
most excellent person—in mind and years much older than
the poet [1]—as it were by profession elderly, able in every
species of preserve, profound in salts, and pans, and jellies—
culinary by taste; by tact and instinct motherly and house-
wifish." Bagehot adds that she was not "without some less
larderiferous qualities"; but the main impression he suggests
is that Mrs. Unwin, in point of mental refinement, was little
more than a superior cook-general. Bagehot alone is patron-
ising towards Mrs. Unwin. Yet his essential view of her is
one which, despite its demonstrable falsity, persists in many
minds, as does the idea that Cowper, pathetically domesticated,
spent most of his leisure hours in holding wool for her to
wind. He *did* occasionally hold her skeins: why, indeed,
should not a man sometimes perform that innocent, useful,
and (when once the necessary skill has been attained) delightfully soothing function? But that is far from being the whole
of the story.

I would not, in this matter of "salts, and pans, and jellies,"
be misunderstood. I have no wish to defend Mrs. Unwin
against the charge of having soiled her hands. From the
allusions in Cowper's letters to "receipts" for cakes and other
comestibles, it is clear that, like many other sensible women,
she was not a stranger in her own kitchen, and that on occasion she could herself prepare the dinner. So much the more
honour to her! From Cowper's references to "servants" and
to his "genteel way" of living, however, it is equally manifest,
and in the interest of a truthful picture must be pointed out,
that the Unwin establishment was a comparatively "polite"

---

[1] Mrs. Unwin was in fact seven years older than Cowper.

one, and that Mrs. Unwin's abilities and interests were many-
sided. The Evangelical movement admittedly drew a large
proportion of its recruits from among the unlettered masses.
But Wesley, its predominant figure, was himself, in every
point of breeding and acquirement, a gentleman and a
scholar; and the Revival had a considerable leaven of culture.
There is ample proof that Mrs. Unwin had studied intelligently the classics of poetry and religion; the Revival had its
own by no means negligible literature; and she could
thoroughly enjoy with Cowper a narrative of travel or
adventure. As she sat bespectacled in her high chair in the
evenings, knitting her stockings with the finest of needles, it
was not as a bored slave that she listened by the hour to
Cowper's reading of Milton or Homer. The poet's sensitiveness would soon have detected the well-intentioned deceit,
and the readings would have been discontinued. The fact
that she was both second mother and boon companion to
Cowper for nearly thirty years would itself be enough to
determine for us alike the quality and range of her character.
But we have, again, abundant direct evidence that she was
homely and practical, yet cultivated; spiritually earnest, yet
gay.

It is with no feeling of discrepancy that, having just written
the word "gay," I now quote part of the familiar letter which,
in October 1766, Cowper addressed to the Major's wife:

"Having told you how we *do not* spend our time, I will next
say how we do. We breakfast commonly between eight and
nine; till eleven we read either the Scripture, or the sermons of
some faithful preacher of those holy mysteries; at eleven we
attend divine service, which is performed here twice every day;
and from twelve to three we separate, and amuse ourselves as
we please. During that interval I either read in my own apartment, or walk, or ride, or work in the garden. We seldom sit
an hour after dinner; but, if the weather permits, adjourn to the
garden, where, with Mrs. Unwin and her son, I have generally
the pleasure of religious conversation till tea-time. If it rains,
or is too windy for walking, we either converse within doors, or
sing some hymns of Martin's [1] collection; and by the help of

---

[1] Martin Madan, who was in his day a well-known hymn-writer.

Mrs. Unwin's harpsichord, make up a tolerable concert, in which our hearts, I hope, are the best and most musical performers. After tea we sally forth to walk in good earnest. Mrs. Unwin is a good walker, and we have generally travelled about four miles before we see home again. When the days are short, we make this excursion in the former part of the day, between church-time and dinner. At night we read and converse, as before, till supper, and commonly finish the evening either with hymns or a sermon, and last of all the family are called to prayers."

Some of Cowper's biographers have expressed sober or mock horror at this revelation. And it must be admitted that the Evangelicals did excessively indulge in religious discourse. Wesley realised the danger, and warned his followers against it. Writing, for instance, to a friend in 1768, he says: "But, were these or those of ever so excellent a spirit, you converse with them too long. 'Three or four hours'! One had need to be an angel, not a man, to converse for four hours at once to any purpose. In the latter part of such a conversation we shall doubtless lose all the profit we had gained before." [1] Nevertheless, it is a common temptation to carry things too far, and history is the record of a swinging pendulum. The Evangelical Revival was a necessary revolt against religious apathy or static faith; its over-emphasis— while, ideally speaking, a weakness—was needed, as things go in this world, to redress the balance. In any case, the question of "gaiety" is unaffected. "I need not tell you," added Cowper in the letter just quoted, "that such a life as this is consistent with the utmost cheerfulness; accordingly we are all happy, and dwell together in unity as brethren." Through all surface changes of time and manners, "'tis in ourselves that we are thus or thus." Essential mirth may underlie outward sobriety no less than outward pleasure may hide inward boredom.

V

Though his shrinking from publicity soon made him abandon the idea, Cowper in 1766 had thoughts of taking holy

[1] *The Letters of John Wesley.* Standard Edition. Edited by John Telford. 1931. Volume V, p. 84.

orders. Not only was he afire with religious zeal, while
lacking definite occupation: he may have been inspired by
the example of several well-known divines, including Maddock, Madan, and Romaine, who, like himself, had studied
for the bar in early life. With two of these clergymen, as also
with the famous Dr. Thomas Haweis,[1] he was personally
associated at this time. Abraham Maddock held a living at
Kettering; while Madan, Cowper's cousin, often visited
Huntingdon in the course of his travels, and Cowper sometimes accompanied him on his preaching tours in the district.
All these clerics were Calvinists.

Madan became involved in two notorious controversies
during his career. Feeling ran strong on both of the opposing
sides, and has so coloured all available estimates of him that it
is provokingly difficult to form a clear impression of the man.
He was the elder son of Colonel Martin Madan, M.P. of
Hertingfordbury, and of Judith, daughter of Judge Spencer
Cowper, the poet's aunt. Born in 1726, he attended Westminster School, and graduated at Christ Church, Oxford, in
1746. He was called to the bar two years later, and joined a
convivial club in London. Being a good mimic, he was
commissioned by his fellow-members to hear John Wesley
preach and to reproduce his antics for their entertainment.
He went to scoff, but remained to pray. On returning to the
club, he was asked if he had "taken the old Methodist off."
"No, gentlemen," he replied, "but he has taken me off."
Though converted by Wesley, he soon became a Calvinistic
Methodist under the influence of David Jones and William
Romaine, and was ordained through Lady Huntingdon's
efforts.[2] With his striking personality and fine voice, the

---

[1] Haweis was born in 1734 and died in 1820. From 1764 onwards he was Vicar
of Aldwinkle, Northamptonshire, but his eloquence and originality secured him
a national reputation. In 1768 he became one of Lady Huntingdon's chaplains
and manager of her newly opened theological college at Trevecca. He was
Madan's curate at the Lock Hospital, and also a director of the London Missionary
Society.

[2] Selina, Countess of Huntingdon (1707-1791), the leader of " the genteel
Methodists," was the daughter of Washington Shirley, second Earl Ferrers. She
joined the first Methodist society in Fetter Lane, London, in 1739, and on the
death in 1746 of her husband, Theophilus Hastings, ninth Earl of Huntingdon,
devoted her wealth and energy to promoting, on its Calvinistic side, the work of
the Revival. She built sixty-four chapels in various parts of England, selected

"lawyer turned divine" at once attracted notice. In 1750 he was appointed Chaplain to the Lock Hospital, near Hyde Park Corner, to which seat-holders were admitted as well as the patients. The services were at first held in a parlour; but Madan's preaching became so popular that a chapel was built for him in 1760. Thenceforward, for many years, it provided the odd spectacle of a building filled partly by the destitute and the depraved, and partly by the most wealthy Evangelical congregation in London.

The first of the two Madan controversies arose in 1767. Kimpton, who held the patronage, had wished to sell the advowson of the living of Aldwinkle, which was about to become vacant. Failing to negotiate a sale, he presented the living to Thomas Haweis, who had been recommended by Madan. Three years later, Kimpton, now in straitened circumstances, received a tempting offer for the advowson, and asked Haweis to resign, declaring that he had been appointed under some such reservation. Haweis, acting on Madan's advice, refused. Madan was widely and violently attacked, being accused of simony and misrepresentation. Finally, Lady Huntingdon bought the advowson from Kimpton for a thousand pounds, the sum named by the other would-be purchaser. Lady Huntingdon wished Madan to make a qualified apology. He refused, and she did not insist. "That Madan's conduct in this matter did not forfeit the confidence of his friends," says one writer,[1] "may be deduced from the action of Lord Apsley (later Lord Bathurst) in soon after appointing him his domestic chaplain; but Lady Huntingdon and others certainly considered that he held to a narrow and

and employed her own chaplains, and converted an old mansion at Trevecca, South Wales, into a theological college, of which Cheshunt College, Cambridge, is the lineal descendant. Her chief aim was to evangelise her own class, and her "spiritual routs," sometimes attended by Chesterfield, Walpole, and Bolingbroke, became recognised social functions. Wilful and imperious, she was fundamentally sincere, and her work doubtless bore some genuine fruit. But John Wesley disliked her theological views and was not alone in regarding with suspicion the alliance between religion and fashion. Till 1779, Lady Huntingdon and her chaplains continued to be members of the Church of England; but circumstances then forced her to take shelter under the Toleration Act, and thus to constitute herself legally a dissenter. See *The Countess of Huntingdon and her Circle*. By Sarah Tytler. 1907.

[1] *Dictionary of National Biography.*

legal view of the circumstances, in opposition to considerations of equity."

The second storm broke in 1780. Madan published his *Thelyphthora, or A Treatise on Female Ruin*, in which he argued that polygamy is a state that was not restricted to the Jews, but had divine sanction for all races and time. The writer may have been prompted by his work as hospital chaplain. "If," says Canon Benham, "he ever looked sorrowfully upon his charge at the Lock, and thought how each fallen woman had been once an innocent child, and might have been a happy wife with children round her knees, is it to be wondered at that he pondered the question, 'On what theory *might* these have been wives?'" Madan, at any rate, turned for justification of polygamy to his Bible, which, like all theologians of his time, he took to be of equal authority in all its parts. This literal view of inspiration, sincerely held as a theory, had in practice one inevitable result. Those portions of Scripture were chosen that suited the seeker's own ends; the rest were ignored. By this process, Madan, citing chapter and verse, was able to build up an impressive "Christian" argument in support of his thesis. In the same manner, as we know, the Devil can quote the Bible to his own purpose, and, though Madan's intention may have been good, his fellow-divines, scared by visions of Turkish harems, and not pausing to weigh the logic of a treatise based upon methods which they themselves put to more conventional uses, thought that in this case the Devil was actually at work. The book provoked hostility and scorn among religious professors of every kind. Lady Huntingdon was indignant, and Madan retired into private life. Cowper, whose regard for his cousin was rudely shaken, wrote a satirical attack entitled *Anti-Thelyphthora*, which was published anonymously in 1781. It is an allegory of lustful lovers, discovered and put to the sword by a true knight; and, though he says that

> "*what old Chaucer's merry page befits,*
> *The chaster muse of modern days omits,*"

the poem shows that the writer could use sensuous imagery when he liked. Some critics have even called it "coarse." It is so only by comparison with Cowper's own normal standard.

In the *Dictionary of National Biography* we are told that obloquy did not sour Madan. The writer of the article, who credits him with "activity, zeal, gentleness, and love of study," and who says that his sermons were characterised by directness and earnestness rather than by rhetorical display, adds that "no impartial reader of the two controversies can fail to acquit Madan of insincerity and of self-seeking." Yet he has to admit that many contemporaries saw the Chaplain of the Lock in a different light. Nor can we ignore the doubts of Wesley. It may be argued that Wesley would naturally be prejudiced against one who, having been converted by himself, had turned to Calvinism. But Wesley, while he vigorously opposed Calvinism as a theology, was charitable towards individual Calvinists, and even ready to use them, if he felt that their hearts were better than their creeds. No one, again, was less swayed by petty personal jealousy. His judgment was usually cool and impartial and, while women might deceive him, he was a shrewd reader of men. Even he, however, was often "at a loss" concerning "Mr. Madan." He found his character a little baffling, and his view of it underwent repeated modifications. One thing is clear: Wesley, long before the *Thelyphthora* episode, distrusted Madan's doctrines and style of preaching, and seems sometimes to have suspected him of trimming his sails to the breeze of personal success. He accuses Madan of making "the imaginary transfer of Christ's righteousness serve as a cover for the unrighteousness of mankind." [1] Elsewhere he includes Madan among several preachers whose followers are "thoroughly conformed to the maxims, the spirit, the fashions, and customs of the world." He dislikes their "*amorous* way of praying" and their "luscious way of talking." [2] In other letters Wesley reveals his impression of Madan as one for whom preaching was a fashionable art, and religion a theory rather than a vital call to "the loving God with all our heart, soul, and strength, and the loving all men as Christ loved us,"

[1] *The Letters of John Wesley.* Standard Edition. Volume III, p. 249.
[2] *Ibid.* Volume V, p. 83.

which made for Wesley himself the sum of "pure religion
and undefiled."

However much Madan's personality may elude us, I claim
that two facts, which bear upon Cowper's history, are incon-
trovertible.   Madan, as all the authorities agree, was more
definitely Calvinistic than John Newton; and, secondly,
Cowper had long been familiar with Madan before Newton
entered his life.   If Cowper had not had previous intimacy
with his cousin, would he have sent for him during the crisis
of 1763?   Despite its conventional references to the ungodli-
ness of his youth and early manhood, the *Memoir* reveals that
Cowper in his student days had thought much about religion
and had "been always an industrious and diligent inquirer
into the evidences."   And though, as he says, he used to think
Madan "an enthusiast," would he have turned to him for
"balm" if he had not already had strong leanings, intuitive
or acquired, towards Madan's own point of view?   At Huntingdon, moreover, he renewed acquaintance with "Martin,"
and sometimes accompanied him on preaching tours.   He thus
became friendly with other Calvinistic clergymen.

It is probable that Madan, Haweis, and others had a considerable influence upon Cowper.   This, in the circumstances,
was almost inevitable.   I do not wish, however, in the absence
of direct evidence, to suggest that Madan, or anyone else,
actually "converted" the poet.   Indeed, though I have said
that Cowper plainly underwent a genuine spiritual experience
in Dr. Cotton's house at St. Albans, I doubt if he were ever
"converted," in the strict sense, at all.   Why he became a
Calvinist may more appropriately be discussed when we
survey the Evangelical Revival as a whole.   Meanwhile, I
have reiterated certain facts because, while they have escaped
the due notice of previous biographers, they are of prime
significance.   They show that Cowper had moved intimately
in Calvinistic circles in the more formative years of his life,
and that, whether the later influence of Newton were on
balance good or injurious, at all events Newton was not
responsible for making Cowper a Calvinist—or even, as we
shall see, for accentuating his Calvinism.

But enough of anticipatory allusions.   The time has now

I

come for Newton himself to enter the scene. On Sunday morning, July 2, 1767—nineteen months after Cowper had taken up residence with the family—the Rev. Morley Unwin, riding to conduct a service at Graveley, fell from his horse while passing through Godmanchester. "At nine o'clock," Cowper wrote to Hill, "he was in perfect health, and as likely to live twenty years as either of us; and before ten was stretched speechless and senseless upon a flock bed, in a poor cottage, where (it being impossible to remove him) he died on Thursday evening. I heard his dying groans, the effect of great agony, for he was a strong man, and much convulsed in his last moments." After a characteristic Evangelical homily, Cowper proceeded:

> "The effect of it upon my circumstances will only be a change of a place of abode. For I shall still, by God's leave, continue with Mrs. Unwin, whose behaviour to me has always been that of a mother to a son. We know not yet where we shall settle, but we trust that the Lord, whom we seek, will go before us and prepare a rest for us."

The new place of abode was decided by a fortuitous (or "providential") event. Within a few days of her husband's death, Mrs. Unwin received a visit from John Newton, then perpetual curate of Olney, in Buckinghamshire, whose absentee rector, Moses Browne, lived at Blackheath. A common friend had told Newton of Mrs. Unwin's bereavement, and Newton, ever ready to answer such calls, rode over to Huntingdon to condole with her. Not only did he and she take to each other; there seems to have been instant sympathy between him and Cowper. It was an odd chance that brought into lasting friendship two men whose lives had hitherto been so totally different, and whose characters, to a superficial view, were so completely dissimilar. Was it a case of the attraction of opposites? Or shall we find, on closer scrutiny, that each was more truly the complement of the other than has yet been recognised?

Be that as it may, Mrs. Unwin, whose son was now at Cambridge, was faced with the necessity of making a move. Naturally she wished to settle in a place where there was an

Evangelical clergyman, as a modern Quaker in similar circumstances would, if possible, select a spot within range of a
Friends' Meeting.   And in one respect, if to a much greater
degree, the Evangelicals in 1767 were like the Quakers of
to-day: their numerical strength was small in comparison
with their influence.   There was not a wide field of choice
open to Mrs. Unwin; and, having prayerfully considered and
rejected several alternatives, she fixed upon Olney, where
she, her daughter, and Cowper could "sit under" an already
much loved friend.   Newton engaged for them a residence in
the market-place; but, pending its readiness, he invited them
to be his guests at the Rectory.   They moved to Olney on
September 14.   On December 9 they took possession of the
house which is now, thanks to the late Thomas Wright, one
of the best literary museums in the world.

Chapter Seven

THE EVANGELICAL REVIVAL

I

THE EVANGELICAL REVIVAL cannot be understood without some knowledge of the general condition of religion in the eighteenth century. By "religion" I mean Christianity; and that, for our purpose, implies Protestantism. As his friendship with the Throckmortons will show, Cowper could tolerate and like Roman Catholics as individuals. But theoretically, in common with all other Protestants of his time, he deemed Roman Catholicism hardly better than heathenism. The Test Act, which prevented both Catholic and Protestant non-conformists from holding State or municipal office, was the cornerstone of the Revolution settlement. Roman Catholics were now allowed freedom of worship; but fear of them, because they were suspected of Jacobitism and later of complicity in the French Revolution, continued throughout our period, and in the Gordon Riots of 1780 woke temporarily again into violent opposition. The full legal emancipation of Catholics, as of dissenters, belongs to the Victorian age.

The discussion of religion is fraught with difficulties. "Christianity" has different meanings for different people. It may, for example, signify adherence to an historical tradition: the acceptance of divine authority as progressively revealed, through the Holy Spirit, to Christ's Church. Another view is summed up in the phrase "Back to Christ Himself." Yet Jesus did not lay down a code of rules, and to assume that He did is to run the danger of falling into a narrow legalism. Jesus set forth general principles, admitting of diverse interpretations in detail. Above all, He revealed a new spirit. But may we gain that spirit by mere emulation, or can we ally ourselves with it only through supernatural means? Do these, again, involve recognised sacraments, or may every man, whether a member of any church or of none, have direct spiritual access to God? And is God one, or three in one? Some of us may be in no doubt respecting our own attitude on these points: but others, with equal sincerity, think otherwise.

Even if we could agree about definitions and implications, we should still have cause to lament with Browning: "How very hard it is to be a Christian!" As William Law says: "the infirmities of human life make such food and raiment necessary for us, as Angels do not want," and, though it is in our normal working life that the spirit should find its truest expression, the business of gaining a livelihood in an imperfect world involves some unavoidable degree of compromise. Furthermore, while religion should imply a vital balance between clear-sighted faith and conforming action, each individual has temperamental peculiarities which make him strong at certain points and weak elsewhere. One may have keen spiritual vision, yet find another law in his members, warring against the law of the mind; another may be warm-hearted and diligent, yet err through lack of insight. There is an infinite number of types and gradations. At our best, we are but "hints and facets of One, the Eternal."

There is a further complication. Religion did not begin with Christianity; it is as old as the race itself. Primitive man, looking about him, found the world inexplicable and sometimes frightening. "To people who had not yet learnt to count," says Mr. Kellett, "even the sun's diurnal course must have appeared mysterious, as beyond doubt his alternating tyranny and tenderness must have been past finding out, and his motives for hiding his face during an eclipse must have been sinister. He was assuredly now angry and now pleased: but *why* was he either the one or the other?"[1] The explanations given were, of course, anthropomorphic. Every natural force was personified; wind and stars and rain became deities, to be flattered, cajoled, or otherwise placated. The idea of an "angry" and "jealous" God, demanding propitiation through the vicarious sacrifice of His Son, bears an obvious likeness to primitive beliefs. Theology is now moving towards a sounder view of the Atonement. But, even where

[1] *A Short History of Religion.* By E. E. Kellett. 1933.

ancient superstition has been discarded in theory, it yet lies upon us with the weight of custom, "heavy as frost." Religion, in Dr. R. H. Moberly's words, is still

> "constantly confused with the quite different attitude towards the same objects, for which the proper name is magic. . . . In magic man is trying to use the gods for his own ends; in religion he is trying to get into touch with them in order that he may understand and appreciate their ends, and so may be used by them. To worship God because one deems Him really worshipful is quite different from paying Him attention mainly because one wants to get something out of Him."

The religion of Christ, seen in the long perspective of time, is comparatively new. It has had an uphill fight against human passions, limitations, and conservatism; and inevitably, after the rapture of the Early Church was spent, it became coloured by ancient myth and contemporary paganism. Add the facts that man is naturally a lover of argument for its own sake, that many people are always ready to use religion as a cloak for ulterior ends, and that organisations, though necessary, tend to stultify their original inspiration, and we have reasons enough why even to-day "Christianity" presents a picture often sadly incongruous with the spirit and teaching of its Founder. If, on the other hand, we consider how formidable the obstacles have really been, the surprise, after all, may be that, "spite of this flesh," Christianity has so impressively "made head, gained ground upon the whole."

II

Many Protestant apologists speak as if Luther immediately introduced a more Christian spirit into Christianity. If he did, it was in very small measure. To say this is not to deny the importance of the Reformation; it is only to point out that the new road begun by Luther took a long time in construction: indeed it is still far from being completed. Luther made possible a more direct spiritual access to God; but Biblical criticism, while it owes its existence to him, did not come even within sight of its true goal until the nineteenth century. Moved by sincere revolt against spiritual corruption,

Luther turned from Rome; but, being a man of his own day, he struck out his new path without having any clear sense of its ultimate destination: and soon it led to Geneva. The reformers left a Church that claimed to be founded upon a Rock. Now, and for long afterwards, another rock stood between themselves and progress.

The Reformed religion had but exchanged an infallible Church for an infallible Book. Little spiritual gain accrued from freedom to read the Scriptures so long as they were regarded as being literally and equally inspired. And if Luther himself showed some glimmering sense of discrimination, his followers displayed none. The laity was mainly illiterate, and clergy and scholars were under the supposed necessity of accepting the imprecatory psalms or the "Chronicles" of slaughter as being no less truly a revelation of God than the loftiest vision of Isaiah or the Sermon on the Mount. It was impossible, in these circumstances, to build up a theology that was at once logical and distinctively Christian. Thus a vast number of competing theologies arose, reflecting the minds of different thinkers. According to the man, so did the choice of Scripture vary. Luther's mellower nature, if still very inadequately, leaned more towards the New Testament than did that of most of his successors; Calvin's religion in its "neat" form—though it was often a cheerful one to those who felt themselves predestined, giving them, as in the case of the Scottish Covenanters, immense assurance and driving power—was essentially Jewish rather than Christian, even though Calvin had but made almost Euclidian propositions from a superficial reading of certain passages in Paul's Epistles, which he falsely regarded as *treatises*.

It is needless to dwell upon the religious disputes and struggles of the two succeeding centuries. If ethics and the social implications of Christianity tend largely to engage us to-day, the reverse was then the rule. The so-called wars of religion were really wars of theology, concerned with questions of belief, ritual, or church government rather than with what we should now deem vital spiritual issues. Faith, while consequently a prolific cause of terrestrial strife, was preoccupied with the world to come. The problem that engaged it was not how to bring the Kingdom of God upon earth, but wherein lay the best specific for personal salvation—and, if needs were, the forcible salvation of others—in the future state. Religion in Tudor and Stuart times, and during the Commonwealth interlude, was in one sense virile and widespread. Theological controversy was as much a matter of popular interest in taverns as football and racing are to-day. But, while every age has had its seers and its saints, it is a fair generalisation that, until towards the close of the seventeenth century, the claim of ethics had hardly been seriously considered. Nor must we

> "*blame*
> *Too much the sons of men and barbarous laws.*
> *These were the rough ways of the world till now.*"

A change came in England, as we have seen, with the Revolution of 1688. Old passions and feuds had spent their fury, and an age of tolerance, soon aided by Walpole's political regime, set in. The new tolerance was far indeed from being complete, but it marked a great advance. The intellectual reaction was sweeping. Religion was brought down from heaven—or, rather, from the clouds of metaphysics—to solid earth. Reason, which had too long been an outcast from men's minds, now established itself as the prime standard of values. The surface vitality of religion inevitably received a check. There was a decline in church attendance and in similar formalities. In every period when theology undergoes rapid modification, many whose allegiance to the older ideas and habits had been merely conventional abandon religious observances altogether. This tendency has been seen again in our own times, and we may take courage from the lesson of history. When Christianity is apparently baffled, it is only that it may soon fight better.

It is true that, during the reigns of the first two Georges, tolerance often declined into apathy, and that many of the clergy—unashamed pluralists, place-seekers, and pleasure-hunters—displayed a spirit anything but commendable. Cowper, whose own sincerity made him abhor the "wolf in sheep's clothing," has described a clerical type then far too common:

> " *But, loose in morals, and in manners vain,*
> *In conversation frivolous, in dress*
> *Extreme, at once rapacious and profuse;*
> *Frequent in park with lady at his side,*
> *Ambling and prattling scandal as he goes;*
> *But rare at home, and never at his books,*
> *Or with his pen, save when he scrawls a card;*
> *Constant at routs, familiar with a round*
> *Of ladyships—a stranger to the poor;*
> *Ambitious of preferment for its gold,*
> *And well-prepar'd, by ignorance and sloth,*
> *By infidelity and love of world,*
> *To make God's work a sinecure; a slave*
> *To his own pleasures and his patron's pride:*
> *From such apostles, oh, ye mitred heads,*
> *Preserve the church! and lay not careless hands*
> *On skulls that cannot teach, and will not learn.*"

But the poet himself reminds us that there was also to be found the kind of clerk

> "*whose heart is warm,*
> *Whose hands are pure, whose doctrines and whose life,*
> *Coincident, exhibit lucid proof*
> *That he is honest in the sacred cause.*"

From other sources, too, we know that there were many individual clergymen who, if they were neither prophets nor saints, at least spread a quiet leaven of morality and culture among their parishioners. And the fact remains that even the prevailing stagnation served a useful end. It provided a breathing-time. It enabled reason to be heard; and its voice was sorely needed.

In many instances, of course, the pendulum swung too far. Reason became isolated and exalted for its own sake. There was a rapid drift towards Socinianism both in the Church of England and among the dissenters, whose many "academies," while admirably promoting general education, had sometimes a less happy spiritual effect.[1] Whatever may be thought of Unitarianism on purely theological grounds, it tends in prac-

---

[1] A good description of a typical dissenting academy will be found in *Philip Doddridge, D.D.*, by Charles Stanford, 1880. For a list of the academies in the days of their prime see *The Cambridge History of English Literature*, Volume X. It is interesting to note that some eminent Churchmen, including Bishop Butler himself, were educated at one or other of these institutions.

tice to the undue enthronement of intellect. Then also there
were the Deists. They discarded Scriptural revelation and
supernatural religion altogether, reducing God to an absentee
Creator, Who, having wound up the mechanism of the
universe, Himself stood apart from it. Eighteenth-century
records abound in allusions to the Socinian and Deistical controversies; but they left little permanent mark upon later
history, except that it was in reply to the Deists, though he
does not mention them by name, that Bishop Butler wrote
The Analogy of Religion.

Butler's vision was hedged in by the common limits of pre-
Victorian times. The Bible for him was a single book, not a
library; and he assumed that personal salvation in a future
life was the aim of religion, which he identified with a scheme
of rewards and punishments. But—inspired by his reading
of Locke—he brought reason to bear upon theology. He
urged that, while we cannot have direct insight into what is
supernatural, we may at least assume the probability that
God's attributes and operations in the supernatural sphere
are not fundamentally different from what we observe them
to be in Nature and in human life. Hitherto, man had too
often seen God through the medium of undisciplined fancy,
or had created Him in his own metaphysical image. That
habit was not immediately subdued: it is not quite unknown
even to-day! Butler, however, exposed its folly, and made
indulgence in it less easy. He did more. Though he accepted
as natural man's preoccupation with personal salvation in the
world to come, he showed that, as rewards in this life are
generally the fruits of virtue, immortal joy must be *earned*.

The *Analogy* introduced sanity into theological discussion.
It gave men a sounder conception of God and a deeper sense
of moral responsibility. Yet the very aim and method of
Butler involved the defects of their virtues. The great need
of the time was for religion to be brought down to earth; but
ere long it showed signs of being content to remain there. And
Butler's influence unconsciously fostered that tendency. The
fantastic representations of God which had often hitherto been
made by those who claimed direct knowledge of Him awoke
in this good, sage, simple man an ineradicable suspicion of all

experimental religion. This misgiving characterised the
Latitudinarians as a whole, and explains their intense dislike
of "enthusiasm."

"Enthusiasm" had a different meaning in the eighteenth
century from that which it carries in popular usage to-day.
In a book which was not published until 1834, but which
nevertheless provides a reliable clue to the understanding of
a period when the ideas in question were more generally
widespread, enthusiasm is defined as being "not a term of
measurement, but of *quality*." [1] An "enthusiast" was not
necessarily one who eloquently declaimed or violently ranted.
He *might* incidentally do either of these things; and, if he
did, so much the worse. But "enthusiasm" in the pulpit was
judged by the *substance*, not the *manner*, of the preaching.
Though most Latitudinarian sermons were in fact polite
moral essays, a Latitudinarian divine could be perfervid in
oratory or gesticulation without, on that account alone,
incurring the dreaded charge.

"Reason" was in the ascendant. It had gained a hardly-
won victory in theology, and it also conformed with the social
taste of the time. If the Latitudinarians had to accept their
Bible whole, they found no more difficulty than their fiery
predecessors had done in selecting texts to prove the truth of
what they wished to believe, And it pleased them to imagine
that, for men of "reason," finality in religious revelation had
been attained, and that its practical obligations were now
clearly defined for all time. "True religion, unlike human
science," as Isaac Taylor put it, "was given to mankind in a
finished form, and is to be learned, not improved; and though
the most capacious human mind is nobly employed while
concentrating all its vigour upon the acquirement of this
documentary learning, it is very fruitlessly, and very per-
niciously, occupied in attempting to give it a single touch of
amendment." A "fictitious piety," again, "corrupts or
petrifies the heart not less certainly than does a romantic
sentimentality"; while through imagination, as distinct from
reason, a man "becomes a visionary, who lives on better terms
with angels and with seraphs than with his children, servants,

---

[1] *The Natural History of Enthusiasm.* By Isaac Taylor.

or neighbours; or he is one who, while he reverences the 'thrones, dominions, and powers' of the invisible world, vents his spleen in railing at all dignities and powers of earth." [1]

One cannot but appreciate the large element of truth in these protests. It is equally impossible not to see the danger of complacency which lurked in them, or to realise how easily Latitudinarianism could be made the tool of *laissez-faire* in politics. Unlike the Deists, whom they scorned, the Latitudinarians did not deny the supernatural. But they liked to keep it in its place. There had been too many men in previous times who had pretended to have private access to God. Such familiarity bred contempt. It was in bad taste, and shocked feelings of "refinement" no less than it offended "reason." One could do one's duty to God without boasting of being His confidant. "Sir," said Bishop Butler to Wesley, "the pretending to extraordinary revelations and gifts of the Holy Ghost is a horrid thing; yes, Sir, it is a *very horrid thing*." It was not the first occasion in history when a great and good man has failed to recognise another who was to reap the field which he himself had ploughed.

III

"Canst thou by searching find out God? Canst thou find out the Almighty unto perfection?" Humanity, at any rate, will never for long abandon the quest. Latitudinarianism, as we have seen, was not always synonymous with apathy; it had a philosophy of its own, based on practical good sense and well suited to the particular conditions of the hour. Its weaknesses were that it appealed almost exclusively to the head and that it lacked the driving force which alone can make ethics fruitful unto life. The heart was bound to reassert itself; but it now did so in a more disciplined manner. The Wesleyan Revival had its ranters and its quacks. But so far was the movement as a whole from being one of superficial emotionalism that its practical benefits to society have nowhere been more vigor-

---

[1] Dr. Johnson in his Dictionary, quoting Locke, defined enthusiasm as " a vain belief in private revelation, a vain confidence in divine favour."

ously proclaimed than in the pages of Lecky,[1] the secular historian, and in those of two distinguished foreigners.[2]

Butler and his colleagues served their own generation well by isolating the claims of reason. Yet "reason" is, after all, a negative quality in itself; and it was not the monopoly of those to whom belongs the credit of having made its voice first clearly heard. Even Butler was compelled to have his hypothesis, though he reduced it to the bare minimum. William Law was more daring in his actual assumptions. But, if he afterwards became somewhat vaguely mystical, he was in earlier days hardly less rationalistic than Butler in the application of his theory. The *Serious Call to a Devout and Holy Life*, which appeared in 1728 and deeply influenced Wesley and other leaders of the coming Revival, had literary graces denied to Butler. Not the least charming feature of the book is the shrewd and quietly ironical portraiture of representative human types. But in pressing home his main argument that practice should conform to prayer, and that mere hypocrisy lies in "adding Christian devotion to a Heathen life," Law was strictly logical. And even he, though favouring experimental knowledge of God, had his feet well set on solid ground.

"Were it not our strict duty [he says] to live by reason, to devote all the actions of our lives to God, were it not absolutely necessary to walk before Him in wisdom and holiness and all heavenly conversation, doing everything in His Name, and for His glory, there would be no excellency or wisdom in the most heavenly prayers. Nay, such prayers would be absurdities; they would be like prayers for wings, when it is no part of our duty to fly."

As for Wesley himself—if again we admit his premise and allow for certain odd touches of credulity in him—no one in that age of reason was more a reasoner than he. Even when he was a child, his father—the warm-hearted but impulsive Rector of Epworth, who, though tracing his line back to notable dissenting theologians, roused the ire of his parish-

---

[1] *A History of the Eighteenth Century.* By W. E. H. Lecky. Volume II.
[2] *A History of the English People.* By Elie Halévy. *La Réaction de John Wesley dans l'Évolution du Protestantisme.* By M. Piette.

ioners by his fierce Toryism and High Churchmanship—said
of John Wesley that he "would do nothing—*non etiam
crepitare*—unless he could give a reason for it."

Wesley was thirty-five before he finally shed his father's
High Churchmanship. He never shed his theoretical Toryism. Quintessentially, however, he was the son of his mother:
he was, says Mr. Vulliamy,[1] "a Methodist from the cradle."
He was the fifteenth child born into that parsonage in the wild
Lincolnshire fens, among a people "drunken, surly, and
violent," though only five sisters and one brother were then
surviving. His mother, who was yet to have four more children, was one of the miracles of history. To be the wife of an
irascible, if affectionate, clergyman-farmer, often abstracted
in literary labours, and often in debt through ill-luck, bad
management, and a vengeful peasantry; not merely to
nurture a large brood of children, but to discipline them,
without cruelty, so that they even learned to "cry softly"; to
find time, amid incessant mundane cares, to give them all a
sound literary, theological, and moral training; and withal to
be able, in emergency, to carry on successfully her husband's
parochial work: such demands would have taxed all but
supreme gifts and character. To the end of her days she
continued to be John's confidante and adviser, and some of his
most important decisions, such as that of employing lay (or
"local") preachers when the Revival outgrew the strength of
the itinerating clergy, were made only upon her recom-
mendation. When we remember that she was also the
mother of Charles Wesley, who was an active preacher in the
earlier days of the Revival and incalculably enriched it with
his hymns, we may call Susannah Wesley, in every sense, the
true parent of Methodism.

Wesley in youth was a Prince Charming, who seemed destined for a conventionally distinguished career. This is not
the place in which to follow his amazing life in detail. I could
expatiate indefinitely about this "Sometime Fellow of Lincoln
College, Oxford," who, obeying (reluctantly at first) the
demands of reason and conscience, ceased to be a fastidious
artist in personal devotion and became the prophet of re-

[1] *John Wesley*. By C. E. Vulliamy. 1931.

generative love to the masses—travelling, though small and
not physically robust, thousands of miles a year on horseback
along execrable roads; preaching several times a day in the
open air, in all weathers and perhaps amid violent hostility;
visiting the sick; encouraging fellow-workers throughout
England and Ireland by letters sensitively framed to their
individual needs; and withal finding time not merely to
continue his classical and theological studies but to keep
abreast with contemporary thought, to interest himself in
science, to promote education, to spread views on medicine
and hygiene far in advance of their time, to found our oldest
surviving publising house, and to write and edit innumerable
books.

Here was no mere "revivalist," but a man truly sent of
God; whose physical and moral courage were so fused with
gentility that his calm eye could quell an angry mob; whose
spirit laid upon itself the lowliest as well as the highest duties,
so that he was not only the master-builder of the Evangelical
Revival, but also its carpenter; whose personality never
coarsened under strain or opposition; whose judgment of
others (save deliberate impostors) became more charitable as
he grew sterner in recognising his own endearingly human
faults; and whose disinterestedness was such that, though his
writings earned him the vast sum for his period of thirty
thousand pounds, he spent nothing on himself, but, Spartan
in habit, died in his eighty-eighth year, after a life of unremitting toil, with eighteen hours for his average working
day, possessed of two silver spoons. "Autocratic," to some
extent, he certainly was. But if ever there were a benevolent
despot, it was John Wesley. Of egotism, in the cruder sense,
he had none. His last thought as he lay dying, a very old
and very happy man, was not of the magnificent life's work
he had accomplished, but of the Master Whom he had served.
"The best of all is—God is with us." Such were his last
lucid words.

Wesley, I would again remind those who speak of eighteenth-century Evangelicalism as if it were a mere upwelling
of primitive emotion, in which a cultivated man like Cowper
could in no case have found real spiritual satisfaction, was a

gentleman and a scholar. Until approaching middle-age, he lived after the straitest sect of High Churchmen, if not a Pharisee, at least a formalist. He was a sacramentalist till the end, and, while the very vitality of the movement he had dominated made ultimate secession unavoidable, the Methodist Societies remained, while he lived, within the Establishment, though "orthodox" opposition made necessary the building of special chapels.[1]

We cannot here follow the successive stages of Wesley's conversion, beginning with his talk with the Moravians on his way to Georgia in 1735, and culminating three years later with the decisive "warming of the heart" which came to him when he went, "most unwillingly," to the meeting of a small religious society in Aldersgate Street, composed mainly of Church of England members, over whom Peter Boehler, the Moravian, presided. Even after his conversion, Wesley was still preoccupied with his own religious difficulties, and, though he was following Boehler's advice to "preach salvation by faith until you have it," he had not yet learnt the doctrine by doing the will. It was by chance that he found his true mission in life, and, through it, his full theological assurance. In 1738, George Whitefield, with his freer and more ebullient temperament, had returned from Georgia, where, unlike Wesley, he had been successful. His oratory now drew vast crowds, but his "enthusiasm" soon closed the churches against him. He started field preaching near Bristol, with amazing results, and appealed to Wesley for help. Every instinct in Wesley abhorred the idea. Nevertheless, even under premonition of death, he went; and, preaching to the savage colliers of Kingswood, John Wesley, by saving others, himself found salvation.

He eventually formulated his beliefs into doctrines. These need not detain us. We cannot give Wesley a place among the great intellectual reformers of the Church. "But if we place what is purely spiritual above what is purely intellectual, if the elevation of philosophy is still below the elevation of

---

[1] One of these new "preaching-houses" would occasionally be built—as by the spirited and unconventional William Grimshaw at Haworth—within a stone's throw of the parish church.

saintliness, then we can surely place him in the highest company of all." Thus, very finely, says Mr. Vulliamy, though elsewhere, of course, he recognises that Wesley, if he were no great or original thinker, had both a very scholarly and very alert mind. It was because until early middle life he was essentially an "intellectual" and an ascetic that emotion, when it was admitted, did not flood out his nature, but found disciplined channels for its true vitalisation. His power lay in the rare balance which he maintained between intellect and feeling; between revelation and experiment; between collective authority and individualism. It was this *oneness* of "the little grey man," neatly dressed in black and with long, silky hair curled over his shoulders, that was sensed by the rudest listener. Whitefield, though he was sincere, commanded every art of the orator. But, while his vast congregations were entranced, he did not make the penetrating and lasting effect which Wesley achieved without rhetoric or histrionics. People listened to Whitefield, said John Nelson, as to "a man that could play upon an instrument." Each individual in a crowd felt that Wesley was speaking directly to him.

Wesley was no more original as an administrator than as a philosopher. All his methods were invented by other people. "He did with other men's suggestions," says Dr. Rattenbury, "what Shakespeare did with other men's plots and Holinshed's chronicles—he made them live." [1] Yet his superbly balanced nature would have been ineffectual if it had not been fired by a selfless devotion, a courage, an independence, and a tenacity for which history provides few parallels. Of faults he had singularly few; his limitations were almost entirely those of his age. And if in some things he remained a man of his time, as in his attitude towards harmless pastimes and his severely disciplinary treatment of children, who nevertheless loved him and owed much to his pioneer zeal for the education of the poor, in other ways, as we shall presently see, he overcame in practice the narrow contemporary theories under which he laboured.

Most of his critics recognise his sense of humour. He could

[1] *Wesley's Legacy to the World.* By J. Ernest Rattenbury, D.D. 1928.

K

certainly have shone, had he wished, among the *beaux* or the
wits. But, as Dr. Johnson, who enjoyed his company,
lamented, he had no time for slippered ease. He knew that
the prime need of his age was for an awakening of religion at
once practical and vital. With this end in view, he appealed
primarily to ordinary people. This fact involved some limitation of his message. Yet, as Dr. Rattenbury reminds us,
"the Evangelical Revival was a watershed from which issued
many streams," of which Methodism, the largest Protestant
sect in the world, is but one. The Revival indirectly re-
invigorated every other religious community, and, as Dr.
Hutton gladly admits, its influence, "even within the Church
of England, radiates far and wide to-day." [1] Wesley's significance, however, extends beyond all boundaries of organised
Christianity. He was no politician in the conventional sense;
but, in their effect, his preaching and example gave a vital
impetus to philanthropy and social reform. His prevailing
charity had an essentially New Testament emphasis. Of his
forty-four *Standard Sermons*, three treat of Hell, which then
had a place on every religious map, while thirty-two deal
with ethics. He insisted, of course, that salvation could come
only through faith. But he held that works were necessary
for *continuance* in grace. Only faith could fully vitalise works;
but faith without works was, for him, a contradiction in
terms. "Does not talking of a justified or sanctified *state*,"
he wrote, "tend to mislead men, almost naturally leading
them to trust in what was done in a moment? Whereas we
are every hour and every moment pleasing or displeasing to
God according to our works: according to the whole of our
inward tempers and our outward behaviour."

By directing the new democratic impulse into religious
channels, Wesley helped to stabilise the national temper
during the period of the French Revolution. Sociologists who
pin their faith to programmes and shibboleths have contended
that he did so only by curbing the rising demand for reform.
This charge does not survive the penetrating analysis of Dr.
Rattenbury and Dr. Maldwyn Edwards,[2] among other writers.

---

[1] *John Wesley*. By William Holden Hutton, D.D. 1927.
[2] *John Wesley and the Eighteenth Century*. By Maldwyn Edwards, Ph.D. 1933.

It is true that, while the main trend of revolutionary thought urged that the individual was to be perfected through changed institutions, Wesley (who, unlike most politicians, had the driving force to make his ideas actually operative) asserted that society could be changed only through individual men. Wesley, in converting his followers, imbued them with new habits of sobriety and industry. Many of them, as he foresaw, became wealthy, and not all remembered his warning against the deceitfulness of riches and his plea for the sense of trusteeship. After his death, the Wesleyan movement did settle down, in measure, into theory and traditionalism, and became entangled in some of the fallacies of post-Industrial Revolutionary thought. On the other hand, many of Wesley's disciples, both in his lifetime and afterwards, were signally loyal to his own precept and example. The balance has certainly swung in the right direction, and the amount of social amelioration inspired by the Evangelical Revival is beyond computation.

Dr. Edwards, in his detailed "study of his social and political influence," reminds us that, while on questions like slavery and smuggling Wesley was in the vanguard of radicalism, upon other issues, such as the War of Independence, his inherited Toryism supported reaction. Nor, while he passionately loved the poor, did he believe in democracy as a political force. Dr. Edwards regrets that he did not more fully see the need for altering man's environment as well as for changing the heart. Yet he realises that, by transforming men from within, Wesley prepared the way for the reforms which he nominally opposed. For, after all, he judged the spirit by its fruits. His central aim was to make men citizens of the Celestial City; but he held that, being such, they must necessarily be better citizens of earth. No man ever preached or exemplified that faith with greater passion, and consequently no actual reformer ever influenced more deeply for good the social life of the world.

IV

Wesley died, full of years and universally respected, in 1791. His evangelistic work had extended over half a century, and until 1760 had been carried on in the teeth of actual violence. Several of his preachers died martyrs' deaths; he himself seemed to bear a charmed life. The change in public opinion is touchingly reflected in the two entries in his *Journal* relating to Falmouth—the scene of one of the worst commotions in 1745, and of an almost royal reception in 1789. It was not merely that people of all ranks had come to reverence a doughty and veteran fighter. Wesley had given his countrymen a new standard of values.

It is impossible to condone the brutal methods which were employed for many years against Whitefield and the Wesleys —methods tacitly and sometimes actively supported by magistrates and even by the clergy. Nevertheless, we can sympathise with the opposition itself. We have seen the apparently good reasons which disposed the Church of England in Walpole's time towards a religion of "common sense"; and this attitude was shared by the dissenters. Not merely, however, was the temper of the age against "enthusiasm": it had been disturbed by the arrival in England in 1706 of three members of the French Prophets, a Protestant sect whose rites were as extravagant as their ideas.[1] They made many converts in this country. One prophet interrupted the service in St. Paul's Cathedral; another prophesied naked in the Roman Chapel in Lincoln's Inn Fields. After prayer these "Camisards" would fall into a trance, and then deliver wild prophecies "under very strange agitations or shakings of the body, loud and terrifying hiccups and throbs, with many odd and very surprising gestures."

This exhibitionism naturally alarmed those who flattered themselves that religion had at last become reasonable; and can we wonder that the Evangelical Revival itself incurred suspicion when its early preaching—conducted, of all unprecedented places, in the open air, by itinerant clergymen "poaching" on the preserves of the incumbents—often produced shriekings, faintings, fits, and other convulsive symptoms among the listeners? Alien as were these manifestations to his quiet, deliberate temperament, Wesley at first accepted

---

[1] For a fuller account of this strange sect, see *A History of the Evangelical Party in the Church of England*. By G. R. Balleine. New Edition. 1933.

them as clear evidence of redemption at work. Ever the rationalist, however, he collected the fullest possible data, and later his attitude towards hysterical phenomena underwent severe modification. After a time, moreover, the symptoms ceased to recur—partly owing, Mr. Vulliamy suggests, to Wesley's own discouragement of them, but more largely because the number of suddenly convertible types had been exhausted: for it is in the crudest natures that conversion is most rapid and explosive, and, when Wesley began his mission, the lower classes of the population, alienated from every religious and cultural influence, were hardly better than savages. Wesley and his followers were to show the mettle of which they were made; but how could the frightened and irritated Latitudinarians distinguish at first between the false prophets and the true?

Wesley's rare combination of reason with emotion, his utter sincerity, and the dominance of his long influence, made the Methodist movement one whose permanent benefits, if they be variously assessed, are recognised by historians of every shade of religious opinion and of none. But Wesley, superhuman as were his activities, could not himself control the whole life of the Revival, and, though he was supported by many worthy co-labourers, itinerant and "local," it was inevitable that some of the tares of Evangelicalism should spring up amid the wheat. "No movement of the kind," says Goldwin Smith,

"has ever been exempt from drawbacks and follies, from extravagance, exaggeration, breaches of good taste in religious matters, unctuousness, and cant—from chimerical attempts to get rid of the flesh and live an angelic life on earth—from delusions about special providences and miracles—from a tendency to overvalue doctrine and undervalue duty—from arrogant assumption of spiritual authority by leaders and preachers—from self-righteousness which fancies itself the object of a divine election."

All that is true, though Goldwin Smith appreciates that in the effects produced by Evangelicalism the good outweighed the evil, and that "had Jansenism prospered as well, France might have had more of reform and less of revolution."

That the Revival incidentally produced emotional extravagance may be taken for granted. What is actually on record, and is more to our point, is the unremitting fight which Wesley waged against those Methodists whose peril was "to overvalue doctrine and undervalue duty" and those who fancied themselves objects "of a divine election." Not that Wesley loved dispute for its own sake: "he must be a madman," he wrote, "that will leap into the fire without necessity." His very rationalism, confronting human realities, made him "beware of the reasoning devil." "We are out," he said, "to fight not notions, but sins." He was drawn unwillingly into controversy, in which, when aroused, he displayed a very different spirit from that of many of his opponents, including Augustus Toplady, the author of "Rock of Ages," who, because he disliked his Arminian views, described Wesley as being compounded of "an equal portion of gross Heathenism, Pelagianism, Mahometanism, Popery, Manichaeism, Ranterism, and Antinomianism, culled, dried and pulverised, and mingled with as much palpable Atheism as you can scrape together." Wesley could be trenchant and even satirical; but personal abuse, then very common in debate, was foreign to his nature.

How reluctant he was to enter upon forensic warfare, or to lose the co-operation of a friend whom he regarded as being better than his theological views, may be seen from his correspondence with Whitefield, extending over many years. In 1743 Whitefield's followers had become known as the Calvinistic Methodists; but not until 1764 did there come a formal cleavage between the two sections of the Revival. It is curious, by the way, to note that it was, generally speaking, the Calvinists who remained in the Anglican fold after Wesley's death, while the Arminians became dissenters, as Wesley, despite his loyalty to the Church, could not himself have avoided becoming had he lived much longer. Calvinism, it will be seen, was still strongly entrenched in the Church of England, though with the coming of "reason" it had lain dormant for some decades. It was Calvinism which the more socially select Evangelicals—including Lady Huntingdon's "genteel Methodists"—espoused. It is an error to associate

Calvinism at this stage of history with the dissenting spirit: and we may have here an additional reason why Cowper, who was a "gentleman" and a disliker of Nonconformity, ranged himself on the Calvinistic side.

I have said that Whitefield reawakened the slumbering element of Calvinism in the Church of England. But Calvinism after all is a relative term. As a *theology* it is, if you grant its hypothesis, logical in the extreme: but logic is not the average man's strong point, or history would never have witnessed the absurd contradiction of Calvinistic evangelism. In strict Calvinism there *is* no possible evangel, as was recognised by Wesley when he summarised the Genevan "Gospel" thus: "One in twenty of mankind is elected; nineteen in twenty are reprobated. The elect shall be saved, do what they will; the reprobate shall be damned, do what they can." That is genuine Calvinism; but it was not held in all its rigour by the eighteenth-century Calvinistic Methodists. They inherited it as a tradition, and diluted it in different degrees, according to the measure of their own light or darkness. Whitefield's Calvinism was hardly more than nominal. He was no lucid thinker, and what tinged his mind with Calvinism was probably the fact that he had been raised to his great position from obscure beginnings, and seemed to see therein special evidence of divine election. But his sincere passion for souls, and his readiness to believe in the possibility of their salvation, refuted in action his avowed tenets.

The Calvinism of Methodists like Hervey, Toplady, and Madan in the early days of the Revival, and of others like Venn, Romaine, and Newton in its later phase, varied considerably. Newton's Calvinism was as mild as Whitefield's, but that of others, including Madan, Cowper's cousin and counsellor, was, while far from being "pure," of a stronger vintage. It went doctrinally to the heads of some of the leaders in question, and through them infected their followers with the idea that salvation, coming by a momentary act of divine grace, was something wholly or relatively independent of conduct. This notion, except when it was held as a mere convention, Wesley could not tolerate, and, much as he disliked the task, his conscience forced him into controversy. His

sermons, letters, and *Journal* abound in persuasive reasoning
against this heresy, and in caustic sallies upon it. He himself
believed in Salvation by Faith. He held, in other words, that
only by supernatural power could "works" become spiritually
vital. But "I have found," he said, "that even the precious
doctrine of Salvation by Faith has need to be guarded with
the utmost care, or those who hear it will slight both inward
and outward holiness. I will go a step farther: I seldom find
it profitable for *me* to converse with any who are not athirst
for perfection and who are not big with earnest expectation
of receiving it every moment." [1] He abhorred, in Dr. John
Brown's phrase, "the religiosity which is at once as like and
unlike the real thing as hemlock is to parsley."

Wesley's Calvinistic opponents tried to confound him with
selected texts of Scripture: and here we see how he surmounted the limits of his time. Theoretically he was bound
by belief in the equal inspiration of the whole Bible; but
when it came to a choice between isolated texts and his own
inward experience of Christ, he accepted the witness of the
heart. In his famous sermon on Free Grace, preached in
1739, he said:

"This is the blasphemy clearly contained *in the horrible decree*
of predestination. You represent God as worse than the Devil;
more false, more cruel, more unjust. But you say you will prove
it by Scripture? Hold! What will you prove by Scripture?
That God is worse than the Devil? It cannot be. Whatever
that Scripture proves, it never can prove this; whatever its true
meaning be, it cannot be this meaning. No Scripture can mean
that God is not love, or that His mercy is not over all His works;
that is, whatever it prove beside, no Scripture can prove predestination."

So much for the purer milk of Calvinism. But Wesley
knew that even a much adulterated Calvinism had in effect an
anti-ethical tendency. Speaking of "what are vaguely called
'Gospel Sermons,'" he said, "let but a pert, self-sufficient
animal, that has neither sense nor grace, bawl out something
about Christ, or His blood, or justification by faith, and his

---

[1] *The Letters of John Wesley*. Standard Edition. Volume V, p. 83.

hearers cry out, 'What a fine Gospel sermon!' *We* know no Gospel without salvation from sin."

While John Wesley argued and preached, Charles Wesley sang. He knew the value of satire, and could tersely expose Calvinism by summarising its implications:

> " *To damn for falling short*
> *Of what they could not do,*
> *For not believing the report*
> *Of that which was not true."*

In more characteristic moods his experimental knowledge of Christ welled up into a positive statement of his own faith. The emphasis is Dr. Rattenbury's:

> "*Father, whose* everlasting love
> *Thy only Son for* sinners *gave,*
> *Whose grace to* all *did freely move,*
> *And sent Him down the* world *to save:*
> *Help us Thy mercy to extol,*
> Immense, unfathomed, unconfined;
> *To praise the Lamb who died for* all,
> *The* general *Saviour of mankind."*

Charles Wesley, once overshadowed by his brother, has of modern years received more of his due at the hands of historians, while critics have increasingly appreciated his full literary stature. The fact is seldom recognised, however, that the greatest *poet* of the Revival—far superior, of course, to Cowper himself in pure lyrical quality—was William Blake, who actually commends by name, in terms of warmest admiration, the work of Wesley and Whitefield,[1] and whose songs, with their evangel of mercy, their humanism and passion for liberty, their love of children and animals, and their strong individualism harnessed none the less to a social gospel, breathe in their own exalted measure the very spirit of the Revival. As hymnologist, however, Charles Wesley is supreme. He not only created a wealth of fresh music; he introduced into hymnology a new spirit. He sounded the death-knell of Calvinism. The Judge, in his song, melts into the Father.

Such was the original force of Calvinism that it still persists,

---

[1] Blake's *Milton*, Book I, Part 21, line 61—Part 22, line 5.

here and there, in attenuated form. The ghost of Calvin may even yet haunt the Scottish kirkyard or the Welsh tabernacle. But, while it had its own Calvinistic party, the Evangelical Revival as a whole dealt Genevan theology a blow from which it never fully recovered. Yet, despite the ever-growing volume of sound literature about the master-builder of the Revival, the idea is still held by ignorant people that Wesley worked upon the fears of the feeble-minded and "preached against a lurid background of eternal conflagration." No conception, says Mr. Vulliamy, could be more "villainously false." Has any single man ever done more than John Wesley to spread abroad the love that casts out fear?

V

Cowper's first volume of poems was published in 1782, when he was fifty-one. It was followed three years later by *The Task*, which immediately became popular. The Revival was now well established and was disseminating an influence out of all proportion to its numerical strength.[1] It had its aristocrats, but was still largely confined to the labouring population. Cowper's poems helped to spread its ideas among the educated of all classes. Blake gave the most vital imaginative expression to the spirit behind the Revival: Cowper, because of his formal alliance with the movement and the practical effects of his work, remains its laureate.

He had been a convinced Evangelical for at least fifteen years before he began to write his moral satires. He was, perhaps, hardly "converted" in the strict sense. His was not the primitive type of nature for which conversion is a sudden and explosive process. Nor, for that matter, was Wesley's. But Wesley did need to be vitalised out of religious formalism, and, if the change were gradual, it had its clearly defined stages and its obvious culmination. Cowper, on the contrary, belongs, as I see him, to the rare company of the "once-born."

---

[1] For details of the geographical distribution of the Revival, with character sketches of some of its representative leaders, see Balleine's *History of the Evangelical Party* and *A History of the English Church*, Volume VII, by John H. Overton, D.D., and Frederick Relton, A.K.C. New Edition. 1924.

Not only was he innately virtuous: he was also a natural zealot, though he possessed qualities to which, in his own day, religious zeal was seldom allied. He was born an heir to Evangelicalism, and much of the suffering of his youth and early manhood was, I fancy, due to the fact that, while he was groping his way, he had not yet found his spiritual home.

The influence of the Methodist Revival was already being widely felt when he was in the Temple, and it could not but attract one who, though he was a "gentleman" and had a strong hereditary fund of "reason," was even more deeply characterised by his religious seriousness, his warmth of heart, and his love of Nature. About his warmth of heart there is no dispute. All his biographers recognise that he craved in friendship a more than normal touch of intimacy. It was hardly likely, then, that one of his devout temperament—as the *Memoir*, intelligently read, reveals him always to have been—could have rested content with the absentee Creator of the Deists, or the formal Governor of the Latitudinarians. He needed a more personal faith, and could not disregard the challenge of those who sang of God in the heart:

> "*What we have felt and seen*
> *With confidence we tell,*
> *And publish to the sons of men*
> *The signs infallible.*"

His love of Nature was a hardly less potent factor in drawing him irresistibly into the Evangelical ranks. When he left St. Albans he wrote the hymn beginning:

> "*Far from the world, O Lord, I flee,*
> *From strife and tumult far ;*
> *From scenes, where Satan wages still*
> *His most successful war.*
>
> *The calm retreat, the silent shade,*
> *With pray'r and praise agree ;*
> *And seem by Thy sweet bounty made*
> *For those who follow Thee.*"

It is indeed possible to read into these lines the poet's relief at not returning to London; but "Retirement" is no song of mere escape. We have already seen, and shall see again, that

Cowper's love of Nature and his Evangelicalism, which gave Nature symbolical significance in his eyes, were closely linked.

By these temperamental necessities, Cowper was inevitably drawn towards "enthusiasm." There remained his gentility and his stubborn vein of reason. The fact that Evangelicalism was not the "polite" religion of his day probably gave him qualms and caused some hesitation. The Revival had outgrown the fiercest opposition by the time he entered the Temple; but it was yet far from being "respectable." That Cowper, being fastidious, had some worldly scruples on this point can hardly be doubted, and when in 1781 he drew a word-portrait of Whitefield, he veiled his identity under a Greek synonym.[1] But at length even the Whig nobility in his blood was overruled by elements still stronger.

What of his "reason"? Had it not been overbalanced by his other qualities, it might have made him a Deist. Mr. Fausset regrets that he did not become a Deist rather than an Evangelical: an extraordinary point to be made by one who complains that Cowper divorced "God" and "Nature"! The Deists *did* divorce them; on the contrary, the Evangelicals, and not least Cowper himself, did to some extent see God working in and through His creation. The fact remains, however, that in the eighteenth century there was not as yet the full material for a synthesis of reason and religion. The Deists and Latitudinarians deserve credit for having liberated religion from mere fantasy or metaphysics. They certainly promoted a cooler spirit of debate by their appeal to common sense. They laid open another avenue of approach to religion. But they erred in wishing to close all the older approaches, and, living before the age of Biblical criticism, they did not know how rightly to utilise "reason" itself. They were justified by their fruits in their own day. But the fruits would soon have withered on the branch if Evangelicalism had not brought the rain of revival.

Cowper was impaled on the horns of an inescapable dilemma. "Reason" pointed to what, for one of his warmth of emotion and religious zeal, would only have proved a stony desert. His heart won the day: but it won it imperfectly.

[1] *Hope*, 554-593.

His nature could not dispense with reason, which was therefore employed to find a rationalistic basis for his Evangelical faith. I have twice stressed the fact that as a young man he had carefully studied the "evidences" of Christianity; we have also seen that he then had intimate relations with Madan, and later with other Calvinistic preachers. It is likely that these divines—especially Madan—influenced him to some extent. But it is equally probable that Calvinism commended itself to his own critical faculties. Calvinism was a system based on logic, and, incredible as it may seem to-day, it attracted many intellectuals on that score. Had Cowper been less rationalistic, he might have become not a Calvinist, but an Arminian. Some have contended that he erred by not giving free rein to reason, instead of to his emotions. It seems to me that he made the opposite mistake.

What made Calvinism harmful to Cowper, even in its then modified form, was its insistence on the need for conversion— or if not precisely for "conversion," which can have no place in strict Calvinism, at least for the "witness" of the "special operation of the Holy Spirit" in the hearts of the "faithful." The Arminians, as they were more logically entitled to do, also believed in conversion; but Wesley cared not whether it was sudden or gradual, dramatic or otherwise. For him the only proof of regeneration lay in a changed life. He would have realised that Cowper needed no violent pangs of rebirth. For the Calvinists, on the other hand, "evidence" of being "joined to Christ" was essential. And though the best of them held, like Calvin himself, that "works," while intrinsically worthless, should conform with faith, they all thought primarily of salvation in theological terms. That many Calvinists rested complacently content with abstract faith is here irrelevant. Cowper, accepting the Calvinistic view, was under the supposed necessity of having "assurance": of knowing himself "a child of grace." He was, however, too sincere and too humble for such assurance to come easily to him, or, having come, to remain ever afterwards undoubted; he was not the type of man who finds no difficulty in thinking himself specially chosen of God.

Perhaps, as *some* of his hymns might suggest, he *did* feel quite satisfied on this point. Yet, while he records various instances of special revelation, going back to the day when, as a schoolboy of six or seven, he heard an inward voice prompting him to spiritual confidence, it seems to me that he found some difficulty in fixing upon one unmistakable spiritual crisis in his life. In the *Memoir* he refers to the moment of his reading the third chapter of Romans, in Dr. Cotton's house, as that in which "a clear opening of the free mercy of God in Christ Jesus" came to him, and he adds: "Whatever my friend Madan had said to me, long before, revived in all its clearness, with demonstration of the Spirit and with power." Elsewhere, however, he gives much of the credit to Dr. Cotton himself; and, in still another place, he ascribes his spiritual change at St. Albans largely to the visit of his brother John, who, though not then an Evangelical, "put to flight a thousand deliriums and delusions." Yet again, he told Abraham Maddock that his "conversion" at the Collegium Insanorum was due to his study of Hervey's writings.[1] All these influences, we may assume, worked together to bring him into the light which he had long been seeking, though the light might have been fuller if the sun of Dr. Cotton had not had the mist of Calvinism—in some measure, perhaps, a mist created by Madan—to battle against in his patient's mind. The sceptic may see in Cowper's spiritual happiness at St. Albans merely a sign of his reviving physical condition. But his returning health was, after all, largely due to his "sweet communion" with Dr. Cotton. Cowper, for the first time, was in the spiritual environment that he needed. He found an even more congenial spiritual home with the Unwins at Huntingdon. He was now definitely an Evangelical. But he had "arrived": he had not been "converted."

Unfortunately, however, he was not content with mere "arrival," as he might have been if he had originally encountered Evangelicalism in its Arminian form. He could not entirely escape from the Calvinism into which outside influences or his own reason had led him before he met Dr. Cotton, the Unwins, or Newton. Yet in his case we find a paradox. It is among the tenets of Calvinism that "once a

[1] *The Life of William Cowper.* By Thomas Wright. P. 118.

child of grace, always a child of grace." There *cannot*, for the
elect, be any falling from divine favour. Cowper claimed to
have been "elected," and yet held—at any rate in his times
of despondency—that he was forsaken of God. In later life
he said that he still believed the *general* "truth" of predestination, but knew himself to be the world's solitary exception to the rule. Was this delusion *wholly* due, as it may well
have been, to morbidity of a physical origin? Or—if only
again in his darker moods—did there lurk some uncertainty
in his mind whether he *had*, after all, received "the spirit's
witness" and gained the "imputed righteousness of Christ"?
In any case, his early association with Calvinism must be
lamented. In one of his sensitive and humble nature, it had
inevitably fostered dangerous habits of introspection.

One wonders, again, what might have been the effect if, in
early life, he had come directly under Wesley's influence. He
never met Wesley, though Walter Churchey, a Methodist
lawyer and minor poet of Brecon, apparently suggested plans
for such a meeting.[1] The plan never matured. Wesley's
time-table probably did not make possible a journey to Weston
Underwood, and Cowper was not easily moved to travel. In
two of Wesley's letters to Churchey there are references to
The Task.[2] "I think," says one, "that Mr. Cowper has done
as much as possible with his lamentable story. I can only
wish he had a better subject." "What a pity it is," runs the
other, "that such talents as his should be employed in so useless a manner!" Hardly an encouraging verdict! But
Wesley, who did his reading in a book-lined chaise instead of
on horseback as formerly, was now eighty-three. In any
case, while he was a man of wide culture, his preoccupation
with his mission made him something of an intellectual
utilitarian, and the discursiveness of *The Task* would hardly
commend itself to one of his energetic and forthright nature.
He and Cowper were in some respects antithetically different.
Cowper would have joined with Dr. Johnson in lamenting
that Wesley, so interesting a conversationalist, had little time

---

[1] *The Letters of John Wesley*. Standard Edition. Volume VIII, pp. 107 and
264.
[2] *Ibid.*, Volume VII, p. 107 ; Volume VIII, p. 74.

for fireside talk. Yet we can well imagine that had the two men met when Cowper was young and Wesley only middle-aged, they would have understood each other and perhaps have formed a lasting friendship. At all events, Wesley would have recognised Cowper's sterling character and would not have urged him to needless penitence.

But there were other men on the Arminian side of the Revival who might better have met Cowper's need. What incalculable joy and assurance might have accrued to him if he had lived at Madeley, in Shropshire, in daily contact with John Fletcher! This learned yet simple man, whose intense humanity and whimsical charm made him the idol of children, was Wesley's favourite disciple. Wesley, who did not require his followers to be mirrors or echoes of himself, designated Fletcher as his successor. But Fletcher was not an itinerant, and no offers of preferment had lured him from the loved scene of his constant labours. While promising that if John Wesley died first he would help Charles Wesley to keep the Methodists together, he rejected the proposal that he should immediately become his leader's co-partner. He died before Wesley, who was not given to indiscriminate eulogy, but who dispensed with reserve when he preached Fletcher's funeral oration from the text, "Behold the perfect man, and mark the upright, for the end of that man is peace." Fletcher, who had lived at Geneva in youth, knew Calvinism too well not to oppose it with all his strength. When he saw its doctrines reviving, he wrote his *Checks to Antinomianism*; but hatred of false beliefs did not tempt him to bitterness. The work has been described as the only controversial book of the period of which the author had no cause to be ashamed. "I know not which to admire most," said Wesley, the sternest of critics, "the purity of the language, the strength of the argument, or the mildness and sweetness of the spirit that breathes throughout the whole." The mellow sanctity of Fletcher is attested by a host of other witnesses. The most striking tribute of all came from Voltaire, who, when challenged to name a character as perfect as that of Christ, instantly answered, "Fletcher of Madeley." One has only to look at the portrait of this "Saint Francis of Methodism"—

astute, yet radiant with love and hallowed mirth—to feel
that he, if any human agent, could have dispelled Cowper's
gloom.[1]

If Cowper, I say, can be assumed to have been fully responsible, the error he made was insufficiently to trust the
heart. To trust the heart too much is, generally speaking, as
dangerous as excessively trusting the head. But much
depends upon the particular heart, and much also upon the
time in which a man lives. Wesley in his own sphere was a
rationalist; but we have seen how, confronted with the
impossibility of squaring his experimental knowledge of
salvation with certain passages of a still uniformly inspired
Bible, he obeyed the deeper logic of his heart. He offended
theoretically against reason as then understood; but it is now
apparent that, in doing so, he displayed but the truer common
sense. If Cowper in his London days had known some good
Arminian friend, he too might have learnt thus to discard
his chains.

Yet, after this necessary discursion, we return to the
fact that Cowper's heart in later years did, if with no full or
final assurance of freedom, break through its prison-bars.
He could not dispense with Evangelicalism altogether. He
needed, at the core of his being, much that it alone, in its
wider form, could supply; and in Methodism, even allowing
for the needless shadow which he clutched, he found the most
joyful and vital influence of his life. It is true that his fits of
morbidity recurred. It is further true that they continued
to have a religious complexion. But granted the madness,
with its probable physical predisposition, it was inevitable that
it should be coloured by his faith. At all events, after he
definitely embraced Evangelicalism, his madness returned
only at intervals and never again in so virulent a form as in

---

[1] It was once suggested to the writer that it might have been best of all if
Cowper had earlier in life met the Quaker, William Crotch, who felt a " concern "
to visit the poet in one of his gloomy hours at Weston Underwood, and who
soothed him by his mere presence. But I doubt if Quakerism could have satisfied
Cowper's " enthusiasm " even if it had helped to satisfy his reason. The great
age of Quakerism was over. The Friends, like the other Nonconformists, had
settled down by this time into quietism and traditionalism. It was only the
influence of the Evangelical Revival itself that later gave a new lease of life to
the religion of George Fox.

L

1763. It is irrelevant to cite the comparatively settled gloom of his declining years. He was then an old man. His own health was shaken; he had, moreover, to face the ordeal of Mrs. Unwin's long illness, followed by the calamity of her death. Less sensitive minds might easily have broken under the strain.

But between his emergence from Dr. Cotton's asylum and Mrs. Unwin's first seizure there spread twenty-six years. During much of that period he enjoyed the truest kind of happiness. Grim clouds from Geneva sometimes obscured the quiet Buckinghamshire landscape: to represent them as having permanently darkened it is to ignore the patent facts. As for John Newton, who now claims our attention, we must regret that he was not an Arminian. But the Calvinism of this benevolent divine was relatively innocuous, and under his influence Cowper's own *well-established* Calvinism diminished rather than increased. Newton may not have been the ideal friend for Cowper: few were fitted for that part. A sincerer or more affectionate friend no man ever had.

Chapter Eight

JOHN NEWTON AND THE "OLNEY HYMNS"

I

"I HAD A good deal of conversation with Mr. N——. His case is very peculiar. Our Church requires that clergymen should be men of learning, and, to this end, have an University education. But how many have an University education, and yet no learning at all! Yet these men are ordained! Meantime, one of eminent learning, as well as unblameable behaviour, cannot be ordained *because he was not at the University*! What a mere farce is this!"

So, in his *Journal* for March 20, 1760, wrote John Wesley.

The reference is, of course, to John Newton, who, in his thirty-fifth year, was then tide-surveyor at Liverpool. "My duty," he had told his wife, "is to attend the tides one week, and visit the sloops that arrive, and such as are in the river; and the other week to inspect the vessels in the docks. . . . I have a good office, with fire and candle, and fifty or sixty people under my direction; with a handsome six-oared boat and a cockswain to row me about in form." We might infer not merely that the position was respectable—it carried, indeed, a good salary and (no doubt) many perquisites—but that its holder regarded it with the complacence of one who had arrived by smooth paths at his destined goal. This latter conclusion would be quite false. Newton's life had hitherto been one of adventure, hardship, and humiliation, suggesting a "thriller" for boys rather than a record of plain fact. And, at the moment, so far from flattering himself upon having at last found "port after stormy seas," he was, behind his characteristic outward cheerfulness, gravely disturbed. He had recently felt an unmistakable call to holy orders, yet could find no Bishop to ordain him.

Newton's father was for many years master of a ship in the Mediterranean trade. He retired from the sea in 1742, and was later appointed Governor of York Fort in Hudson's Bay, where he died in 1750. He was a man of wide experience, good sense, and practical morality; but, having been educated at a Jesuits' college in Spain, he had an air of "distance and severity" which, despite his fundamental kindness, overawed his son. The mother was a pious dissenter. She was delicate and retiring, and lavished affection upon her only child, whom in her mind she had already dedicated to the Non-conformist ministry. The child himself was fonder of learning than of play, and, under her tuition, could read well at the age of four, besides knowing his Shorter Catechism and Dr. Watts's hymns. When he was six, however, his mother died.[1] His father, when next he returned from sea, married again. John's stepmother, the daughter of a substantial grazier at Aveley, near Tilbury, soon had a son of her own, who exclusively engrossed her attention. John was sent to a boarding-school at Stratford, in Essex, where he remained until he was ten, and where the sternness of his master so broke his spirit that, instead of making progress, he became almost a "dolt."

On his eleventh birthday he went aboard his father's ship in Long Reach. He made five voyages with him to the Mediterranean, and then spent some months at Alicante, in Spain, with a paternal friend, a merchant, with whom he might have stayed and prospered if he had "behaved well." He returned to England, and his father secured an appointment for him in the West Indies. But, being first despatched upon a business errand into Kent, he there visited some distant relatives of his mother, and fell in love with Mary Catlett, who, seven years later, became his wife. In his autobiography he says that "almost at the first sight of this girl (for she was then under fourteen) I was impressed with a deep affection for her, which never abated or lost its influence a single moment in my heart from that hour." As an old man, gazing at Shooter's Hill from the house of a friend at Blackheath, he recalled how in youth he had often travelled several miles thither that he might look *towards* the far distant spot where his beloved lived. "Why," said his friend, "this is more like one of the vagaries of romance than of real life."

[1] In 1731, the year of Cowper's birth.

"True," replied Newton, "but real life has extravagances that would not be permitted to appear in a well-written romance—they would be said to be *out of nature*":[1] an observation which applies to the whole of his own amazing career.

Meanwhile, lingering in Kent, he lost his ship to the West Indies. His father, angry but forgiving, sent him on a voyage to Venice. Back home again, John repeated the offence. He was now impressed into the Navy, on the outbreak of war with France, and was soon made a midshipman. Having yet again overstayed his leave, he was arrested as a deserter, publicly flogged, and degraded to the rank of a common sailor. One day, however, he saw a man leaving the ship for another vessel bound for Guinea. He obtained permission to join him. On reaching the African coast, he took service under a slave-dealer, whose negro wife, a woman of local importance, brutally ill-treated him during her husband's absence:

"I was sick when he sailed in a shallop to Rio Nuna, and he left me in her hands. At first I was taken some care of; but as I did not recover very soon, she grew weary, and entirely neglected me. I had sometimes not a little difficulty to procure a draught of cold water when burning with a fever. My bed was a mat spread upon a board or chest, and a log of wood my pillow. When my fever left me, and my appetite returned, I would gladly have eaten, but there was no one who gave unto me. She lived in plenty herself, but hardly allowed me sufficient to sustain life, except now and then, when in the highest good humour, she would send me victuals in her own plate after she had dined; and this, so greatly was my pride humbled, I received with thanks and eagerness, as the most needy beggar does an alms. Once, I well remember, I was called to receive this bounty from her own hand; but, being exceeding weak and feeble, I dropped the plate. Those who live in plenty can hardly conceive how this loss touched me: but she had the cruelty to laugh at my disappointment; and though the table was covered with dishes (for she lived much in the European manner), she refused to give me any more. My distress has been at times so great as to compel me to go by night and pull up roots in the plantation, though at the risk of being punished as a thief, which I have eaten raw upon the spot for fear of discovery."

[1] *Memoirs of the Rev. John Newton.* By Richard Cecil, A.M. 1808.

This passage, transparently honest in its simplicity, is taken from *An Authentic Narrative of some Interesting Particulars in the Life of John Newton,* which the writer published in 1764.[1] Here may be read in detail the rest of the saga of Newton's earlier life; how, even in the circumstances above described, he studied Euclid and drew his diagrams on the African sand; how he later taught himself Latin by means of a Horace and a Latin Bible; how he had other voyages and several hairbreadth escapes; how he was converted through the combined influences of Thomas à Kempis and a shipwreck that nearly cost him his life; and how his fortunes then improved, until at length he became the master of a slave-ship. Interspersed with the plain records of fact are the author's reflections upon the almost total depravity into which he fell, though never quite to the extent of forgetting his mother's influence and his love for Mary Catlett. On this point his confessions must perhaps be read with caution: it is impossible to judge from the conventional idiom of Evangelical self-accusation whether Newton actually yielded to the manifold temptations by which he must have been assailed, or whether his "sins" were mainly or merely those of youthful high spirits, rebelliousness, swearing, and lack of definite religious faith. His later career and the fact that he lived to be eighty-two suggest that both physically and morally he must have been innately robust.

Newton tells us that, when he became captain of a slave-ship, he tried to deal both justly and mercifully with crew and cargo. To modern ideas, there is something incongruous in the thought of a Christian being in charge of a slave-ship at all, and Newton has further played into the hands of hostile critics by declaring that he never experienced "sweeter and more frequent hours of divine communion" than during his last two voyages to Guinea. That, however, is not the end of the story. He admits that at first he had no scruples about the slave trade, which was, indeed, counted "genteel." But soon, he says, "I considered myself a sort of gaoler or turnkey,

---

[1] "To-day I gave a second reading to that lively book, *Mr. Newton's Account of his own Experience.* There is something very extraordinary therein; but one may account for it without a jot of predestination."—Entry in Wesley's *Journal* for August 14, 1769.

and I was sometimes shocked with an employment that was perpetually conversant with chains, bolts, and shackles. In this view I often petitioned that the Lord would be pleased to fix me in a more humane calling." Newton is subsequently found, like Wesley and Cowper, in the vanguard of opposition to slavery. But even if he had died in the belief that slavery were a divinely ordained institution, there would still be no cause for surprise or scorn. Slavery was in his day the biggest vested interest in England; the whole fortunes of Liverpool and Bristol were based upon it; and many of the sincerest religious people, clerical and lay, were financially implicated in this human traffic. Newton's conscience was in fact in advance of contemporary Christian opinion. That Christianity and slavery were ever deemed compatible is in itself a humiliating reflection. But it will be time enough for us to deride our eighteenth-century forebears when there are no longer any Christian stockholders in armament firms, when war has been abolished, and when industrial serfdom is no more.

We may smile, again, at Newton's belief in the special mercy of Providence in rescuing him from physical perils to which others, taking his place, succumbed. His repeated escapes were indeed so remarkable that his faith in divine interposition is the more understandable. But his attitude was, after all, the common one of his time; the rising sun of a new day had not yet dispelled the mists of ancient magic. Newton was just as ready to see the hand of God in the fit of apoplexy which struck him one afternoon in 1754 as he was drinking tea with Mary, now his adored and devoted wife, two days before he was due to sail again. And the stroke, which was never repeated, was, in fact, the means of freeing him from further direct engagement in the slave trade. Unfortunately, the shock so affected Mrs. Newton that, although she was to enjoy many years of married happiness, with two adopted nieces to liven an otherwise childless home, she remained a semi-invalid.

Newton himself recovered quickly, and settled in Liverpool, where, as we have seen, he was appointed tide-surveyor. Having now resolved, however, to become a clergyman, he

abandoned his study of Latin, French, and mathematics for a
closer reading of Scripture. For several years his applications
were refused. Dr. Gilbert, Archbishop of York, told him
bluntly that he should be satisfied with that state of life into
which God had called him, and even insinuated that he was a
fool to contemplate resigning a good worldly position for an
uncertain clerical prospect. Other leading ecclesiastics were
no more helpful. At last perseverance was rewarded.
Through the influence of Lord Dartmouth, a convert to
Evangelicalism, Newton was ordained by Dr. Green, Bishop
of Lincoln; and Lord Dartmouth, the patron of the living,
installed him as curate at Olney, the insignificant Buckinghamshire village which was destined to be associated with
two other leading Calvinistic "lights" of the Revival.

II

Newton took up residence at Olney in 1764. He remained
there for sixteen years, the last thirteen of which were spent
in constant intimacy with Cowper. It is this middle period
of his career that most definitely concerns us. But, since a
character can be understood only when seen in the round, it
may be best to glance at Newton's later history before we
resume the narrative of Cowper's life. In 1780, owing to
circumstances to be explained in due course, Newton, who
shared Cowper's love of the country and had previously
declined an offer of preferment to Hampstead, accepted, at the
hands of John Thornton,[1] the living of St. Mary Woolnoth,
Lombard Street, London. Here he remained until his death
in 1807, living for a time in Charles Square, Hoxton, then a
pleasant suburb, and afterwards moving to Coleman Street
Buildings, close to the scene of his labours.

Whitefield's tabernacle had been opened, amid the fields
and market-gardens of Tottenham Court Road, as far back as

[1] John Thornton (1720-1790) was a well-known city merchant, who, in addition to his many extensive benefactions, bought the advowsons of livings in order
to install clergymen of his own Evangelical persuasion. His son, Henry Thornton,
became a member of the Clapham sect of business men, including Wilberforce
and Zachary Macaulay, who were identified, early in the nineteenth century,
with the anti-slavery campaign.

1756. Wesley, besides acquiring West Street Chapel and several lesser ones, had in 1778 built the "cathedral" of Methodism in City Road. Lady Huntingdon's chaplains preached regularly at the Lock Hospital. But as yet there were in London few Evangelical clergymen engaged in normal parochial work, the most notable at the time of Newton's arrival being Henry Venn. There had been fierce opposition against the earlier settled "enthusiasts," as against their itinerating brethren. In 1750, for example, William Romaine had been dismissed from his appointment as morning preacher at St. George's, Hanover Square, because he attracted too large and ungenteel a congregation, to the discomfort of the regular attenders. There was even worse trouble, involving scenes of riot, when he became "lecturer" at St. Dunstan's-in-the-West. By 1780, however, the period of active hostility was over, though it remained for John Newton to show that an Evangelical incumbent—in the very heart of the City, close to the Bank of England and the Royal Exchange—could win the respect, soon ripening into affection, of all classes of his parishioners.

Nor was his influence confined to these. In a then comparatively small London he became a metropolitan figure, and, through his spreading fame as preacher and as writer, a national one. He never outgrew a sense of marvel at his position.

"That one of the most ignorant, the most miserable, and the most abandoned of slaves should be plucked from his forlorn state of exile on the coast of Africa, and at length be appointed Minister of the parish of the first magistrate of the first city in the world—that he should there not only testify of such grace, but stand up as a singular instance and monument of it—that he should be enabled to record it in his history, preachings, and writings to the world at large—is [he said] a fact I can contemplate with admiration, but never sufficiently estimate."

He would have been less than human had he not felt a certain pride; and human, above all things else, this burly, bluff, hearty ex-seaman was.

Therein lay the secret of his success. He was no great preacher. The matter of his sermons was original and sound;

but his voice did not carry well, and his mannerisms were awkward. He pandered neither to the plutocracy nor to the "gallery," though he mixed a little of the serpent's guile with the harmlessness of the dove. He knew that some of the "bankers" in his congregation were, spiritually speaking, but infants who needed to be fed with milk. For their benefit he preached more briefly and with greater "caution" on Sunday mornings: he dissented from those "that are not only for forcing strong meat, but *bones* too, down the throat of a child." He cared not if this application of the apostolic principle laid him open to misunderstanding. He knew that he was "*apparently* inconsistent," but was satisfied with the knowledge, in his own conscience, that he was no "trimmer." The fact that his church was crowded mainly with humble listeners speaks for itself. Some of the wealthiest merchants in the world lived within a small radius of St. Mary Woolnoth. Had Newton kept his church select, he could have enjoyed ease and luxury. But that there was no pose in his attitude towards money is revealed in the anecdote of the lady who stopped him one day on the steps of his church and said: "The ticket, of which I held a quarter, has drawn a prize of ten thousand pounds. I know you will congratulate me upon the occasion." "Madam," Newton replied, "as for a friend under temptation, I will endeavour to *pray* for you." We have seen that he gave up a good position in Liverpool for the curacy of Olney, with its salary of sixty pounds a year. He could neither be patronised nor bought, and in consequence some of the richer members of his flock absented themselves from his services. With such he retained contact through printed pastoral addresses, assuring them that, though they had left an already overfilled church, he had not lost his concern for their own spiritual welfare.

Important as his preaching may have been, it was in personal relationships and through his letters—spontaneous, human, and understanding—that his truest service was rendered. If he had a measure of childish vanity, it was only the spray on the surface of a nature essentially *childlike*. Many sailors have the same characteristic. It is Newton's glory that, though he became a considerable scholar and a public character in the City of London, surrounded by the perils of affluence and flattery, he retained unimpaired the wisdom and simplicity of one who had seen God's wonders in the deep.

It is the tenderness of this strong man that shines most clearly through all the records of his ministry. He and his wife kept open house for rich and poor alike; no cry of distress, physical or spiritual, reached him in vain; he was never, like Venn, the Church official, but always the friend, thoroughly approachable. The humble and illiterate intuitively turned to him for advice or help; Wilberforce and Hannah More were among the many famous people who made him their confidant. His childlikeness instantly melted reserve, and his keen interest in life was but another aspect of that trait, which made him a magnet for people in joy or sorrow. "I see in this world," he said,

> "two heaps of human happiness and misery; now if I can take but the smallest bit from one heap and add to the other, I carry a point. If, as I go home, a child has dropped a halfpenny, and if, by giving it another, I can wipe away its tears, I feel I have done something. I should be glad to do greater things, but I will not neglect this. When I hear a knock on my study door, I hear a message from God; it may be a lesson of instruction; perhaps a lesson of penitence; but, since it is *his* message, it must be interesting."

One of Cowper's biographers briefly admits that Newton was "a downright, homely man, with a warm heart, a genial humour, and an ardent sensibility." But he reproduces a few "typical" sayings which, he says, "will be enough to controvert" those who still imagine Newton's Calvinism to have been moderate:

> "We find depravity so deep-rooted in our nature, that, like the leprous house, the whole fabric must be taken down before we can be freed from its defilement."
> "I believe that sin is the most hateful thing in the world; that I and all men are by nature in a state of wrath and depravity, utterly unable to sustain the penalty, or to fulfil the commands of God's holy law; and that we have no sufficiency of ourselves to think a good thought."

These are among six selected specimens of the "rabid sentiments" which, we are told, are "not exceptional," but which
"dominate all Newton's writings."

I have not myself read all Newton's works. I have read
enough, however, to know that such utterances represent
merely the *formal* voice, not of Newton alone, but of his age.
When Newton spoke with his own very individual accent, his
words have quite another ring. It would be possible to fill
the rest of this chapter with the samples of his "familiar
conversation" appended to Cecil's *Memoir*. A few examples
must suffice:

"If three angels were sent to earth, they would feel perfect
indifference as to who should perform the part of prime-minister,
parish-minister, or watchman."

"Love and fear are like the sun and moon, seldom seen
together."

"God's word is certainly a restraint, but it is such a restraint
as the irons which prevent children getting into the fire."

"One reason why we must not attempt to pull up the tares
which grow among the wheat is that we have not the skill for
the work: like a weeder whom Mrs. N. employed in my garden
at Olney, who for weeds pulled up some of Mrs. N.'s favourite
flowers."

"A wise man looks upon men as he does upon horses, and
considers their caparisons of title, wealth, and place, but as
harness."

"Some Christians, at a glance, seem of a superior order, and
are not; they want a certain quality. At a florists' feast the
other day, a certain flower was determined to bear the bell, but
it was found to be an artificial flower: there is a quality called
GROWTH which it had not."

"Don't tell me of your feelings. A traveller would like fine
weather, but if he be a man of business, he will go on."

Vigorous, bold, and independent as Newton was, he had
an almost feminine sensitiveness. "We see the reason," he
whimsically observed, "why women are forbid to preach the
Gospel, for they would persuade without argument, and
reprove without giving offence." It was surely no "God-
assured egoist" who could thus quietly banter about religion,

or who, despite his theoretical hostility to Roman Catholicism, could say: "I have read of many wicked Popes, but the worst Pope I ever met with is POPE SELF." Nor was that man a sour, militant Calvinist who could tell the following story against his own creed: "Some preachers near Olney dwelt on the doctrine of predestination; an old woman said—'Ah! I have long settled that point, for if God had not chosen me before I was born, I am sure He would have seen nothing in me to have chosen me for afterwards.'"

Newton had been drawn to Evangelicalism through the influence of Whitefield.[1] That fact no doubt determined the Calvinistic bias of his faith; and his remarkable early history predisposed him, like Whitefield, to see a special intervention of Providence in his case. Yet his innate charity and catholicity are apparent enough in his letters and conversation, as in many of his hymns; and we know that he deplored the Antinomian tendency fostered by the more pronounced Calvinism of preachers like Romaine and Venn. He had a long controversy with Madan; "but reasons of delicacy led him to commit the whole to the flames." That he failed to satisfy the standards of Calvinism as preached at the Lock is shown by a remark he once made, "smiling," to Richard Cecil. "I hope," he said, "I am upon the whole a Scriptural preacher; for I find I am considered as an Arminian among the high Calvinists, and as a Calvinist among the strenuous Arminians." And in this connection it is deeply interesting and instructive to read the correspondence between Newton and Wesley.

Specially illuminating is the letter which Wesley addressed to Newton from Londonderry on May 14, 1765, when Newton had only recently begun his ministry at Olney and was less mellow than he afterwards became. The letter is too long for quotation, but the main points may be summarised. Newton had apparently stated that his Calvinistic doctrines were *indispensable* articles of faith. Wesley replies that he once similarly maintained that his own doctrine of

---

[1] Newton told how, as a young man, he used to rise at four o'clock in the morning to hear Whitefield preach at his five o'clock service, and how he had seen Moorfields " as full of the lanterns of the worshippers before daylight as the Haymarket was full of flambeaux on opera nights."

"perfection" was *essential* to salvation. Now he has learned
that the doctrine either of predestination or of perfection may
be held as a mere *opinion*. He still insists that the doctrine
of predestination has wrought much evil; "I can name time,
place, and persons." But he cannot ignore a certain plain
fact: namely, that "Mr. Newton"—he playfully introduces
the name of his correspondent—holds this doctrine, and yet
has "real Christian experience." Manifestly, therefore, continues Wesley in effect, he (Wesley) was mistaken in supposing
that the doctrine of predestination must necessarily be incompatible "with a love to Christ and a genuine work of grace
—here is clear proof to the contrary." Not only does "Mr.
Newton" hold that doctrine, but others "at whose feet I desire
to be found in the day of the Lord Jesus." "I leave *you* in
your calm and retired moments," Wesley concludes, "to
make the application." [1]

In what a sane, tolerant, and gracious light Wesley is here
revealed! We could wish that Newton had emerged into the
full Arminian sunshine. Yet this very letter provides striking
testimony both to the comparative mildness of his Calvinism
and to the sincerity and charm of his character. Except,
indeed, among certain biographers of Cowper, there is general
agreement about this sagacious, gentle, and lovable man.
His friend, Richard Cecil, said that he was the living prototype of the ideal clergyman described by Goldsmith in *The
Deserted Village*. The later Church historians, with whom it
is a sore point that Newton was so "broad" in his ecclesiastical
views that he might easily have been a dissenter,[2] unite in
recognising his fine spirit. Nor is appreciation confined
to religious critics. No writer has paid higher tribute to
Newton's memory than Lecky, the rationalist, who, not content with having called him "one of the purest and most
unselfish of saints," describes him again on a later page as

---

[1] *The Letters of John Wesley*. Standard Edition. Volume V, pp. 297-99.

[2] Newton " may be considered one of the chief founders of the Low Church
party which was then, through the influence of Methodism, rapidly rising in the
Establishment, and of the great ' Benevolent Enterprises ' which, organised in
the latter part of his life in London, embodied there the moral energies of
England to be put forth in the ends of the earth."—*History of Methodism* By
Abel Stevens, LL.D. 1878. Volume II, p. 70.

"one of the most devoted and single-hearted of Christian ministers."

In 1776, while still living at Olney, Newton came to London for a surgical operation, then an extremely painful and dangerous affair. He admitted afterwards that his heart was "sadly reluctant and dull in secret"; but rejoiced that he had been able to carry on his duties till the last moment, and said that the fact of his having had strength to face the ordeal "with tolerable calmness and confidence was a greater favour granted to him than the deliverance from his malady." In this spirit he met all the troubles of his later years, which, if they were not numerous, struck him at the most vulnerable point. For he was primarily a man of strong domestic affections; he was in this respect, Cecil tells us, an "original." Soon after he settled in London, one of his adopted nieces, of whom he wrote a memoir, died at the age of fourteen. "He loved her," says Cecil, "with the affection of a parent, and she was, indeed, truly lovely." Then he had to see his wife suffer a long and torturing illness before she died in 1790. His devotion to her was so rare in an age when true companionship between the sexes was little known that even Cecil, who never doubted the utter sincerity of the affection, thought his friend carried matters to extremes.

It was the age of "the tender passion." "The fair," as may be seen in the poetry of Pope, were treated by men with a tinsel chivalry: they were seldom deemed worthy of being partners. Even an Evangelical like Cecil was suspicious of "enthusiasm" in the domestic realm, and Newton provoked a little mirth or the charge of bad taste by his public references to his wife: though Wesley, himself "polite" and reserved, was, in this as in other respects, before his time. "The objection current here," he wrote to Newton in 1765, "that you talk too much of Mrs. Newton, seems to me of no force at all. I cannot apprehend that you could well have spoken less or any other wise than you do." [1] Wesley here incidentally reveals again his generous spirit, for his own marriage had proved as unfortunate as Newton's was ideal.

Newton, after his wife's death, enjoyed no more fine

[1] *The Letters of John Wesley.* Standard Edition. Volume IV, p. 282.

weather. But, being a traveller on business, he went on. He was in his pulpit as usual on the Sunday morning following his bereavement, that his flock might know he believed the Gospel he preached. The last years of his life were further darkened by the illness of his other niece, who could no longer be his devoted comrade and helper. But to the world he still turned a smiling face; he was still ready to share the happiness or grief of others; and when it was suggested that he should rest, "What," he said, "shall the old African blasphemer stop while he can speak?" Over eighty years of age, deaf and partially blind, he yet appeared in St. Mary Woolnoth, driven thither in Alderman Lea's carriage and supported in the pulpit by Mr. Bates's servant. And though he was now almost inaudible, people flocked to the church that they might have the joy of "seeing his person." "However they *admired* some ministers," said Cecil, "they all *loved* him."

Newton had obvious faults, not least among which was a sailor-like gullibility that made him sometimes credit plausible scoundrels with his own integrity. He had, too, his limitations. He was not eloquent. His knowledge of books was extensive but somewhat haphazard. He was no profound or systematic thinker. He never fully escaped from the Scriptural fetters of his age. He confessed that he could preach from any single text, but that he often found difficulty—no wonder!—in correlating them. With other Evangelicals, again, he frowned on many innocent amusements, and, unlike the Wesleys, a highly gifted musical family, who did not see why the Devil should have all the best tunes, he thought music, other than simple hymn-singing, an exclusive prerogative of Satan. In 1784 and 1785, when Handel's *Messiah* was arousing widespread enthusiasm, he preached a series of sermons in which he protested against a Scriptural message being made into an *entertainment*. Yet his first-hand experience of the world, his warm heart, his shrewd native sense and homely humour, more than atoned for his lack of other equipment, and in "practical meekness, tenderness, and piety" few Christian leaders, as Lecky says, have surpassed him. He stood the test of his own "square measure" for ministers. "I have no idea," he said, "of the size of a table, if you only tell me how *long* it is; but if you also say how *wide*, I can tell its dimensions. So when you tell me what a man is in the pulpit, you must tell me what he is out of it, or I shall not know his size." On another occasion he remarked: "Tell me not how the man died, but how he lived." Yet it is worth recording that, as he neared the end of his gradual decline, "the old African blasphemer" was heard praying for "more light, more love, more liberty."

Such was the man of whom most writers on Cowper have spoken with condescension, if not with scorn!

III

Olney, though it belongs geographically to Buckinghamshire, lies between the towns of Northampton and Bedford. It is to-day a minor satellite of Northampton in the manufacture of shoes, and factory sirens disturb, at regular intervals, its ancient peace. Yet it retains the air of a quiet country town, and the surrounding landscape has changed little since Cowper roamed across the fields with Newton or Mrs. Unwin to Emberton, Weston Underwood, Clifton, or Lavendon. The valley of the Nen has been unpleasantly metamorphosed; its ash-trees stand solitary about the coal-fields between the towns and the iron-ore furnaces. But the broad Ouse still winds slowly and tortuously through rich pastures, primrose woods, and the pink, white, and yellow washed villages with their water-mills.[1]

[1] " Here Ouse, slow winding through a level plain
      Of spacious meads with cattle sprinkled o'er,
      Conducts the eye along its sinuous course
      Delighted. There, fast rooted in their bank,
      Stand, never overlook'd, our fav'rite elms,
      That screen the herdsman's solitary hut;
      While far beyond, and overthwart the stream
      That, as with molten glass, inlays the vale,
      The sloping land recedes into the clouds;
      Displaying on its varied side the grace
      Of hedge-row beauties numberless, square tow'r,
      Tall spire, from which the sound of cheerful bells
      Just undulates upon the list'ning ear,
      Groves, heaths, and smoking villages, remote."
                                    The Task, Book I.

M

In Cowper's day, as now, Olney consisted mainly of one long, broad street widening into a spacious triangular market-place, on the south side of which stood, and still stands, the red-bricked house, somewhat prison-like in appearance, in the western half of which the poet lived for sixteen years. Along one side of the High Street, with its thatched cottages and bow-windowed shops, there ran, in his time, a raised cause-way, supported by posts; on the other side flowed a stream. Amid the many projecting signs was the pole of William Wilson, the barber. The fact that Wilson, who ranked among "the best society in Olney," was Cowper's friend and confidant speaks well for the barber himself: it also reflects, by contrast, the illiteracy and coarseness of the population as a whole. The main occupation was lace-making. The women and children still plied needle and bobbin in their own cottages, continuing by candlelight when the winter sun declined. They were waging a losing battle against the newer methods of industry, and their condition was poor in the extreme.

As always amid destitution, public-houses were numerous. Among the most notable were the Saracen's Head, with its signpost standing out in the High Street, and the old Swan, which, with its large wooden balcony, was the inn associated with Cowper's immortal post-boy. Here the mail was brought and sorted, and, in the conduct of this side of their business, mine host and hostess were, the poet complained, "excessively careless." The old Swan—there is now another inn of that name—and the Saracen's Head have vanished; but the Bull, in the market-place, remains much as it was when Cowper and Mrs. Unwin, one of whose maids had contracted small-pox, lived there for a few weeks in 1771.

In the market-place itself, overshadowed by three great elms, stood the Shiel (or Town) Hall, a two-storied stone building, and the small hexagonal "Round House," or prison. Through his windows, Cowper could also see a blacksmith's forge. Hard things have been said about his residence— "Orchard Side"—and he himself sometimes spoke disrespect-fully of it, especially after his removal to Weston Underwood. It was, indeed, far from being an ideal habitation. Externally it was then made grimmer by the imitation battlements which hid the roof. Inside it was neither convenient nor commodious; the celebrated "parlour"—where may now be seen the tiny sofa which inspired *The Task*, and other personal relics of Cowper and Mrs. Unwin—is only thirteen feet square. The house, moreover, was unhealthily situated. Pestilential mists crept up from the Ouse in the winter, and, though Mr. Wright assures us that Cowper was guilty of slight exaggeration in describing his abode as "deep in the abyss of Silver End," [1] it was at least in close proximity to the most squalid part of the town.

Yet in one respect Orchard Side suited Cowper's temperament. He could be an innocent Peeping Tom. If Olney were duller than Huntingdon, he was at least in its centre. He could see a little bustle without himself becoming involved in it. He could watch—a sympathetic yet detached spectator—the comedies and tragedies of everyday life, which are everywhere much the same. His letters show that for him, with his keen, whimsical vision and his imaginative transmutation of things local and trivial into things universal and permanent, the tide of existence flowed, in one sense, as fully through Olney market-place as it did for Johnson at Charing Cross.

In the summer the country was accessible and pleasant enough. In winter the "roads" and fields were often impassable. Cowper's "locomotive faculty" had then to satisfy itself with a gravel walk, thirty yards long, which threaded the garden. The building of his greenhouse and summerhouse, and his cultivation of lettuces and cucumbers, belong to a slightly later date. The motive that brought Cowper and Mrs. Unwin to Olney, in 1767, was to be near John Newton, who had settled three years previously in the Vicarage, which, soon afterwards, Lord Dartmouth converted from "one of the most inconvenient" into "one of the best and most commodious houses in the country." The prospect from Newton's study on the top floor embraced the church, a perpendicular building with tall spire and bulging sides; Olney Mill; and the stone bridge of many arches—Cowper's "bridge of wearisome but needful length"—which then bestrode the

---

[1] *The Town of Cowper.* By Thomas Wright. 1893.

whole valley of the Ouse. Bleak, and a little sordid, if also
engagingly animated, might be the view from Cowper's
north windows into the market-place. Yet Orchard Side deserved its name. Only an orchard divided its garden from
the Vicarage garden, in whose wall Newton made a doorway.
The proprietor of the orchard charged Cowper and Newton
a guinea a year for the privilege of passing through this
"Guinea Field," as they called it, and so of visiting each other
without taking a circuitous journey by lane and street.

Newton had not engaged Orchard Side for Mrs. Unwin and
Cowper without first giving them the option of a more
capacious and pleasantly situated house at Emberton, a mile
away; and he had promised that, if they took the latter, he
would visit Mrs. Unwin whenever the weather was too bad
for her to reach Olney, and the state of the road did not make
walking impossible for him. Faced with the choice, the
strangers from Huntingdon soon made their decision. Far
better, they were agreed, a less convenient house and *more*
Newton than *less* Newton and a better house! They were
not "dominated" or mesmerised by Newton's personality.
They were drawn towards Newton by sheer affection no less
than by respect for him as an Evangelical clergyman. It is
only a biased or hasty judgment that can decide otherwise.
The evidence is abundant and unequivocal.

Newton's rare and *genuine* chivalry towards women [1] would,
among other qualities, commend him to Mrs. Unwin. As for
Cowper and Newton, how could two such men fail to understand and love each other? Their differences were all on the
surface. Beneath his reserve, his caution, and his feminine
fastidiousness, Cowper hid an essential, and in some respects
a tough, masculinity. Newton externally was bluff, vigorous,
and sometimes a little stern; but his heart was tender as a
child's. That Cowper went somewhat in awe of him is true.
The feeling, however, was based, not upon fear, but upon
admiration. It was no bullied or reluctant Cowper who spent
several hours a day in Newton's company, and who scoured

---

[1] See the charming letter written on July 28, 1764, by Newton, then settling
in at Olney Vicarage, to his wife, who was remaining in London for several
weeks. *The Town of Cowper*. By Thomas Wright. P. 76.

with him the surrounding country, now visiting Kettering, now riding to Winslow, now walking to Lavendon Mill, or now going on a pastoral errand to Weston. "On September 19," wrote Newton in his pocket-book for 1768, "breakfasted at Yardley, spoke from Matt. v. 6, at Denton, from Phil. iv. 4. Mr. Cowper went with me, a pleasant walk both ways." Entries like "a pleasant walk with Mr. Cowper" recur frequently in Newton's diary during the period.

What a feast of talk these friends must have enjoyed as they strode together across the fields! Each was in large measure the temperamental complement of the other. Each had lost his mother in childhood and had known strange and bitter experiences. Newton would lend an intensely sympathetic ear to Cowper's record of misfortunes; Cowper, to whose imagination the sea always strongly appealed, would in turn be as much fascinated by Newton's reminiscences as was the wedding-guest by the Ancient Mariner's tale. Both of the men were fond of Nature; both were keenly interested in everyday life and character; both had plenty of whimsical humour and philosophy; both were good teasers, and found enough idiosyncrasies in each other for sly sallies and retorts. Thus, Newton liked his pipe, which rather shocked Cowper,[1] though he had to allow that Newton, unlike many votaries of tobacco, was at least the pattern of courtesy in not venting his fumes upon the ladies. Both men, again, were classical scholars. And, not least, they had both had their innate spiritual zeal fanned by the Revival that was sweeping across England. Here, however, there were differences in degree. Newton, a disciple of Whitefield, was, as we have seen, milder in his Calvinism than Cowper, whose religious views, some-how and somewhen, had acquired a grimmer tinge. Newton, again, was broad-minded enough to associate with dissenters; Cowper at this time was not.[2]

Newton had great physical energy. This must not in his case be confused, in the cruder sense, with "strong animal spirits": his tenderness refutes that glib assumption. If

[1] See his attack on smoking in *Conversation*, 245-268.
[2] It was through Newton that the poet later became intimate with the Rev. William Bull, of Newport Pagnell, who was an Independent—and " smoke-inhaling! "

energy were entirely dependent upon animal spirits, Wesley would not have come near to holding the world's record for sustained physical activity. Newton, though his early sufferings had left their mark upon him,[1] *was* constitutionally robust; but his heart was in his work and he was methodical. His driving power, therefore, appeared the greater because it was fully utilised. He soon made his influence felt at Olney. His congregation increased so largely that a gallery —long afterwards known, until it was demolished, as "Newton's Gallery"—was added to the church. It was said that he sometimes "preached people mad." Possibly he did. The population of Olney was very primitive, and he was newly ablaze with religious fervour. He was less mature than he afterwards became. Yet it is scandalously untrue to suggest that he took a pride in preaching people mad, or made that his aim. His sermons, if well garnished with Scriptural allusion, were in substance practical and homely; his style was far from being impressive. That his intense earnestness was nevertheless sensed by the rudest listener, and sometimes provoked hysterical symptoms in natures unaccustomed to the impact of such a force, we may well believe. Even John Wesley's early preaching, which was deliberately calm, produced similar disturbances.

Newton did not confine his services to Sunday or to his own sanctuary. Between the church and the mill stood an empty mansion known as "The Great House." He obtained leave from Lord Dartmouth, the owner, to use it. He himself preached there on week-days, and secured the co-operation of other clergymen, neighbouring and itinerant, in addition to that of "dear Taureau," as he called his dissenting friend Bull. Then there were lectures at "the Mole Hill"—his nickname for the cottage of Molly Mole. There were also special services and lectures for children, and frequent prayer-meetings. It is easy for us to smile, and perhaps the early Evangelicals did, as Wesley said, talk religion too often and too long. Yet we must remember that there were then no travelling facilities for the poor, few schools, no free libraries,

---

[1] In his *Cardiphonia* he states this fact as one of the reasons why he chose to remain in parochial work, instead of undertaking itinerancy.

and no village institutes: to say nothing of popular news-papers, cinemas, or broadcasting. Even if we choose to discount liberally the direct religious value of the work of men like Newton, such men exercised in their day a socialising and, in the broadest sense, an educational influence.

Despite his many meetings, Newton found time for study and literary work, and his flock knew him not only as preacher and lecturer, but as pastor and friend. His own means were slender; but Thornton allowed him two hundred pounds annually for the relief of distress in the neighbourhood. He is well revealed in the following anecdote from Thomas Scott's once famous book, *The Force of Truth*. Scott was deeply influenced by Newton, whom he succeeded at Olney. He lived, indeed, to add new lustre to the Olney tradition, though at the time to which reference is here made he was still the formalist curate of Weston Underwood:

"In January, 1774 [he says] two of my parishioners, a man and his wife, lay at the point of death. I had heard the circum-stances, but, according to my general custom, not being sent for, I took no notice of it; till one evening, the woman being now dead, and the man a-dying, I heard that my neighbour Mr. N. had been several times to visit them. Immediately my conscience reproached me with being shamefully negligent, in sitting at home within a few doors of dying persons, my general hearers, and never going to visit them. Directly it occurred to me that, whatever contempt I might have for Mr. N.'s *doctrines*, I must acknowledge his *practice* to be more consistent with the ministerial character than my own."

To this incident Scott traced his ultimate conversion to Evangelicalism.

Whether through Newton's persuasion or through his own desire to emulate the man he reverenced, Cowper, soon after settling in Olney, was drawn, against all his previous habits, into action. Contemplative by nature, he now undertook sick-visiting; his voice, even, was heard at prayer-meetings. Though he was among those "to whom a public exhibition of themselves on any occasion is mortal poison," he showed great ability (if the word may be allowed) in his new role. Actual records and popular tradition are agreed upon this point.

Newton thought Cowper spoke "as if he saw the Lord whom
he addressed face to face." Mr. Greatheed, a local contemporary, said he gave his hearers "an awful yet delightful
consciousness of the presence of the Saviour." Another
villager remarked years afterwards: "Of all the men I ever
heard pray, no one equalled Mr. Cowper." But the price
paid was too heavy for Cowper's sensitive constitution.
Though his nervousness disappeared when he rose in the
assembly, he confessed that "his mind was always greatly
agitated for some hours preceding."

If Newton's perception had been a little more penetrating,
he might have seen the danger involved. To *blame* Newton,
however, is beside the point. Subtle intuition is a gift of the
gods, which a man either has or has not. Newton's vision was
by no means blunt, and, while wishing that it had been
slightly keener, we must remember that *we* know Cowper as
revealed in his poems: to his friends, at this time, he was
only an occasional amateur in verse. It is quite understandable that Newton should have seen in his friend an earnest,
yet unoccupied and introspective, gentleman, who needed, in
modern parlance, to get outside himself. In finding Cowper
"a job of work," Newton acted on a sound enough general
principle, and he certainly felt already the loving concern
which, even amid the distractions of his later life in London,
he never ceased to show for one of whom he said that he was
indeed an "*alter idem*." But every rule has its exception,
and in this instance the method was probably wrong: though,
as we shall presently see, a number of other factors were at
this time combining to depress Cowper's spirits again.

IV

In 1771, observing his friend's increasing gloom, Newton,
who had resolved to write some hymns for Evangelical use,
now sought to divert Cowper's thoughts by engaging his
collaboration. The proposal was doubly congenial to Cowper:
it offered a prospect both of spiritual service and, as he admitted, of satisfaction to his modest literary ambition. But
his full share of the task was never completed. Two years

later he was again seriously afflicted in mind. Newton hung his own "harp upon the willows" for some time, not wishing to proceed further by himself. At length, however, he resumed his part of the work, and the *Olney Hymns* appeared in 1779,[1] almost simultaneously, as it happened, with the Wesleys' great collection.

Newton's character is well mirrored in his Introduction, which is a model of charity, humility, and good sense. His motive in writing hymns is easily understood. The evangelical Revival had given a new impetus to *congregational* singing and had occasioned a demand for popular religious song embodying its own spirit and tenets. Charles Wesley was supplying the needs of the Arminians, and, though in fact most of Newton's own hymns could have been sung in Arminian churches, the Calvinists naturally wished to sound their distinctive voice. But hymn-writing cannot be an industry. Even Charles Wesley produced much literary dross; and the amount of alloy in Newton is, of course, vastly greater:

> "*When Jonah sunk beneath the wave*
> *He thought to rise no more;*
> *But God prepared a fish to save,*
> *And bear him to the shore.*"

Lines like these might well find a place in any anthology of "verse, or worse": or these, again, on David:

> "*His eyes on fair Bathsheba fix'd,*
> *With poison fill'd his soul;*
> *He ventured on adultery next,*
> *And murder crown'd the whole.*"

Much of Newton's verse is definitely bad. Much, however, while crude, has in its breezy colloquialism a certain vividness and vitality.

It is indeed a mixed vintage, theological no less than literary, which Newton gives us. Most of his hymns are merely rhymed versions of Scriptural stories, with a moral appended, and they corroborate his own statement that he

---

[1] Newton contributed 280 hymns, Cowper 68. A few of Cowper's contributions may have been written after his recovery in 1774; but it seems more likely that they were all composed between 1771 and 1773.

could preach from any one text, but found difficulty in "correlation." Theoretically, like all his contemporaries, he was in bondage to a Bible of uniform inspiration. We must, therefore, judge him by the passages of Scripture to which his inmost being instinctively responded. His native impulse was all on the side of love, and, moved by a congenial text, he soared sometimes into the true firmament of song. Hymns like "Glorious things of thee are spoken," "How sweet the name of Jesus sounds," and "Come, my soul, thy suit prepare" are as universal in their appeal as they are imperishable.

The same may be said, of course, of Cowper's best contributions. "Sometimes a light surprises," "Hark, my soul! it is the Lord," "God moves in a mysterious way": these hymns, with others from the same source, are among the common and permanent riches of the whole English-speaking race. They sufficiently prove that, though they were written more or less under the shadow of impending mental disorder, the Evangelical impulse in Cowper had suffered no essential reaction. It may be that his best hymns are those in which he voices his love of Nature. Yet Cowper was not using the *form* of an Evangelical hymn to *escape* from Evangelicalism as he wrote:

> "*When, like a tent to dwell in,*
> *He spread the skies abroad,*
> *And swathed about the swelling*
> *Of Ocean's mighty flood.*"

Evangelicalism itself fostered a warmer feeling for Nature, and it is very questionable indeed if Cowper would have become so true a natural poet had he not experienced the influence of the Revival. He always needed the touch of intimacy. An impersonal Nature he could never have loved, and he lived before the time when it was possible for one of his temperament to think of "something far more deeply interfused" in other than theological terms.

The *Olney Hymns* supply further proof that Cowper's *mind* had been preoccupied with Calvinism long before his *heart* was fired by Evangelical zeal, and even longer before he encountered Newton. By asking the collaboration of his muse, Newton, who had then known Cowper a comparatively brief time, was the indirect means of making his friend's Calvinism vocal. But the Calvinism itself had been of long development. This will become plain to anyone who carefully and impartially examines the *Olney* volume. Hints of pure Calvinism—or, in milder degree, of an Old Testament religion based upon fear—are proportionally much more evident in Cowper's than in Newton's contributions. Cowper's hymn entitled "Not of Works," of which I quote the final stanza, is Calvinism almost undiluted:

> "*Still the boasting heart replies,*
> '*What! the worthy and the wise,*
> *Friends to temperance and peace,*
> *Have not these a righteousness?*'
> *Banish every vain pretence*
> *Built on human excellence;*
> *Perish everything in man,*
> *But the grace that never can.*"

Take, again, the last verse of his "Sardis":

> "'*Yet I number now in thee*
> *A few that are upright;*
> *These My Father's face shall see,*
> *And walk with Me in white;*
> *When in judgment I appear,*
> *They for Mine shall be confest;*
> *Let My faithful servants hear,*
> *And woe be to the rest!*'"

And here is part of a hymn designed to be sung "before annual sermons to young people, on New Year's evenings":

> "*Ye careless ones, O hear betimes*
> *The voice of sovereign Love!*
> *Your youth is stain'd with many crimes,*
> *But mercy reigns above.*
>
> *True, you are young, but there's a stone*
> *Within the youngest breast,*
> *Or half the crimes which you have done*
> *Would rob you of your rest.*"

There are ample traces of "Calvinism" in the more colloquial sense. "Old Testament Gospel" supplies a characteristic example. I quote the second and fourth stanzas:

> " *The paschal sacrifice*
> *And blood-besprinkled door,*
> *Seen with enlightened eyes,*
> *And once applied with power,*
> *Would teach the need of other blood*
> *To reconcile an angry God.*
>
> *The scape-goat on his head*
> *The people's trespass bore,*
> *And to the desert led,*
> *Was to be seen no more:*
> *In him our Surety seem'd to say,*
> *'Behold! I bear your sins away.'*"

These lines are in sharp contrast to many of Newton's references to the Cross. I am not pretending that allusions to "the threatening law" or an angry God do not occur in Newton, as in the conclusion of "Malachi":

> " *Assembled worlds will then discern*
> *The saints alone are blest,*
> *When wrath shall like an oven burn,*
> *And vengeance strike the rest.*"

There are other similar passages in his hymns,[1] though none more deeply tinctured; and the doctrine of "imputed righteousness" finds expression in "A Brand Plucked from the Burning." But I repeat, without fear of contradiction, that, while Cowper is *characteristically* preoccupied with personal salvation and *characteristically* stresses the need of a vicarious sacrifice to appease a jealous God, Newton in practice often gives an ethical interpretation to the Atonement:

> " *In evil long I took delight,*
> *Unaw'd by shame or fear,*
> *Till a new object struck my sight*
> *And stopped my wild career.*
>
> *I saw One hanging on a tree*
> *In agonies and blood,*
> *Who fix'd His languid eyes on me,*
> *As near His cross I stood.*

---

[1] See, for instance, " The Believer's Safety."

> *Still never till my latest breath*
> *Can I forget that look;*
> *It seemed to charge me with His death*
> *Though not a word He spoke."*

In these lines, which Palgrave said are of such power and intensity that Bunyan might have been proud to own them, the appeal of the Cross is not to self-interest or fear, but to conscience and love. Cowper, in a typical couplet, sings:

> *"Comfortable thoughts arise*
> *From the bleeding sacrifice;"*

but Newton repeatedly breaks into strains like this:

> *"When on the cross my Lord I see,*
> *Bleeding to death for wretched me,*
> *Satan and sin no more can move,*
> *For I am all transform'd to love."*

Cowper, pathetically concerned with his own case, seeks a spiritual amulet: Newton, gazing upon the crucified Christ, sees an example of love that calls for reciprocal devotion and for emulation.

Throughout Newton's pages there is far more of love than of fear; there is an ethical emphasis often greatly in advance of its time; and even in some of the relatively few hymns in which the doctrine of election finds a place, he refutes it in spirit with such questions as:

> *"Can His pity or His power*
> *Suffer thee to pray in vain?"*

Nor is there much of the grim Calvinist in this by no means unrepresentative stanza:

> *"O sinners, hear His gracious call,*
> *His mercy's door stands open wide!*
> *He has enough to feed you all,*
> *And none who comes shall be denied."*

And it is illuminating to compare the number of his references to God as Judge with that in which he uses his favourite appellations of "Father," "Husband," "Brother," or "Friend." Beneath his proselytising fervour there lay an essential

humility, tolerance, and gentleness that make him among
the most lovable of saints:

> "*Quiet, Lord, my froward heart:*
> *Make me teachable and mild,*
> *Upright, simple, free from art,*
> *Make me as a weanèd child:*
> *From distrust and envy free,*
> *Pleased with all that pleases Thee.*"

That is his true voice; and if to be childlike is to approach
most nearly to Christian perfection, then John Newton was
not far from the Kingdom.

Cowper's long classical training saved him from the worst
of Newton's *literary* pitfalls. But Cowper's excesses in other
respects are, as I have said, both more numerous and more
pronounced. The worst aspects of Evangelicalism, on its
Calvinistic side, are seen in some of his hymns. Many of his
contributions to the *Olney* volume are, by the way, hardly
hymns in the strict sense. Though he usually wrote with a
purpose essentially indistinguishable from that of hymn-
writing, his feelings were too deep and individual, and he was
innately too much of an artist, for him to be able to frame
his message, except by chance, in a form suitable for public
worship. Some of his "hymns" are *poems* of personal doubt
and conflict rather than *songs* of faith and assurance. *As*
poems they are sometimes laboured and flat; at other times
they are poignant enough:

> "*Ah, whither shall I fly!*
> *I hear the thunder roar;*
> *The law proclaims destruction nigh,*
> *And vengeance at the door!*"

That may move us as poetry, but it is hardly suitable for
congregational singing! Still less so is this:

> "*Thy saints are comforted, I know,*
> *And love Thy house of prayer;*
> *I therefore go where others go,*
> *But find no comfort there.*"

In judging the Cowper of the *Olney Hymns* we must bear
several facts in mind. He was forty when he began writing

his contributions to the collection. He had reached what is a critical age in any man's life—an inevitable time of stock-taking. He was simultaneously passing through an inescapable phase of his Evangelical experience. It is reflected in one of his earliest, most beautiful, and still most frequently sung hymns: for his self-questioning was here put into a form which makes a general appeal:

> *" Where is the blessedness I knew*
> *When first I saw the Lord ?*
> *Where is the soul-refreshing view*
> *Of Jesus and His Word ?"*

It may be that his impending derangement gave to these lines their special intensity, or perhaps he was merely expressing, with a poet's emphasis, the feeling of "staleness" which comes to all sincere pilgrims after the first rapture of morning has faded.

Cowper had, in any case, reached that stage of his spiritual journey. Seven or eight years had passed since, at St. Albans, the sunrise had kindled his heart. His enthusiasm, as he later admitted, had then been excessive: it could not have failed to be in one of his temperament. The temporary reaction was for him correspondingly bitter. And it synchronised not merely with the advent of middle age but with the approach of his third attack of insanity. The spiritual reaction may have aggravated his mental condition: or, conversely, his mental condition may have coloured more darkly the inescapable spiritual reaction. But the disorder which was once more threatening his mind is mainly traceable, as we shall now see, to causes not directly connected with religion at all.

Chapter Nine

LIFE AT ORCHARD SIDE

I

" A VERY ALARMING turn aroused us from our beds and called us to Orchard Side at four in the morning. I stayed there till eight, before which time the threatening appearance went entirely off, and now things remain much as they were. My dear [Mrs. Newton] was there the whole day." Thus runs Newton's journal for January 24, 1773. Cowper had again been seized with madness; he was plunged, as he himself afterwards wrote, "into a melancholy that made him almost an infant."

A month later his condition became even worse. One night he had a "fatal dream." In the significance of ordinary dreams he did not believe. But this dream, like two or three others in his experience, was different: it made a lasting impression on him. He does not tell us precisely what it was: only that a "Word" was spoken, which reduced him to spiritual despair. "It is all over with thee, thou art lost," would seem to have been its purport. Thomas Wright, who discovered the record of this dream and who was tempted on that account to attach undue importance to it, suggests that while Cowper had hitherto believed that God was afflicting him for some ultimately good purpose, he now finally lost hope. "Henceforth," says Wright, he was "a doomed man. God had forsaken him for ever."

In a restricted sense this may be true. Several times, in later life, the poet recalled this particular nightmare. "I had a dream twelve years ago," he wrote to Newton in 1785, "before the recollection of which all consolation vanishes, and, it seems to me, must always vanish." Again, not very long before his death, he told Lady Hesketh: "In one day, in one *minute* I should rather have said, she [Nature] became a universal blank to me; and though from a different cause, yet with an effect as difficult to remove, as blindness itself."

192

The "fatal dream" was never completely forgotten, and the memory of it accentuated the gloom of Cowper's despondent periods.

It is absurd, nevertheless, to represent his melancholy as having been other than intermittent. There is a chronic hypochondria which makes a permanent physical or mental invalid of its victim. But Wright's own account of Cowper's later career contradicts in essence his assertion that "the fearful delusion never left him except for very brief intervals during the remainder of his life." The facts, indeed, speak for themselves. All Cowper's major poetry, and many of his sprightliest letters, were written after 1773; and, though grief and pain may put on a smiling face, unmitigated *despair* cannot so mask itself. Anyone who has had intimate experience of nervous disorders knows how strangely fluctuating, from day to day, and even from hour to hour, the spirits of some neurasthenics can be. A task or social engagement from which they shrink at one time will be fulfilled without effort at another; and their feelings are as variable as an April sky.

Any degree of nervous tension must, it is true, prevent the integration of personality. This, however, few even among so-called "normal" people actually attain. In most natures there are unresolved tangles of some kind; and many hypochondriacs have their own compensations. If their dark hours are darker than those of other folk, their bright hours may be correspondingly brighter: the inn fire is cosier to the man who has been out in the storm than to him who has not left his seat in the ingle-nook. And while lassitude or timidity may sometimes reduce a nervously unstable person to impotence, at other times his faculties may be abnormally alert. It was thus with Cowper. One has only to contrast some of the letters in which he speaks in retrospect of his "fatal dream" with others written a few days before or afterwards, in a very different spirit, to realise how much he was a man of moods. Nor is it a contradiction to add that he often represented his moods as being a little darker or lighter than they were. No one was ever more fundamentally truthful. But he was, after all, an essayist in temperament. He wrote

N

spontaneously what he thought and felt *at the moment*, and whimsically deepened or heightened his effects.

But the "fatal dream"—if, strictly speaking, it were a symptom of his disorder, not its cause—had serious enough consequences for a time. In considering Cowper's third derangement, it is necessary to repeat that his malady was probably constitutional, and that in his earlier life there had been almost every possible irritant. It is not for an *origin*, but for fresh *exciting causes*, that we must now look. And if we glance back over the years immediately preceding 1773, what do we find? In 1769 Cowper had visited Cambridge, where his brother lay seriously ill. At about the same time William Unwin became rector of the pleasant village of Stock, in Essex. His sunny personality was sorely missed at Orchard Side. Early in 1770 John Cowper was again ill. He died in March. William sat with him during the last days, and afterwards wrote, under the title of *Adelphi*, an account of his brother's painful yet spiritually triumphant end.[1] Since William had moved to Olney he had necessarily seen John less often. But John's death was a deep sorrow to him:

---

[1] Some biographers have accused Cowper of having taken advantage of John's condition to wring from him a death-bed confession of Evangelical belief. They have also condemned Newton, who preached a joyful sermon at Olney, in which he gave thanks for John Cowper's ultimate, if belated, " salvation." At this time Newton and Cowper, like many other " enthusiasts," may have attached too much importance to death-bed conversions. Newton largely outgrew this weakness in later life, and Cowper, in a letter written in 1786, admitted that " eagerness of spirit, natural to persons newly informed, and the less to be wondered at in me, who had just emerged from the horror of despair, made me imprudent." But the charge that Cowper stimulated his sinking brother into a merely nominal acceptance of Evangelical truth is nevertheless unjustified. John acknowledged a few days before his death that, though full conviction had only just come to him, he had for some time been moving steadily towards the Evangelical position. John's character remains a little obscure. Bishop Bennet called him " the best classic and most liberal thinker " at Cambridge. He was kindly and " a perfect gentleman " ; but he was in religion a formalist. When visiting Olney he conformed to the rules of Mrs. Unwin's household. He went to church and listened to Newton ; he attended, but took no share in " leading," the family prayers. He avoided religious discussion. He was subject, we also know, to moods of depression, which the fortune-telling of a gipsy had served to foster. He was perhaps, like William, a little abnormal. We must allow for that possibility in trying to assess the value of his conversion ; and the Evangelical idiom of the period does not help us to judge more clearly. Yet we cannot ignore the fact that, a few hours before he died, he said smilingly, though in great pain : " Brother, I am as happy as a King." Was the new light that had come to him all an illusion ?

moreover, such a vivid reminder of the fact of dissolution was itself, as always, disturbing to his mind. As is the case with many potential suicides, the idea of death alternately terrified and attracted him. It is not without significance that each of his own attempts at self-murder was made soon after the passing of some relative or intimate friend. Financial worry further aggravated his condition. He was actually the loser by a small bequest from his brother, who had evidently given him an annual allowance of greater value than the legacy, invested, would now yield.

There were other anxieties. Susanna Unwin had become engaged to Matthew Powley, a clergyman of Huddersfield. Mrs. Unwin and Cowper would soon have only servants in the house beside themselves. Wholly innocent as was their relation to each other—founded on the truest spiritual companionship and suggesting that of mother and son rather than any other physical bond—they knew that the tongue of scandal had already been heard in the town, and that it was now likely to be more active. Late in 1772, therefore, they were betrothed. Were they "in love"? It is possible, but unlikely. Cowper was now forty-one; Mrs. Unwin was forty-eight. They were to live together for another twenty-four years without any strain and with ever-deepening affection. The nature of their friendship was apparent to everyone who knew them. Innuendo was confined to the vulgar village gossips; nor has any literary muck-raker among the love stories of the world ever thought Orchard Side worth his attention. Cowper called Mrs. Unwin "Mary"; but she, to the end of her days, addressed him as "Mr Cowper." It seems almost certain that the proposed marriage was to be one of pure convenience or worldly prudence. The project nevertheless agitated Cowper. It may have stirred memories —as also may the engagement of Miss Unwin—of the time when he *was* "in love"—with Theodora. In any case, marriage for him was something new and untried; he may well have been in two minds about the wisdom of it; and, at the best, he hated things that needed planning and preparations. Following upon the loss of his brother, the excitement was too much for his nerves. The season of the year, moreover, was against him; January was always his worst month. The marriage ceremony was arranged for the February or March of 1773. It never took place. On January 24, as we have seen, Cowper again lost the kindly light of reason.

Newton, by encouraging (or, at all events, by not discouraging) his friend in sick-visiting and public prayer, had perhaps unwittingly played a minor part in provoking this fresh attack of madness. Nor were he and Mrs. Unwin before their time in knowing how to deal with lunacy. They cannot be blamed for that. The only possible ground for criticism is that they were tardy in sending for Dr. Cotton: but, again, they lived in an age when, especially in the country, doctors and "specialists" had small part in the conventional routine of life. Even if its aid were invoked, medical science was often of questionable benefit. Dr. Cotton seems to have been uncommonly wise and skilful for his day. Yet the reports suggest that when he was at last summoned for consultation, his prescribed treatment was not this time wholly successful. Cowper had owed the recovery from his previous derangement largely to his long rest at Cotton's home at St. Albans and to daily intercourse with the cheery doctor himself. The little physician's *medicines*, by themselves, appear to have been only partly efficacious. Rest and the passage of time again wrought the cure. Nor must we forget that it was at the Vicarage that Cowper recovered.

If Mrs. Unwin and the Newtons were inclined to think that his madness would yield to prayer alone, their practical kindness was devoted and selfless. At first Cowper had turned against Newton and had refused to visit him. Single-handed —for so she chose to undertake the task, while Susanna prepared for her marriage with Mr. Powley, which took place in May [1]—Mrs. Unwin tended him day and night. Her task

[1] Some few years afterwards Susanna Unwin, now Mrs. Powley, visited Olney with her husband. Cowper's regard for her, as hers for him, seems to have undergone a change. During her stay at Orchard Side he wrote to her brother: " Your poor sister !—she has many good qualities, and upon some occasions gives proof of a good understanding; but as some people have no ear for music, so she has none for humour. Well, if she cannot laugh at our jokes, we can, however, at her mistakes, and in this way she makes us ample amends for the disappointment. Mr. Powley is like herself: if his wife overlooks the jest, he will never be able to find it." The fact was that, while she concealed her true feeling under

was grimmer because Cowper soon fancied that she hated him and intended to poison his food. Then, on April 12, wishing to avoid the noise of the annual fair, he suddenly resolved to seek refuge at the Vicarage. Once there, he decided to stay—and remained for thirteen months! "Equally regardless of her own health and of the uncharitable construction of censorious and malicious tongues," as Newton said, Mrs. Unwin gave up her own home and joined the Vicarage household. Newton, for his part, declined to regard her and Cowper as "boarders": not a penny would he accept.

In October the patient seemed so much better that Newton and his wife felt justified in travelling to Warwickshire. While they were away, however, Cowper, conceiving it to be the divine will that he should "after the example of Abraham, perform an expensive act of obedience, and offer not a son, but himself," attempted suicide: we do not know in what manner or by whom the plan was defeated. The Newtons hurried home, and decided never again to be both away for long at a time until their guest were healed. The idea now obsessed Cowper that he was sentenced by God "to a state of desertion and perpetual misery" *because* he had failed to make the sacrifice demanded. He still accepted the *general* "truth" of predestination, but insisted on deeming himself the sole exception to the rule. Further attempts at suicide were expected of him, but—owing, probably, to the vigilance of his guardians—none was made.

Months went by. He was still at the Vicarage. "Mrs. Unwin," wrote Newton in March 1774, "has often tried to persuade him to return to their own house, but he cannot bear to hear of it. He sometimes begs, and weeps, and pleads to stay with such earnestness that it must be submitted to." Newton, on at least one occasion, spoke of the "cross" imposed on himself. But patiently and gallantly he bore it, and when at last, with the coming of Spring, Cowper's spirits began to revive, Newton, as is plain from the tender phrasing of the entries in his diary, recording the convalescent's

an apparent coldness towards his poetry and his personal " sallies in the way of drollery," Mrs. Powley resented her mother's financial generosity to Cowper. At a later date she complained that Mrs. Unwin had wasted eighteen hundred pounds upon him. See *The Life of William Cowper*. By Thomas Wright. P. 253.

pleasure in gardening and in feeding the chickens, felt far more of affectionate joy on his friend's behalf than of relief on his own. By the middle of May, Cowper's condition had greatly improved. At the end of the month he went back, at his own wish, to Orchard Side.

His third derangement had, on the whole, been less severe than the second one, ten years earlier. Sanity had frequently returned to him during sleep; many of his dreams had been "gracious and comfortable." Newton tells us that, in everything which did not concern his own peace, his judgment had often been normally "sensible" and "quick." And—a sure sign that despondency had not been unrelieved—he had written several poems, very different from the morbid sapphics of 1763:

> "*Come, peace of mind, delightful guest!*
> *Return and make thy downy nest*
> *Once more in this sad heart!—*
> *Nor riches I, nor pow'r, pursue,*
> *Nor hold forbidden joys in view;*
> *We therefore need not part.*
>
> *Where wilt thou dwell if not with me,*
> *From av'rice and ambition free,*
> *And pleasure's fatal wiles?*
> *For whom, alas! dost thou prepare*
> *The sweets that I was wont to share,*
> *The banquet of thy smiles?*"

The tune is plaintive indeed. Yet there is an undertone of quiet satisfaction: of a joy in craftsmanship which itself partially contradicts the theme. A man in complete despair lacks both the will and the capacity to express his feelings; or, at least, as Coleridge once said, "When a man is unhappy he writes d—— bad poetry." And Cowper, though forty-one, was but upon the threshold of his poetical career. He was soon to enjoy a long period of sustained productiveness.

II

His convalescence was steady, if slow. For some time after his return to Orchard Side he felt no inclination to read and did little writing, though his gloomy verses in Latin—"Heu! quam remotus"—belong to this period. He was fortunate, however, in being a man of hobbies. He had first taken pleasure in gardening while at Huntingdon; he had further cultivated the taste during his residence at Olney Vicarage; and now he was to turn his interest to excellent account. I can do little more than record the important fact; for though I know that

> "*gardens are not made*
> *By singing 'Oh, how beautiful!',*
> *And sitting in the shade,*"

I am among those who wish that such a miracle were possible. Cowper, happily for him, was not. By practising "the arts of pruning, sowing, and planting," and "enterprising everything in that way, from melons down to cabbages," he nursed himself, with the wise encouragement of his friends, back to health of body and spirit.

"I have a large garden to display my abilities in," he had written to Hill from Huntingdon, "and were we twenty miles nearer London I might turn higgler, and serve your honour with cauliflowers and broccoli at the best hand." He informed Mrs. Cowper about the same time that he had become "a great florist and drug-doctor," and begged of the Major a small packet of seeds that would make a figure in a garden where there was "little else besides jessamine and honeysuckle." He promised to take special care of any "natives" of Hertingfordbury Park that might be sent him, but requested that "they be not such as require great skill in the management." Now, at Olney, he speaks with the confidence of the expert:

". . . I made Mr. Wright's gardener a present of fifty sorts of stove plant seeds; in return, he has presented me with six fruiting pines, which I have put into a dark bed, where they thrive at present as well as I could wish. If they produce good fruit, you will stand some little chance to partake of them. But you must not expect giants, for being transplanted in December will certainly give them a check, and probably diminish their size. He has promised to supply me with still better plants in October, which is the proper season for moving them, and with a reinforcement every succeeding year. Mrs. Hill sent me the seeds; which perhaps could not have been purchased for less than three guineas. 'Tis thus we great gardeners establish a beneficial intercourse with each other, and furnish ourselves with valuable things that, therefore, cost us nothing."

A little later he is training his vines and raising his cucumbers, and these activities, combined with his growing interest in tame pigeons and other pets, have made him also a carpenter and general handyman. "There is not a squire in all this country," he writes, "who can boast of having made better squirrel-houses, hutches for rabbits, or bird-cages." The Government having laid a tax upon glass, he forms a scheme "to cheat the glazier," who has "trebled it," by building his own hot-house frames. He erects, too, his famous "greenhouse," which, he tells Newton, "Lord Bute's gardener could take upon his back and walk away with." This "sunny shed," in which *John Gilpin* and portions of *The Task* were to be written, was later furnished as a second parlour. It offered a pleasant retreat in hot weather from the voices of squalling children in the market-place and the odours of Silver End. It must not be confused with the still existing "summer-house" at the end of the gravel path. This was the property of Cowper's apothecary and neighbour, Mr. Aspray, who used it as his smoking-room, and kept his bottles concealed under a trap-door. Cowper was not given the use of the summer-house, which he described as being "not much bigger than a sedan-chair," and which commanded a prospect both of his own "pinks, roses, and honeysuckles" and of his neighbour's orchard, until 1785, some time after Aspray's death.

In *The Task* the poet says:

> *How various his employments, whom the world*
> *Calls idle; and who justly, in return,*
> *Esteems that busy world an idler too!*
> *Friends, books, a garden, and perhaps his pen,*
> *Delightful industry enjoy'd at home,*
> *And Nature in her cultivated trim*
> *Dress'd to his taste, inviting him abroad—*
> *Can he want occupation who has these?"*

The Third Book of the poem is devoted to "The Garden."
Some hundreds of lines are, it is true, engaged with an
attempt to justify the ways of God to phlox and lettuces, and
conversely, to show that gardening is not only compatible
with moral innocence, but of positive value to the Christian
who, through Nature, may come to a better understanding
of Nature's God. With the philosophical aspect of Cowper's
gardening we may deal later. It is enough to remark here
that the long succession of English poets who have celebrated
the gardens they have loved owe much to his example.

It cannot be said that his efforts were, as poetry, always
successful: they were, to use an appropriate metaphor, spade-
work. It may be that the ambition to praise "the prickly
and green-coated gourd"—an ambition then "unassay'd in
song"—was in itself no less "sublime" than many themes
which had stirred the Mantuan or Grecian bards: but sublime
the result did not always prove:

> " The stable yields a stercoraceous heap,
>   Impregnated with quick fermenting salts,
>   And potent to resist the freezing blast."

The verse is here blank indeed, and, though these lines provide
an extreme example, it must be confessed that Cowper rises
to a higher level when he dilates in general terms upon the
pleasure of gardening—one of those simple domestic joys
which move him to reflect that

> " The only amaranthine flow'r on earth
>   Is virtue"—

than when he deals with garden lore in detail. Yet his descriptions, if they fail as song, show much prosodial ingenuity,
and supply an intimate picture of the poet himself amid his

> "grateful mixture of well-matched
>   And sorted hues."

And if some passages resemble a seedsman's catalogue rather
than an epic, I suspect that many gardeners may like them
none the less on that account.

But in giving a composite impression of Cowper as gardener
—as well as by reference to *The Task*—I have done some slight

violence to chronology. By the end of the period with which
this chapter deals he had, indeed, become the complete horti-
culturalist. He reached that status through successive stages;
but the year 1773 marked the serious beginning of the enterprise. It was then, too, that he began his lifelong habit of
keeping pets. The circumstances are familiar to every reader.
Puss, Tiney, and Bess—"notwithstanding the two feminine
appellatives, I must inform you that they were all males"—
have been immortalised by the account their master wrote of
them in the *Gentleman's Magazine*.[1] And if any reader
would plumb the depths of human tenderness let him refresh
his memory of that essay, in which Cowper tells how, having
just recovered from his third mental disorder, and needing
diversion without fatigue, he received from neighbours the
timely gift of three leverets; how he "commenced carpenter"
on their behalf and built a house for them with three separate
compartments; how "in the day time they had the range of
a hall, and at night retired each to his own bed"; how Puss
"grew presently familiar," would leap into the writer's lap,
and bite the hair from his temples, and what gratitude the
creature showed on being nursed back to health after an
illness; how Tiney, on the other hand, was ferocious on
receiving the same attention, but was none the less entertaining in his very surliness; and how, while Puss was tamed
by gentle usage, and Tiney was not to be tamed at all, Bess—
"a hare of great humour and drollery"—was tame from the
beginning, and, being remarkably strong and fearless,
"proved himself the Vestris of the party."[2]

Of the whims, the habits, the diet, and the distinguishing
characteristics of these hares, each of which their owner came
to identify by its peculiar facial expression, one may read fully
in a paper which makes one regret that Cowper did not more
fully cultivate the art of the essay. For ourselves, we are only

---

[1] June 1784.

[2] Bess died soon after attaining full growth. Tiney lived to be nine ; and Puss,
who was on the friendliest terms with the dog Marquis, reached "the age of
eleven years eleven months." She died, notes Cowper, on March 9, 1786,
"between twelve and one at noon, of mere old age, and apparently without pain."
See also Cowper's poem "Epitaph on a Hare," written on the death of Tiney in
1783, and again the passage in *The Task* (Book III, 334-351) ending "I knew
at least one hare that had a friend."

partially the losers by his neglect, for his letters, which were written without the slightest intention or prevision of publication,[1] are perhaps even better "essays" than any he might have written in the essay form. But his prose contribution to the *Gentleman's Magazine* shows what he could have done, had he chosen, for his own additional pleasure, as well as for the sake of contemporary reputation and reward.

The essay, indeed, was in one respect a medium more suited than poetry to the needs of a writer who, while he had in plenty the gifts of description, fancy, and humour, was yet a born moralist. His didacticism often fails to blend artistically with the other *motifs* in his verse. How naturally, on the contrary, and with what a positive access of unity to the work, homily creeps into the essay on his pets:

> "It is no wonder that my intimate acquaintance with these specimens of the kind has taught me to hold the sportsman's amusement in abhorrence; he little knows what amiable creatures he persecutes, of what gratitude they are capable, how cheerful they are in spirits, what enjoyment they have of life, and that, impressed as they seem with a peculiar dread of man, it is only because man gives them peculiar cause for it."

A moral, by the way, which was vastly in advance of the general conscience of a century when the baiting of bulls, with cats tied to them, and fireworks tied to the cats, was a popular "entertainment."

III

By 1776 Cowper was so much better, and his financial condition so much worse, that he thought of "taking two, three, or four boys" under his care for instruction, according to "the Westminster method," in Greek and Latin. "They would lodge and board under our roof," he told Joseph Hill, whom he regarded as the most likely agent for securing candidates, "and be in all respects accommodated in a manner that would well warrant the demand of a hundred guineas per annum." Hill's efforts were unsuccessful, and the project

---

[1] Cowper destroyed the letters he received, and commended the practice to his correspondents.

was soon abandoned. "If it were to rain pupils," said Cowper, "perhaps I might catch a tub full; but till it does, the fruitlessness of my inquiries makes me think I must keep my Greek and Latin to myself."

He fell back for occupation upon his gardening and carpentry. He was also for a time, until the effect on his eyes proved too severe, an amateur artist. "I draw mountains, valleys, woods, and streams, and ducks, and dab-chicks," he told Newton. "I admire them myself, and Mrs. Unwin admires them; and her praise and my praise together are frame enough for me." Nor was he dependent wholly upon hobbies. He was the type of man to whom plenty of *unpaid* work always finds its way. The following letter to Hill, who in turn freely put his advice at his friend's disposal, explains itself:

"I know less of the law than a country attorney, yet sometimes I think I have almost as much business. My former connection with the profession has got wind, and though I earnestly profess, and protest, and proclaim it abroad that I know nothing of the matter, they cannot be persuaded to believe that a head once endued with a legal periwig can ever be deficient in those natural endowments it is supposed to cover. I have had the good fortune to be once or twice in the right, which, added to the cheapness of a gratuitous counsel, has advanced my credit to a degree I never expected to attain in the capacity of a lawyer."

Cowper busied himself, too, on behalf of the lace-makers of Olney, who, indeed, comprised practically the whole population. "The lace trade had declined so much," says Thomas Wright, "that the poor lace-makers could only earn just enough to keep body and soul together even in summer-time, while in winter, when there was the additional difficulty of being compelled to procure fuel, their hardships can scarcely be imagined." "We make none but the cheapest laces," wrote Cowper himself, "and the price of them is fallen almost to nothing." Through correspondence at first with Lord Dartmouth, then with Joseph Hill, who was made Secretary to Thurlow when that fiery and obscene Tory became Lord Chancellor in 1778, and later with Newton after he had moved to London in 1780, the poet strove to get petitions considered in Parliament. William Unwin also helped him by providing an introduction to Robert Smith, afterwards Lord Carrington, a wealthy Nottingham banker, who on several occasions sent funds for Cowper to administer as he thought best.

"We shall use our best discretion," Cowper told his benefactor,

"in the disposal of the money; but in this town, where the gospel has been preached so many years . . . it is not an easy thing to find those who make no profession of religion at all, and are yet proper objects of charity. The profane are so profane, so drunken, dissolute, and in every respect worthless, that to make them partakers of the bounty would be to abuse it. We promise, however, that none shall touch it but such as are miserably poor, yet at the same time industrious and honest, two characters frequently found here, where the most watchful and unremitting labour will hardly procure them bread."

It will be seen that, in some matters at least, Cowper's heart did not run away with his head. I suspect, indeed, that his head was still a little obstinately doctrinal, and that "profession of religion" by candidates for relief may perhaps have unduly biased him in the work of distribution.

It is significant, by the way, that the above letter was written in 1782. It is obvious that Cowper was *voluntarily* undertaking this social service, which must have involved much actual contact with the poor and ailing. Indeed, it seems plain from his letters describing (apparently at first hand) the lacemakers' gratitude, that such was the fact. One woman, he says, "carried home two pairs of blankets, a pair for herself and husband, and a pair for her six children. As soon as the children saw them, they jumped out of their straw, caught them in their arms, kissed them, blessed them, and danced for joy." Another woman, "a very old one, the first night that she found herself so comfortably covered, could not sleep a wink, being kept awake by the contrary emotions of transport on the one hand, and the fear of not being thankful enough on the other." As Newton had left Olney two years previously, Cowper, I say, was acting on his own impulse; and we should think the less of him if, despite his sensitiveness, he had not been moved to practical pity at sight of the distress around him. But, seeing that he *was* so moved, what right have some biographers to declare that the sick-visiting undertaken by him some years previously had been "forced" upon him by Newton?

Cowper was not the man to be driven: he was mentally far too obstinate. He was legalistic in his religious and other views; and, as we have just seen, he could be coolly detached even in the allocation of charitable funds among people in the mass. But his heart was very sensitive to the influence of individuals who in any way kindled his esteem. Admiration soon became affection, and affection (to him) meant intimacy. This susceptibility had its dangers; but, on the whole, it served him well, especially as he was fortunate in the strangely varied friends of his later years. The influence of those friends in some measure broadened and mellowed even his ideas; but it is truer, in the main, to say that, in drawing forth the qualities of his heart, his friends broadened and mellowed him *in spite of* his reason. "Narrow in opinion and wide in sympathy," is Mr. Harold Child's accurate reading of Cowper's character.[1]

How eagerly Cowper responded to individuals may be judged from a letter to Unwin in which, long after the time alluded to, he recalled his interchange of letters with Smith, the Nottingham philanthropist. "We corresponded," he says,

"as long as the occasion required, and then ceased. Charmed with his good sense, politeness, and liberality to the poor, I was indeed ambitious of continuing a correspondence with him and told him so. Perhaps I had done more prudently had I never proposed it. But warm hearts are not famous for wisdom, and mine was too warm to be very considerate. . . . I have not heard from him since, and have long given up all expectation of it. I know he is too busy a man to have leisure for me, and I ought to have recollected it sooner." [2]

[1] *Cambridge History of English Literature.* Volume XI.
[2] In another letter Cowper told Unwin that his bosom burned to immortalise Mr. Smith. "How I love and honour that man!" he said. Smith is commemorated in *The Task*, Book IV, 424-428.

A revealing letter in more ways than one! Cowper's humility, no less than his avid need of affection, shines through it.

But we must return to 1777. On June 9 of that year, the bells of Olney were set ringing. Lord Dartmouth had arrived in the town on a business errand. Newton dined with him and other gentlemen of the county, at the Swan, "upon a committee to inspect and report the ruinous state of our bridge." There was "a sumptuous dinner," with a man cook and a bill of fare from London. "Sixteen at table," runs Newton's diary; "the ordinary came to nine shillings, but I suppose a guinea apiece would not have defrayed the expenses. The town makes good the rest." Cowper was not among the diners, and I suspect that on the following morning Newton made his mouth water by describing the fish course or courses. For Cowper was "the most ichthyophagous of Protestants," and his fondness for fish had recently found characteristic expression in a letter to Hill:

"The very agreeable contents of your last came safe to hand in the shape of two notes for thirty pounds. I am to thank you likewise for a barrel of very good oysters, received about a fortnight ago. One to whom fish is so welcome as it is to me, can have no great occasion to distinguish the sorts. In general, therefore, whatever fish are likely to think a jaunt into the country agreeable, will be sure to find me ready to receive them: butts, plaice, flounder, or any other. If herrings are yet to be had, as they cannot be had at Olney till they are good for nothing, they will be welcome too. We have seen none this year, except a parcel Mrs. Unwin sent for, and the fishmonger sent stale ones, a trick they are apt to play upon their customers at a distance."

Cowper missed Lord Dartmouth's "sumptuous dinner"; but he received a visit from his old schoolfellow. He conducted him round the garden at Orchard Side; the two men spoke, among other topics, of the recent voyages of discovery that were exciting public interest, and his lordship promised to lend his friend the books of Captain Cook and of Forster.[1] As for Newton, he was seldom happier than when he sat conversing with Lord Dartmouth under his "favourite great

[1] Cook's companion.

tree" in the Vicarage garden. We have seen that he owed his admission to holy orders and his appointment at Olney to this Evangelical nobleman, who, if he could on occasion enjoy the good things of this life, was genuinely devout and a great philanthropist. Newton (never a sycophant) called him simply "the good Earl." Cowper, whose sense of humour must have been slumbering at the moment, commemorated him, in *Truth*, as "one who wears a coronet and prays."

The first sentence of the above-quoted letter to Hill reminds us that Cowper was still living by the sale of his capital.[1] The death, in 1778, of Sir Thomas Hesketh brought him some pecuniary relief. "Poor Sir Thomas!" he wrote, "I knew that I had a place in his affections, and from his own information, many years ago, a place in his will; but little thought that after the lapse of so many years I should still retain it. His remembrance of me, after so long a season of separation, has done me much honour, and leaves me the more reason to regret his decease." Hesketh seems to have been a solid, honest, kindly man. But we should like to know more about him, if only because we might then see his wife a little less vaguely. Her character is more elusive than is generally imagined. Cowper's references to her, and the joy and benefit he derived from her letters and society, show that she was a woman of sterling character, combining vivacity with good sense. Her practical benevolence to him and to Mrs. Unwin during their declining years stands greatly to her credit. But, while she was fond of Cowper—how could she help that?— and while she appealed strongly to one side of his nature, I doubt if she ever fully *knew* him.

Her vision, unlike her sister Theodora's, was the limited one of her class and time. She thought Cowper's Evangelicalism a mere fad; she failed to see how *inevitable* was his association

---

[1] A will which Cowper made at this time shows that he now had only three hundred pounds standing to his name in the Bank of England. This, or whatever sum might be left at the time of his death, he bequeathed to Mrs. Unwin. Joseph Hill, who acted as his "Chancellor of the Exchequer," was to keep whatever funds he might have in hand, arising from the bond of the testator's chambers in the Temple : and "my desire is," the document concludes, "that such money as he may have received on my account in the way of contributions, and not remitted to me, may be returned to those who gave it, with the best acknowledgments I have it in my power to render them for their kindness."

with the Revival. She understood neither it nor him. She had been irritated into a severance of relationships by his excessive religious zeal at Huntingdon. She did not realise that there was depth beneath the outward commotion. Like most of the other members of her family, she gave William up as a bad job. His regular allowances were sent him—presumably through his friend Hill, who was a lawyer by profession—but direct intercourse ceased. Even when Hesketh died, his legacy reached Cowper through the formal channel. Harriet, as we shall see, needed actual demonstration that her cousin was not merely unbalanced or a ne'er-do-well, with whom it was best not to renew intimacy.

Meanwhile, if still excluded from intercourse with his own kin, Cowper was again taking pleasure in correspondence. Necessity and choice had alike moved him to communicate first with Hill. Now he was to find some compensation for William Unwin's having left Olney: there was another sympathetic friend to whom he could address his "talking letters" and express his "uppermost thoughts." He informs the new incumbent of Stock that Mr. Morley, the grocer, has been guilty of such neglect and carelessness that Mrs. Unwin has had to transfer her custom to Mr. Rawlinson. He thanks the rector for his political intelligence, but regrets that it cannot be repaid in kind. He exhorts him to continue to send such information as cannot be gleaned from the newspaper, and promises in return to report anything at Olney "which is not in the threadbare style of daily occurrences." Nothing of this sort has happened lately, he adds, except that a lion was imported at the annual Cherry Fair in the market-place, seventy years of age, and as tame as a goose.

"Your mother and I saw him embrace his keeper with his paws, and lick his face. Others saw him receive his head in his mouth, and restore it to him again unhurt—a sight we chose not to be favoured with, but rather advised the honest man to discontinue the practice—a practice hardly reconcilable to prudence, unless he had a head to spare."

Out of the strong, on this occasion, there certainly came forth sweetness. Not only was Cowper inspired to a letter, but

o

Newton was able to tell Bull: "I got a hymn out of this lion, which you shall see when you come to Olney if you please me." [1]

In July 1779, William Unwin is spending a holiday at Margate. "We envy you your sea breezes," writes Cowper.

> "In the garden we feel nothing but the reflection of the heat from the walls, and in the parlour from the opposite houses. I fancy Virgil was so situated when he wrote those two beautiful lines:
>
> '*Oh quis me gelidis in vallibus Hœmi*
> *Sistat, et ingenti ramorum protegat umbra!*'
>
> The worst of it is that, though the sunbeams strike as forcibly upon my harp-strings as they did upon his, they elicit no such sounds, but rather produce such groans as they are said to have drawn from those of the statue of Memnon."

He recalls for Unwin's benefit—and his own—the visit he himself paid to Margate years ago, when he fled from London under the impending shadow of his examination in the House of Lords. From a comparison of Thanet with the Isle of Wight he passes to the question of sea-bathing, against which, though it may be suitable for Unwin's wife, he cautions Unwin himself, as the practice "is not safe for thin habits, hectically inclined." "I remember," he continues, again changing the note, "that Sam Cox, the counsel, walking by the seaside as if absorbed in deep contemplation, was questioned about what he was musing on. He replied, 'I was wondering that such an almost infinite and unwieldy element should produce a *sprat*.'" A postscript requests his friend "to purchase three pounds of sixpenny white worsted, at a shop well recommended for that commodity. The Isle of Thanet is famous for it, beyond any other place in the country."

Three months later he asks Unwin to buy him a glazier's diamond pencil:

> "I have glazed the two frames designed to receive my pine plants. But I cannot mend the kitchen windows till by the help

---

[1] "The Lion, though by nature wild." See the *Olney Hymns*, Book II, No. 93.

of that implement I can reduce the glass to its proper dimensions.
If I were a plumber I should be a complete glazier; and possibly
the happy time may come when I shall be seen trudging away
to neighbouring towns with a shelf of glass hanging at my back.
If Government should impose another tax upon that commodity,
I hardly know a business in which a gentleman might more
successfully employ himself. A Chinese of ten times my fortune
would avail himself of such an opportunity without a scruple;
and why should not I, who want money as much as any mandarin
in China?"

He reports a visit by post-chaise with Mrs. Unwin to Gayhurst,
a fine Tudor mansion and park four miles from Olney. It was
then the seat of George Wright, who, knowing that Cowper
"did not much affect strange faces," had, on going away to
Leicestershire, informed the poet that he might view the
gardens "without danger of seeing the proprietor." In the
same epistle he tells Unwin about his pigeons, and adds: "If
your wish could be accomplished, and you should find yourself with the wings of a dove, I shall undoubtedly find you
amongst them. Only be so good, if that should be the case,
as to announce yourself by some means or other. For I
imagine your crop will require something better than tares
to fill it."

Cowper had also taken up reading again. His own library
was wretchedly meagre, as most of his books had apparently
been sold, lost, or otherwise scattered when he made his tragic
exit from the Temple. But through the munificence of
friends he was kept to some extent in touch with current
literature, and he read the first volume of Johnson's *Lives of
the Poets* when it appeared in 1779. The following letter to
Unwin, expressing indignation against the Doctor, reveals
his own enthusiasm for Milton, his chosen master:

"I have been well entertained with Johnson's biography, for
which I thank you: with one exception, and that a swingeing
one, I think he has acquitted himself with his usual good sense
and sufficiency. His treatment of Milton is unmerciful to the
last degree. A pensioner [1] is not likely to spare a republican,
and the Doctor, in order, I suppose, to convince his royal patron

---

[1] Johnson in 1762 had been granted a State pension of £300 per annum.

of the sincerity of his monarchical principles, has belaboured that great poet's character with the most industrious cruelty. As a man, he has hardly left him the shadow of one good quality. . . . As a poet, he has treated him with severity enough, and has plucked one or two of the most beautiful feathers out of his Muse's wing, and trampled them under his great foot. He has passed sentence of condemnation upon Lycidas, and has taken occasion, from that charming poem, to expose to ridicule (what is indeed ridiculous enough) the childish prattlement of pastoral compositions, as if Lycidas was the prototype and pattern of them all. The liveliness of the description, the sweetness of the numbers, the classical spirit of antiquity that prevails in it, go for nothing. I am convinced, by the way, that he has no ear for poetical numbers, or that it was stopped by prejudice against the harmony of Milton's. Was there ever anything so delightful as the music of the *Paradise Lost*? It is like that of a fine organ; has the fullest and the deepest tones of majesty, with all the softness and elegance of the Dorian flute: variety without end, and never equalled, unless perhaps by Virgil. Yet the Doctor has little or nothing to say upon this copious theme, but talks something about the unfitness of the English language for blank verse, and how apt it is, in the mouth of some readers, to degenerate into declamation. Oh! I could thrash his old jacket till I made his pension jingle in his pockets."

Not only was Cowper reading again: his muse, after several years of sleep, had reawakened. His poems written between 1777 and the beginning of 1780 are, it is true, but elegant trifles. Though now in his late forties, he was still the dilettante in verse, with apparently little sense of his own potentialities. "Alas!" he wrote to Unwin,

"what can I do with my wit? I have not enough to do great things with, and these little things are so fugitive, that while a man catches at the subject, he is only filling his hand with smoke. I must do with it as I do with my linnet: I keep him for the most part in a cage, but now and then set open the door that he may whisk about the room a little, and then shut him up again."

Several poems of this period, like *The Pineapple and the Bee*, are fables, furnishing with a moral some whimsical observation of garden life; but *The Modern Patriot* breathes a robust faith in political freedom, while *The Yearly Distress* anticipates the manner of *John Gilpin*.

IV

Neither in the letters nor the poems of this time is there any direct reflection of Cowper's Evangelicalism. We know, moreover, that for some years after his breakdown in 1773 he abandoned his habit of prayer, and sat, knife and fork in hand and with eyes open, when grace was said at table. Yet the inference that he had permanently reacted against Evangelicalism is superficial and false. The streak of morbidity in Cowper made him often gloomy, in varying degrees, about his own salvation, and for a time he regarded prayer as unavailing, and therefore a mocking formality, in his case. He never despaired, however, about anyone else, or questioned the efficacy of prayer in general. And, despite his obsession, he became in fact far less preoccupied with himself. Like all spiritual pilgrims, he passed through a phase of temporary reaction, which happened to coincide with his third attack of insanity. But he had not done with the Revival because, after the first flush of enthusiasm, he had ceased to be a revivalist. If he had not outgrown the rather unctuous and assertive piety of his late thirties and early forties, he would have been not a better, but a worse, Evangelical. Methodism would never have "changed the face of England" unless the emotional forces it set free had flowed, after the initial excitement, into ethical channels. To say that Cowper ceased to be an Evangelical because he no longer prated about the fact is as foolish as it is to declare that married *love* ends with the honeymoon.

"A Christian," said Newton, "is like a young nobleman who, on going to receive his estate, is at first enchanted with its prospects; this in course of time may wear off, but a sense of the value of the estate grows daily." It is the normal experience of every soul that has ever been truly quickened, and one cannot read Cowper's major poetry without perceiving how greatly he developed under Evangelicalism when the phases of ecstasy and of reaction were followed by the period of steady application. He was, to begin with, a considerable egoist, even if he were a charming one, whose self-engrossment was due not to conceit but, in everything save the social sense, to a feeling of inferiority. He was of gentle lineage, and in earlier life he was very conscious of the fact. His courtesy extended impartially to people of every rank; but it was the courtesy of "good breeding" rather than of vital sympathy. At St. Albans his egoism was transferred to the spiritual plane. He remained a spiritual egoist for some years. The best of his hymns are those in which his love of Nature drew him temporarily out of himself. But in vain we search his contributions to the *Olney* collection for evidences of the broad and deep humanity which characterises *The Task.*

Goldwin Smith, while allowing that Cowper attended too many prayer meetings, holds that his sick-visiting during his early days at Olney was beneficial to him. "The effect of doing good to others," says Smith, "was sure to be good; and the sight of real suffering was likely to banish fancied ills." Certainly Cowper gained "a practical knowledge of the poor, and learned to do them justice": so that he became at length the pioneer voice of the "human" and domestic impulse in English poetry. If the price which his nervous sensibility had to pay was heavy, he supplies but one more example of the rule that the poet learns in suffering what he tells in song. But, whatever may be said about the advisability or otherwise of his having ministered to the humble and the sick of Olney, it is self-apparent to my mind, if the characters of the two men be really understood, that Cowper's nature owed much of its gradual broadening to his long and close intimacy with Newton. I believe that Newton, a man of wide experience and a great lover of his fellow-kind, drew Cowper's mind out of itself to a far greater degree than he may incidentally have turned it in. We may regret, again, that Newton was a Calvinist at all. We may wish that his professed theology had been Arminian, as were the instincts of his generous heart. But that he made Cowper a Calvinist, or even imbued him with stronger Calvinistic notions than he already possessed, is patently untrue. He was the means of softening rather than of hardening the tenets to which Cowper, with his obstinate vein of logic, had clung. And where the more mundane aspects of friendship were concerned, Cowper might well have adapted one of Newton's best hymns to secular use, and have said of Newton himself:

> "*One there is above all others*
> *Well deserves the name of friend.*
> *His is love beyond a brother's,*
> *Costly, free, and knows no end.*"

V

"My race at Olney is nearly finished," wrote Newton to Bull in September 1779 ; "I am about to form a connection for life with one Mary Woolnoth, a reputed London Saint in Lombard Street." Newton's farewell sermon at Olney was preached in January 1780. He was sorry to leave the town in which he had laboured for sixteen years. He had already rejected at least one opportunity of preferment, and he always said that he would have declined Lord Dartmouth's offer of the living of St. Mary Woolnoth but for the fact that difficulties had arisen between himself and his parishioners.

The cause of the trouble did him credit. In October 1777, a fire—the successor of many previous ones—had broken out in Olney. It wrought speedy havoc among its wooden cottages, with their straw thatch, and, but for a sudden change of wind, half the town might have been burned. Newton ascribed the extinction of the fire to prayer rather than to water. But he was active in measures of relief for the homeless, at once promising to raise sixty pounds and actually obtaining two hundred. At a meeting to consider precautions for the future, he recommended " the discontinuation of the custom, almost peculiar to this town, of illuminating the houses on the 5th November"; he likewise stressed the danger of bonfires and guns. His suggestions were approved by all his fellow committee-men, but when notice of them was given at church there was bitter opposition. On the next Guy Fawkes evening

"many put candles in their windows who had not done so in former years; and some who had, doubled their number. This gave encouragement to the sons of Belial, and when night came on there was much riot and confusion. A wild lawless mob paraded the streets, breaking windows, and extorting money from one end of the town to the other."

Forty or fifty men, deep in liquor, marched upon the Vicarage. Newton received warning, and, having been in many tighter corners in his life, was for facing his assailants. But the excitement so affected Mrs. Newton, whose health was poor, that counsels of worldly prudence prevailed. He sent out an envoy with money, and thus made peace with his adversaries while they were yet on the way.

He was human enough for his pride to be ruffled. But the episode caused him deeper grief and concern. He had sincerely and indefatigably laboured for the true good, as he saw it, of the people of Olney, and, primitive and rough as they were, he had real affection for them. He revisited them a number of times after London had opened to him a very different sphere of influence, and he spoke of "dear Olney" to the end. Plainly, however, the events of that unhappy Guy Fawkes night had put him into an almost impossible position, and, for that reason alone, he accepted the call to Lombard Street a year or so later. He had wished Thomas Scott, then curate of Weston Underwood, to succeed him at Olney. The townspeople were so hostile to the suggestion that a Mr. Page was appointed instead. But in Page, says Thomas Wright, they caught "a veritable Tartar," who quarrelled with his patron, his absentee vicar, his parishioners, and even on one occasion with the auctioneer who was in the act of selling his goods. Opposition to Scott soon vanished. The curate of Weston was transferred to Olney, and took up residence at the Vicarage in 1781. "Methinks," Newton wrote to him,

"I see you sitting in my old corner in the study. I will warn you of one thing. That room—(do not start)—used to be haunted. I cannot say I ever saw or heard anything with my bodily organs, but I have been sure there were evil spirits in it and very near me—a spirit of folly, a spirit of indolence, a spirit of unbelief, and many others—indeed their name is legion.

But why should I say they are in your study when they followed me to London, and still pester me here?''

Newton was sorely missed by the people of Olney. Although they had been responsible for driving him away, they seem to have had far less affection for any of his immediate successors. Cowper was miserable after his departure. He saw the smoke issuing from the Vicarage chimneys as he paced his garden in the evenings, and lamented, with a feeling of bitter loneliness, that his old friend no longer sat at the familiar desk. His long and intimate association with Newton did not predispose him to regard Thomas Scott favourably; and, while the two men sometimes met on amicable terms, the poet never greatly liked the future author of the *Commentary*. Scott, indeed, whose life from the humblest of origins to his position as Lock preacher in London and his international success as a theological writer, makes a remarkable record of courage and determination,[1] does not seem, when Cowper knew him, to have been a very attractive character. The son of a Lincolnshire grazier, he had known the hardest of menial labour in youth, and, with his ambition of taking holy orders, had had to face the opposition of his family no less than that of the Bishops. His health was never good, and his spirit was somewhat soured. He started his ministry as an obstinate doctrinaire, and we may well believe that he had a militant and rasping manner. He was, during his Olney days, precisely what Newton was not, but is sometimes accused of having been. Indeed, it was through Newton's influence, as we have already seen, that Scott began to mellow. Nowhere are Newton's gentleness, tolerance, and concern with ethical values more clearly demonstrated than in his controversy with Scott. In his autobiography, *The Force of Truth*, Scott admits that Newton by his sweet reasonableness in argument, no less than by practical example, led him to a more spiritual view of religion.

It was, perhaps, because he realised that Scott would not be congenial to Cowper that Newton, before leaving Olney, asked William Bull to call at Orchard Side. The Independent

[1] For an account of Scott's career, see *The Early Evangelical Fathers*. By M. Seeley. 1879. Also *The Town of Cowper*. By Thomas Wright.

minister of Newport Pagnell obeyed the request; and he and
Cowper immediately became friends. Newton's fundamental
broadmindedness is again revealed; for Bull was not merely
a dissenter: he was something of a religious quietist, who
later inspired Cowper to make his graceful translations from
the poems of Madame Guyon.[1] From the *Bletchley Diary* of
William Cole, the friend of Horace Walpole and a characteristic Tory cleric of his age, whose main interests seem to have
been his antiquarian researches and his stomach, we learn
that Bull was the son of a tailor at Higham Ferrers. Cole
mentions the fact in the spirit of one who reveals a dark and
hardly credible secret, and elsewhere he calls the young
minister of Newport Pagnell "an impertinent coxcomb."
This was because Bull had dared to establish a nonconformist
academy at Newport, and had even had the effrontery, as he
walked one day in the very elegant garden of Mr. Pomfret,
the Bletchley attorney, to make use of the expression, "when
I was at college." Mr. Pomfret, who afterwards related the
incident to Cole, thereupon asked the upstart "if he had been
educated in either of our two Universities, or in one of the
Scottish Universities: but he said, he only meant when he
was upon his studies in the Academy at Daventry in Northamptonshire." "So forward," Cole remarks, "are these
People to give Honourable Titles to themselves and their
unlawful and factious Seminaries, and will scruple to give
due Titles of Honour to whom the State allows them."

Here we have, perhaps, a better reflection of the eighteenth-
century Tory mind than of the personality of William Bull.
Cole incidentally tells us that Bull was tall, thin, and pale-
faced, "with a starched and formal Gait, a white wig combed
into nice Ringlets, with a large cocked Hat, and a Cane in his
Hand." It is true that Bull was some years older when
Cowper first met him; but, if Cole's "Appearance of the
Man" were correct, he must rapidly have put on middle-age
spread, for the familiar portrait of him suggests a loose, portly
figure, with a full face and double chin. And Cowper's
description of this "Delphic oracle"—whose erudition, he

---

[1] These were dedicated to Bull and were first published at Newport Pagnell
in 1801, the year after Cowper's death.

said, was a bank upon which he drew at pleasure—gives us a very different impression of his character from that insinuated by Cole:

"You are not acquainted with the Rev. Mr. Bull, of Newport; perhaps it is as well for you that you are not. You would regret still more than you do, that there are so many miles interposed between us. He spends part of the day with us to-morrow. A dissenter, but a liberal one; a man of letters and of genius; master of a fine imagination, or rather not master of it,—an imagination which, when he finds himself in the company he loves, and can confide in, runs away with him into such fields of speculation, as amuse and enliven every other imagination that has the happiness to be of the party. At other times he has a tender and delicate sort of melancholy in his disposition, not less agreeable in its way. No men are better qualified for companions in such a world as this, than men of such a temperament. Every scene of life has two sides, a dark and a bright one, and the mind that has an equal mixture of melancholy and vivacity is best of all qualified for the contemplation of either; it can be lively without levity, and pensive without dejection. Such a man is Mr. Bull. But—he smokes tobacco. Nothing is perfect,—

Nihil est ab omni
Parte beatum."

Thus the poet wrote to Unwin, and another interesting glimpse of Bull is given in a letter to Newton:

"Mr. Bull is an honest man. We have seen him twice since he received your orders to march hither, and faithfully told us it was in consequence of those orders that he came. He dined with us yesterday; we were all in pretty good spirits, and the day passed very agreeably. It is not long since he called on Mr. Scott. Mr. Raban came in. Mr. Bull began, addressing himself to the former: 'My friend, you are in trouble, you are unhappy; I read it in your countenance.' Mr. Scott replied he had been so, but he was better. 'Come, then,' says Mr. Bull, 'I will expound to you the cause of all your anxiety. You are too common; you make yourself cheap. Visit your people less, and converse more with your own heart. How often do you speak to them in the week?' 'Thrice.' 'Ay, there it is! Your sermons are an old ballad; your prayers are an old ballad; and you are an old ballad too.' 'I would wish to tread in the steps of Mr. Newton.' 'You do well to follow his steps in all other instances, but in this instance you are wrong, and so was he. Mr. Newton trod a path which no man but himself could have used so long as he did, and he wore it out long before he went from Olney. Too much familiarity and condescension cost him the estimation of his people. He thought he should ensure their love, to which he had the best possible title, and by those very means he lost it. Be wise, my friend; take warning; make yourself scarce if you wish that persons of little understanding should know how to prize you.' "

Bull had some curious habits. He cut a niche in his garden wall, where, almost completely and very closely secluded by brickwork, he sat and meditated; and, having measured the circumference of his garden, he walked five miles round it every day, marking each revolution by moving a bit of shot along a groove made for the purpose. He was, indeed, what Cecil would have called an "original." He was richly endowed with many qualities, some of which are seldom found together. But he made little attempt to correlate them. He allowed each in turn its idiosyncratic play, though his erratic flights of fancy and changes of mood sometimes followed one another so rapidly that he could be deeply emotional and sternly "realistic" almost at the same moment. It is not surprising that he and Cowper quickly responded to each other. Bull soon established the custom of dining once a fortnight with the poet. The two cronies sat in the summer-house, conversing at large upon matters grave and gay, spiritual and terrestrial, or enjoying silent fellowship while "smoke-inhaling Bull"—who, for us, will indeed be "always filling, never full" [1]—puffed placidly at the pipe which, following the precedent of Mr. Aspray, the apothecary, he kept (for his use when visiting Olney) under the trap-door in the ground. Occasionally he persuaded Cowper to undertake the five-mile journey to Newport Pagnell and there to visit *him*. But that was not very often: and it speaks volumes for *Carissime Taurorum* that the miracle was achieved at all.

[1] See Cowper's poem, *An Epistle to the Rev. William Bull.*

Chapter Ten

LADY AUSTEN AND "THE FROGS"

I

A TRUE LYRICAL impulse will brook no denial, and usually asserts itself early in life. Blake was thirty-two when *Songs of Innocence* appeared. Wordsworth was twenty-eight and Coleridge twenty-six when the *Lyrical Ballads* were published. Shelley was of similar age when he wrote *Prometheus Unbound,* and it was an even younger Keats who sang of the nightingale and of melodies still sweeter, though unheard. Many of Tennyson's best poems formed part of the volumes issued in 1842, when he was thirty-three. Cowper, on the other hand, was forty-eight when he wrote the first of the poems by which, apart from a few hymns, he is now remembered: and it was only in response to outside stimulus that he took seriously to literary composition even then. Here, surely, is further proof that he was not a born lyrist.

He had during the past few years indulged his "whisking wit" in short excursions; and in 1780, as we have noted in an earlier chapter, indignation moved him to write *Anti-Thelyphthora,* a satirical reply to Madan's defence of polygamy. This was the longest poem he had yet attempted, and Mrs. Unwin, who had witnessed his pleasure in the occupation, suggested that he should undertake another sustained effort. She even gave him a subject. *The Progress of Error,* running to over six hundred lines, was quickly finished, and was followed by other poems of similar length, entitled *Truth, Table Talk, Expostulation, Hope, Charity, Conversation,* and *Retirement.* Such was the origin of the moral satires.

The origin? Well, hardly! As we reflected when discussing the *Olney Hymns,* a poem is not the growth of a moment. Even the lyric that is "dashed off" in half an hour may have been developing in the subconscious mind for months or possibly years; and with longer poems, compact of thought rather than of simple emotion or impressionism, the process

221

is correspondingly longer. Any chance match will start a fire—where there is combustible matter. But for Mrs. Unwin's happy and timely idea, the moral satires might not have been written. Had Lady Austen not later drifted into the poet's life, *John Gilpin* and *The Task* might never have been. It seldom occurred to Cowper to light his own fires. All honour to those two women who (so fortuitously and oddly allied in this good work) kindled the blaze! Yet gratitude should not blind us to the fact that they were, after all, but match-strikers.[1] The fire was already laid: and in that essential preparation John Newton, however unconsciously, had lent a hand.

Newton, indeed, had himself nine years earlier wakened Cowper's literary impulse by setting him to write hymns. The practice and discipline involved were not less valuable to the future development of the poet's art because Newton was more concerned with the hymns as religious propaganda than as literature. And though Newton would never have thought of prompting his friend to write poetry for its own sake, yet the long years of intimacy between the two men had broadened and humanised Cowper's mind, so that, when stimuli came from elsewhere, it had richer material upon which to work. It happened that Cowper's literary career began in earnest within a few months of Newton's leaving Olney. But the inference sometimes drawn from this coincidence—namely, that Cowper burgeoned forth *because* he was no longer in "bondage" to Newton—runs contrary to what we know of Newton's character, and shows a naïve faith in the power of poetry to blossom suddenly without roots. The legend that Newton had clung excessively to Cowper will not, of course, bear investigation. Cowper himself had been the leech. Newton had had many duties, many interests, and many friends; Cowper had been lonely and unoccupied. Deeply fond as Newton was of the future poet, Cowper, in the nature of things, had been the more *dependent* upon the friendship; and, since he was temperamentally prone to such concen-

---

[1] I am speaking, of course, of their purely literary influence. In every other respect Mrs. Unwin was certainly a fire-layer, and but for her maternal care and intuitive understanding Cowper might never have been a poet at all.

trated enthusiasm, he was at least well served by the one on whom his affection had fastened itself.

Probably, nevertheless, it was to his ultimate advantage that Newton, in 1780, was called to London. The very intensity of Cowper's attachment would certainly have had a restricting effect in the long run, if circumstances had not decreed otherwise. One may have too much even of a really good thing. Variety of intercourse is essential to psychic health; and though after his breakdown of 1773 Cowper seems to have discontinued his former habit of spending several hours a day in Newton's company, he had yet seen more of him, *to the exclusion of other society*, than was, after a time, salutary. There comes the moment when a brilliant pupil should not be restrained by loyalty to his master, to whom he owes his progress hitherto, from going forward into fields of achievement where the master himself may not be able to follow.

Newton was the antithesis of a pedant, a Pharisee, or a prig. But he was, after all, a clergyman, and, as such, held that somewhat suspicious view of the arts which was an almost unavoidable element in the reaction against vice, luxury, and religious formalism. Poetry and music might indeed be the handmaids of religion, but only as they contributed, deliberately and obviously, to edification. It was, intrinsically, a narrow attitude. Yet it was perhaps a necessary one at the time. Certainly it was an understandable attitude, and was common to many of the truest spiritual leaders—including men of wide learning and culture—both within Evangelicalism and without. Cowper himself still shared it, in 1780, to the full. He wrote the first of his moral satires partly to please Mrs. Unwin, partly for the sake of occupation, and partly for the direct propagation of his religious views.

"It will not be long," he wrote to Newton in December 1780, "before you will receive a poem called *The Progress of Error*. That will be succeeded by another, in due time, called *Truth*. Don't be alarmed. I ride Pegasus with a curb. He will never run away with me again." The explanation of this letter is that though Newton had praised *Anti-Thelyphthora*, he had taken exception to certain parts of the

poem. Critics with a bias against Newton have made the
most of this fact, and, in doing so, have shown a lack of fairness or discrimination. For *Anti-Thelyphthora* is, as we have
seen, the least characteristic of all Cowper's works. It was,
we may guess, not merely the imagery which Newton disliked, though that was calculated to shock many seriously
minded readers of the day. The poem displayed bad taste in
another respect. Its motive was sincere, but it was written
in a mood of pique against Madan. Cowper doubtless felt
that he had been sadly "let down" by the cousin in whom
he had once placed such confidence.

If Newton were indeed the means of preventing repetitions
of *Anti-Thelyphthora*, we should be grateful to him. Neither
the sensuousness—mild and harmless as it may seem to us—
nor the slight venom of that poem was true Cowper. The
poet himself regretted having published it, and was always
glad that his name had not appeared on the title-page.
Newton's disapproval is fully justified. He never seriously
criticised any of Cowper's subsequent work, except in matters
of detail, as when—let it be noted—he objected to a passage
in *Expostulation*, which he considered too bitter against
Roman Catholicism, and for which Cowper, "working like a
tailor who sews a patch upon a hole in a coat," substituted
twenty-four lines on another theme.[1] To the end Newton
followed the poet's work with deep interest and warm
appreciation; and, since actions speak louder than words, it
is well to remember that he conducted the initial arrangements with the publisher. It is nevertheless likely that, had
he remained in Olney, his influence might have tended to
keep Cowper in even graver singing robes than he naturally
assumed.

For, while his "whisking wit" *would* break out when he
took pen in hand, and while in *Anti-Thelyphthora* his Pegasus
had run away with him, Cowper's idea of the main purpose
of poetry was quite as solemn as Newton's own. His history
from this point is, however, the record of the growing, if never
perfectly sustained, triumph of his sympathies over his mental

[1] Lines 390-413. The cancelled passage may be seen in *William Cowper*.
By Thomas Wright. P. 273.

preconceptions. His Pegasus, though it never carried him
again into regions of questionable taste, was not so easily to
be curbed, after all. And this was a happy thing not only for
himself and for English poetry, but even for Evangelicalism,
which was far wider in its implications than many of its own
exponents realised. The leaders of the Revival were necessarily concerned, in great measure, with framing a theology,
creating an organisation, and working among the illiterate
masses. Men of their own time, they thought of religion
primarily in terms of individual salvation in a future world.
It is true that the Arminians—and, in despite of their own
cold logic, the best of the Calvinists—recognised the inevitable
corollary: that the spirit can be judged only by its fruits. But
though the practical effect of this view was to foster a new
sense of moral and social responsibility, the fruits were deemed
more valuable as indications of saved souls than they were for
their own sake. It needed a poet to hold up the mirror to
that new spirit, and to show its humanising influence actually
at work.

II

The Progress of Error, Truth, and *Table Talk* were completed by February 1781; and since Cowper had hitherto felt
most inclined for verse-writing in winter,[1] he resolved to
hang up his harp for the remainder of the year, and

> "*Since Eighty-one has had so much to do*
> *Postpone what yet is left till Eighty-two.*"

But the poetic impulse was now asserting itself too vigorously
to be denied. *Expostulation* immediately followed, and
thoughts of making the four poems into a book entered the
poet's mind. Through the good offices of Newton, Joseph
Johnson, the bookseller in St. Paul's Churchyard, undertook
to publish the volume at his own risk. Johnson, says Gilchrist,[2] was "an open-hearted tradesman of the eighteenth

---

[1] " When I can find no other occupation, I think, and when I think I am very
apt to do it in rhyme. Hence it comes that the season of the year which generally
pinches off the flowers of poetry, unfolds mine, such as they are, and crowns
me with a winter garland." Letter to Hill, May 1781.

[2] *The Life of William Blake.* By Alexander Gilchrist. 1863.

P

century, of strict probity, simple in habits, liberal in his dealings, living by his shop and in it." His interest in books and ideas was not confined to them as merchandise. Cowper was not the only famous author who found in him a sage literary counsellor. The company at his "plain but hospitable weekly dinners" included Dr. Price, Dr. Priestley, Blake, Fuseli, Godwin, and Paine.

In May 1781, Cowper announced the forthcoming event to Unwin:

"In the press, and speedily will be published, in one volume octavo, price three shillings, Poems, by William Cowper, of the Inner Temple, Esq. You may suppose, by the size of the publication, that the greatest part of them have been long kept secret, because you yourself have never seen them; but the truth is, that they are most of them, except what you have in your possession, the produce of the last winter. Two-thirds of the compilation will be occupied by four pieces, the first of which sprung up in the month of December, and the last of them in the month of March. . . . Mr. Newton writes a Preface, and Johnson is the publisher. The principal, I may say the only, reason why I never mentioned to you, till now, an affair which I am just going to make known to all the world (if *that* Mr. All-the-world should think it worth his knowing), has been this,— that, till within these few days, I had not the honour to know it myself. This may seem strange, but it is true; for, not knowing where to find underwriters who would choose to insure them, and not finding it convenient to a purse like mine to run any hazard, even upon the credit of my own ingenuity, I was very much in doubt for some weeks whether any bookseller would be willing to subject himself to an ambiguity that might prove very expensive in case of a bad market. But Johnson has heroically set all peradventures at defiance, and takes the whole charge upon himself. So out I come."

Unwin was chagrined at having been kept in the dark, but accepted Cowper's explanation that "the obvious and only reason" why he had resorted to Newton, and not to his "friend Unwin," was that "the former lived in London, and the latter at Stock." A reconciliation was soon effected. Meanwhile, Hill had heard a rumour, and wrote for confirmation. There is a touch of childlike pleasure in Cowper's reply:

"I am in the press, and it is vain to deny it. But how mysterious is the conveyance of intelligence from one end to the other of your great city! Not many days since, except one man, and he but a little taller than yourself, all London was ignorant of it; for I do not suppose that the public prints have yet announced this most agreeable tidings, the title-page, which is the basis of the advertisement, having so lately reached the publisher: and now it is known to you, who live at least two miles distant from my confidant upon the occasion."

A little earlier, in sending to Newton the manuscript of his third moral satire, the poet had written:

"I send you *Table Talk*. It is a medley of many things, some that may be useful, and some that, for aught I know, may be very diverting. I am merry that I may decoy people into my company, and grave that they may be the better for it. Now and then I put on the garb of a philosopher, and take the opportunity that disguise procures me, to drop a word in favour of religion. In short, there is some froth, and here and there a bit of sweet-meat, which seems to entitle it justly to the name of a certain dish the ladies call a trifle. I did not choose to be more facetious, lest I should consult the taste of my readers at the expense of my own approbation; nor more serious than I have been, lest I should forfeit theirs. A poet in my circumstances has a difficult part to act: one minute obliged to bridle his humour, if he has any, and the next, to clap a spur to the sides of it: now ready to weep from a sense of the importance of his subject, and on a sudden constrained to laugh, lest his gravity should be mistaken for dulness. If this be not violent exercise for the mind, I know not what is; and if any man doubt it, let him try. Whether all this management and contrivance be necessary, I do not know, but am inclined to suspect that if my Muse was to go forth clad in Quaker colour, without one bit of riband to enliven her appearance, she might walk from one end of London to the other, as little noticed as if she were one of the sisterhood indeed. . . ."

Similarly he told Mrs. Cowper that his "sole drift" was to be "useful"—a point, he added, which "I should in vain aim at, unless I could be likewise entertaining."

In the case of Newton and the Major's wife, some such explanations were possibly needed. It is one thing, however,

to admit this; it is quite another to assume that, in writing to
his old Calvinistic friends, Cowper was insincere: that he was
now finding more satisfaction in what *they* would deem mere
adornment or entertainment, and that, while representing
his bits of sweetmeat as a lure to attract worldly readers to
religion, he was actually including the religious passages as a
sop for his godly acquaintances. Cowper could be tactful;
but hypocrisy was utterly alien to his nature. Nor *was* it only
to his Calvinistic correspondents that he wrote in this vein.
William Unwin has never been accused of being strait-laced.
Yet to him we find Cowper saying, a few years later, apropos
of *The Task*:

> "What there is of a religious cast in this volume I have
> thrown towards the end of it, for two reasons: first, that I
> might not revolt the reader at his entrance, and secondly, that
> my best impressions might be made last. Were I to write as
> many volumes as Lope de Vega, or Voltaire, not one of them
> would be without this tincture. If the world like it not, so much
> the worse for them. I make all the concessions I can, that I
> may please them, but I will not please them at the expense of
> conscience."

And, a little later still, he spoke of himself, in his *Poetical
Epistle to Lady Austen*, as

> "*I, who scribble rhyme,*
> *To catch the triflers of the time,*
> *And tell them truths divine and clear*
> *Which, couched in prose, they will not hear.*"

Are we *still* to suspect him of not meaning substantially what
he said?[1] Let us admit, if we like, that his view of poetry is
artistically indefensible. That is not the point. We see him
entirely out of focus if we fail to realise that his principal
object in writing verse was moralistic, and that, by throwing
in his "sweetmeats," much as he enjoyed them himself, he
was merely acting on the apostolic principle of becoming weak
to the weak that he might gain the weak.

---

[1] In certain moods, it is true, Cowper said that he wrote poetry merely to amuse
himself. But he admitted that if he did not publish what he wrote he would
have no inducement to write at all. Plainly he wanted his voice to be heard, and
his chief pleasure itself lay—since he was relatively free from purely personal
ambition—in being the mouthpiece of Evangelical truth.

Newton saw the legitimacy of this method in his own profession. But he failed sufficiently to see how "useful" to the cause of religion it might be in poetry. He and Cowper held different views about what was expedient in literature; but that their fundamental purpose was the same is shown by the fact that Cowper asked Newton to write an introduction for his first volume. It *was* Cowper who made the request; Newton did not (as one might gather from some biographies) foist the preface on an unwilling author. The "Introduction," which greatly pleased Cowper, lies before me as I write. It is couched in the most generous terms, and Newton's affection for his *alter idem* shines unmistakably through it. But Johnson—wisely from his own point of view, and, incidentally, from that of Evangelicalism in the larger sense—suggested that it should be omitted from the first edition, as its definitely theological emphasis might limit the sales. His proposal was adopted, and there is nowhere any hint that Newton was even momentarily piqued.

Meanwhile, on May 23, Cowper had to inform Unwin that the publication of the book was postponed:

"If a writer's friends have need of patience, how much more the writer! Your desire to see my muse in public, and mine to gratify you, must both suffer the mortification of delay. I expected that my trumpeter would have informed the world by this time of all that is needful for them to know upon such an occasion; and that an advertising blast, blown through every newspaper, would have said—'The poet is coming!'—But man, especially man that writes verse, is born to disappointments, as surely as printers and booksellers are born to be the most dilatory and tedious of all creatures. The plain English of this magnificent preamble is, that the season of publication is just elapsed, that the town is going into the country every day, and that my book cannot appear till they return—that is to say, not till next winter."

The misfortune, he said, had its attendant advantage, as three more poems—*Hope, Charity*, and *Conversation*—could now be included. And, indeed, when Johnson heard in September that *Retirement* was on the stocks, he recommended that it too should go to swell the collection. The volume appeared at last in February 1782.

No author was ever fundamentally freer from personal pride than Cowper; but, having launched his first literary venture, he was surprised, as he told Unwin, to find himself and vanity not utter strangers:

"Every extraordinary occurrence in our lives affords us an opportunity to learn, if we will, something more of our own hearts and tempers than we were before aware of. . . . Before I had published, I said to myself—You and I, Mr. Cowper, will not concern ourselves much about what the critics may say of our book. But having once sent my wits for a venture, I soon became anxious about the issue, and found that I could not be satisfied with a warm place in my own good graces, unless my friends were pleased with me as much as I pleased myself. Meeting with their approbation, I began to feel the workings of ambition. It is well, said I, that my friends are pleased, but friends are sometimes partial, and mine, I have reason to think, are not altogether free from bias: methinks I should like to hear a stranger or two speak well of me."

The book was rather savagely attacked, in a manner then common, by the *Critical Review*, which described the "verses" as being "in general weak and languid," and as having "neither novelty, spirit, nor animation to recommend them." Happily, a tribute from Benjamin Franklin, to whom Thornton had sent the *Poems*, came as a salve to Cowper's wound. Franklin said that the relish for reading poetry had long left him; "but there is something so new in the manner, so easy and yet so correct—the language, so clear in the expression, yet concise, and so just in the sentiments, that I have read the whole with great pleasure, and some of the pieces more than once." He begged Thornton, to whom his letter was addressed, to convey his thankful acknowledgments and respects to the author.

Thornton lost no time in performing that pleasant office, and Cowper immediately sent a copy of Franklin's letter to Newton, who, for his part, reported that the book was likely "to run, spread, and prosper"; that the grave could not help smiling at it, and that the gay were struck with the truth of it; and that it might find its way into His Majesty's hands, "being put into a proper course for that purpose." Cowper retailed this news to Unwin, and said that if the King should fall in love with his muse, the event would make ample amends for the Chancellor's indifference; for the volume had been sent to the poet's old associate Thurlow, and had, to his mortification, evoked no response. Nor was George the Third moved, at this juncture, to declare his august approbation.

With the warm approval of his intimate friends, the un-expected appreciation from Dr. Franklin, and favourable notices in the *London* and the *Gentleman's Magazine*, the poet was reasonably content; though one suspense still kept him "in hot water." The *Monthly Review*, the "most formidable" of his judges, had not yet spoken.

"Alas! when I wish for a favourable sentence from that quarter (to confess a weakness that I should not confess to all), I feel myself not a little influenced by a tender regard to my reputation here, even among my neighbours at Olney. Here are watchmakers, who themselves are wits, and who at present perhaps think me one. Here is a carpenter, and a baker, and, not to mention others, here is your idol Mr. Teedon, whose smile is fame. All these read the *Monthly Review*, and all these will set me down for a dunce, if those terrible critics show them the example. But oh! wherever else I am accounted dull, dear Mr. Griffith, let me pass for a genius at Olney! . . ."

At length the "critical Rhadamanthus" delivered itself. Mr. Cowper, it said, "is a poet *sui generis*; for, as his notes are peculiar to himself, he classes not with any species of bards that have preceded him; his style of composition, as well as his modes of thinking, are entirely his own." His language is "plain, forcible, and expressive," and though his predominant tone of mind is devotional, it is "at the same time duly humorous and sarcastic. Hence his very religion has a smile that is arch, and his sallies of humour an air that is religious." Cowper breathed again: he could now look the carpenter, the baker, and the schoolmaster in the face.

The book, if not a great success, was by no means a failure. Its novelty was far more widely recognised and welcomed than fresh voices usually are. The explanation probably is that it appeared at a moment when poetry was much in fashion—anthologies of verse (the first works of their kind) were being published with much success—but when nothing of value was being produced. Pope had died as far back as 1744; Thomson had followed him in 1748, and Collins in 1759. Chatterton, Gray, and Goldsmith had more recently passed away, and had left no successors. Dodsley in his *Miscellany* and Pearch in his *Collection of Poems by Several Hands* reprinted "specimens" by these buried favourites. "But the crowd," says Humphry Ward,[1]

> "the forgotten crowd that fill the bulk of the volumes, they are the writers who represent the average poetical level of the time, the level out of which Cowper suddenly emerged to charm Dr. Franklin. Mr. Cawthorne, Mr. Emily, Mr. Cunningham, Miss Carter, Mrs. Greville, and a hundred others, are the channel into which the river of eighteenth-century verse diffused itself before it was finally lost in the sands. It is harmless enough, this verse . . . but it is incurably *banal*, it wholly lacks distinction."

"The Dutch," said John Constable, "were a stay-at-home people; hence their originality." And Chesterton might have had Cowper in mind when he observed that "travel narrows the mind." The poet attributed his own freshness of vision to the fact of his having few books:

> "I reckon it among my principal advantages, as a composer of verses [he told Unwin] that I have not read an English poet these thirteen years, and but one these twenty years. Imitation, even of the best models, is my aversion; it is servile and mechanical, a trick that has enabled many to usurp the name of author, who could not have written at all, if they had not written upon the pattern of somebody indeed original. But when the ear and the taste have been much accustomed to the manner of others, it is almost impossible to avoid it; and we imitate in spite of ourselves, just in proportion as we admire."

It is true that remaining in one place and abstention from reading will not of themselves make a man original. But it is equally true that many a potentially original mind becomes

[1] *The English Poets.* Edited by Thomas Humphry Ward. Volume III. 1928.

conventionalised through too much surface activity. He who goes everywhere, reads everything, and knows everybody "worth knowing" has little time to see, read, or know himself. He is in a perpetual condition of escape. It is not a mere coincidence that many of the world's truest prophets or interpreters have been semi-recluses. The traveller sees merely *peoples* and differences of custom. The man who has to rely upon his own resources learns not only, in Cowper's borrowed phrase, to "gather honey from a weed": he has leisure to commune with himself, and by familiarity with the secrets of one heart to understand what is common to the race.

III

Conversation and *Retirement*—the last two poems in Cowper's earliest volume—owed something to the same influence which was soon to "inspire" *The Task*. One summer's day in 1781, as the poet gazed through his window, he saw two ladies enter the draper's shop on the opposite side of the market-place. One of the ladies he knew: she was Mrs. Jones, wife of the clergyman at the neighbouring village of Clifton Reynes. But who was her companion? Her face and deportment immediately aroused his interest, and he soon learned, from discreet inquiries, that she was Mrs. Jones's sister and the widow of Sir Robert Austen, Bart. With characteristic impulsiveness, innocent as a child's, he requested Mrs. Unwin to ask the two ladies to tea. No sooner had the invitation been accepted than he was filled with regret and apprehension. When the appointed afternoon arrived, he shrank from the ordeal of meeting the guests, and all Mrs. Unwin's mingled tact and firmness were needed to prevail against his shyness. But when the ceremony of introduction was over, and tea had set the conversation flowing, he felt uncommonly happy and at rest. Lady Austen's sensibility and vivaciousness quickly thawed his reserve. He found himself telling her all about his own concerns, while she, for her part, talked of France, in which she had lived much.

In the evening he escorted Mrs. Jones and her sister home, and a week or so later he and Mrs. Unwin returned the call. Acquaintanceship soon ripened into intimacy, until there were few days when, if Lady Austen did not find occasion to visit Olney, Cowper failed to take the pleasant two miles' walk through the meadows intersected by narrow arms of the river, past the water-mill described in the Fifth Book of *The Task*, and then up the steep path to Clifton, which, with its group of cottages, its antiquated dove-house, and its Georgian trinity of church, rectory, and manor, commanded the tranquil countryside for miles around.

Things moved so quickly that Cowper, evidently in "hop-o'-my-thumb" spirits, was able to convey the following intelligence to Newton:

"Mrs. Jones proposes, ere July closes, that she and her sister, and her Jones mister, and we that are here, our course shall steer, to dine in the Spinnie; but for a guinea, if the weather should hold, so hot and so cold, we had better by far stay where we are. For the grass there grows, while nobody mows (which is very wrong), so rank and long, that, so to speak, 'tis at least a week, if it happens to rain, ere it dries again."

Heaven smiled, however, upon the occasion. The picnic duly took place in the grounds of Mrs. Throckmorton, of Weston Hall. Dick Coleman and Lady Austen's lackey drove a wheelbarrow full of eatables and drinkables into the Spinney—"a most delightful retirement." A board laid over the wheelbarrow provided the table; the dining-room was "a root-house, lined with moss and ivy." At six o'clock the servants, who had dined at a little distance under a great elm, boiled the kettle, and the wheelbarrow was again brought into service. After tea, the revellers—for so at least one of the guests must have deemed himself—took a walk through the park. By eight o'clock all the members of the party were safely home, "having spent the day together from noon till evening without one cross occurrence, or the least weariness of each other."

By October, when Lady Austen had to return to London, she had become "Sister Anne" to Cowper, while he was "Brother William" to her. Before leaving Olney she made

arrangements for settling there permanently in the winter of
1783, when the lease of her town house expired; and though
two years intervened, Cowper's fancy readily leapt the gulf.
"Here," he wrote to Newton, "is a new scene opening, which,
whether it perform what it promises or not, will add fresh
plumes to the wings of time. If the project take effect, a
thousand varieties will attend the change it will make in our
situation at Olney." He told Newton that Lady Austen was
"very desirous of retirement, especially of a retirement near
her sister," and that she was "an admirer of Mr. Scott as a
preacher, and of your two humble servants now in the greenhouse." Her plan, he continued, was to renovate and inhabit
that part of Orchard Side "at present occupied by Dick
Coleman, his wife and child, and a thousand rats."

The news was also sent to Unwin with this commentary:

"You will be pleased with this intelligence, because I have
already told you, that she is a woman perfectly well bred,
sensible, and in every respect agreeable; and, above all, because
she loves your mother dearly. It has in my eyes (and I doubt
not it will have the same in yours), strong marks of providential
interposition. A female friend, and one who bids fair to prove
herself worthy of the appellation, comes, recommended by a
variety of considerations, to such a place as Olney. Since Mr.
Newton went, and till this lady came, there was not in the
kingdom a retirement more absolutely such than ours. We did
not want company, but when it came, we found it agreeable.
A person that has seen much of the world, and understands it
well, has high spirits, a lively fancy, and great readiness of conversation, introduces sprightliness into such a scene as this,
which, if it was peaceful before, is not the worse for being a little
enlivened. In case of illness too, to which all are liable, it was
rather a gloomy prospect, if we allowed ourselves to advert to
it, that there was hardly a woman in the place from whom it
would have been reasonable to have expected either comfort or
assistance. The present curate's wife [Mrs. Scott] is a valuable
person, but has a family of her own, and though a neighbour,
is not a very near one. But if this plan is effected, we shall be
in a manner one family, and I suppose never pass a day without
some intercourse with each other."

Lady Austen had lost her heart to Sir Cowper—or, at least,

had come to regard him as a possible successor to the late
Baronet. The chances are that she was genuinely in love with
him, for her attachment to Cowper serves to remind us, if
another reminder be needed, that he was not merely an uncommonly fascinating person in himself, but that he bore
every outward hallmark of gentility. Lady Austen can hardly
be blamed for thinking that he reciprocated her feeling.
Cowper belonged to that rare type of man whose courtesy
and geniality, while in fact habitual, are mistaken by every
woman who encounters him for an exceptional compliment
to herself. Such a man is himself quite ignorant, as he walks
unselfconsciously through life, that he leaves a trail of
(temporarily) broken hearts. He is undesirous and unaware
of exceeding ordinary politeness, and is at once surprised and
pained when he learns that his merely natural demeanour has
been misinterpreted. Cowper was obviously attracted to
Lady Austen, and his attitude towards her would have been
blameably indiscreet if it had not been so utterly guileless.
That it certainly was. One has only to compare his descriptions of her with the equally glowing accounts he wrote of
other friends, male and female alike, to realise that he deemed
"Sister Anne" a very pleasant addition to his circle of friends,
but nothing more.

And in another way his letters about her reveal his innocence. He takes her statements at their face value. He really
believes that this society woman, accustomed to French salons,
is deciding to settle at Olney because she now needs "retirement"—especially "a retirement near her sister." He even
credits her statement that she has conceived a deep admiration
for the preaching of the lugubrious Mr. Scott! And could
childlike blindness to feminine wiles be more vividly apparent
than in these further remarks to Unwin?

"She has many features in her character that you will admire;
but one, in particular, on account of the rarity of it, will engage
your attention and esteem. She has a degree of gratitude in her
composition, so quick a sense of obligation, as is hardly to be
found in any rank of life. . . . Discover but a wish to please her,
and she never forgets it; not only thanks you, but the tears will
start into her eyes at the recollection of the smallest service."

Another, and slightly less agreeable, trait in Cowper's character emerges from these letters. Lady Austen, if she could have seen them, would have smiled a little ruefully as she read of herself, in an epistle to Unwin, that "she loves everything that has any connexion with your mother"; but she might positively have resented the revelation that "Brother William" was already envisaging her in the capacity of sicknurse, should necessity arise at Orchard Side! Cowper, while he was the soul of courtesy, and while the years after Mrs. Unwin's seizure were to show that he could repay a selfless devotion with a like one of his own, had still at this time a keen eye for his personal interests. Helpless as he might himself be in many of the ordinary affairs of life, he had at least the gift of knowing how to turn his friendships to practical account. His deep need of help may perhaps be his sufficient excuse, as his genuine devotion to his friends was certainly their ample reward.

Cowper's rapid changes of mood are also revealed, once again, in his letter to Newton of August 21, 1781. We have seen, from its opening sentences, that his imagination had immediately flown the two years' interval which must elapse between Lady Austen's decision to live at Olney and her actually settling there. For the moment, in his mind, the plan was already achieved, and he drew a purer pleasure from fancy than the reality itself could ever have brought him. By the time he reached the end of the letter, however, his wings had failed him. The two intervening years now loomed before him like two centuries. "But these things," he says, "are all at present in the clouds—in two years not only this project, but all the projects in Europe, may be disconcerted." This last note has an ominously modern ring. And, indeed, the world in 1781 was, by its own standards, gravely disturbed. The American War was dragging along, for this country, its "disastrous" course, and in Europe, with England at the moment standing "at bay" against the Armed Neutrality of almost all the Powers, the evening sky of the eighteenth century was lurid with presage of coming storm.

But it was not political convulsions which, in the following February, shook the friendship between Cowper and Lady

Austen. "Sister Anne," as we have seen, had returned to London a few months earlier. In December Cowper had sent her his *Poetical Epistle*, in which he sees in her advent to Olney

> "*th' allotment of the skies,*
> *The hand of the Supremely Wise.*"

God, for him, had again moved in a mysterious way to perform His wonders: and, having marvelled that "Dear Anna," though she

> "*must needs prefer*
> *The fairer scenes of sweet Sancerre,*"

should have

> "*come from distant Loire, to choose*
> *A cottage on the banks of Ouse,*"

he proceeds:

> "*This page of Providence, quite new,*
> *And now just op'ning to our view,*
> *Employs our present thoughts and pains,*
> *To guess, and spell, what it contains:*
> *But day by day, and year by year,*
> *Will make the dark enigma clear,*
> *And furnish us, perhaps, at last,*
> *Like other scenes already past,*
> *With proof, that we, and our affairs*
> *Are part of a Jehovah's cares.*"

It is questionable whether Sir Robert Austen, deceased, had made his advances in this style, and probably his widow much preferred the lines in which her new suitor spoke of the "itching" and "tingling" he felt to express her "intrinsic merit true." Still, even while she must have recognised that if she took Cowper she would have to take his Evangelicalism also, the *Epistle*, on the whole, seemed promising.

Within two months, however, there was a rupture. The circumstances were thus related to Unwin:

> "My letters have already apprised you of that close and intimate connexion that took place between the lady you visited in Queen Ann Street, and us. Nothing could be more promising though sudden in the commencement. She treated us with as much unreservedness of communication, as if we had been born in the same house, and educated together. At her departure,

she herself proposed a correspondence, and because writing does not agree with your mother, proposed a correspondence with me. This sort of intercourse had not been long maintained, before I discovered, by some slight intimations of it, that she had conceived displeasure at somewhat I had written, though I cannot now recollect it: conscious of none but the most upright inoffensive intentions, I yet apologised for the passage in question, and the flaw was healed again. Our correspondence after this proceeded smoothly for a considerable time, but at length having had repeated occasion to observe that she expressed a sort of romantic idea of our merits, and built such expectations of felicity upon our friendship, as we were sure that nothing human could possibly answer, I wrote to remind her that we were mortal, to recommend it to her not to think more highly of us than the subject would warrant, and intimating that when we embellish a creature with colours taken from our own fancy, and, so adorned, admire and praise it beyond its real merits, we make it an idol, and have nothing to expect in the end, but that it will deceive our hopes, and that we shall derive nothing from it but a painful conviction of our error. Your mother heard me read the letter, she read it herself, and honoured it with her warm approbation. But it gave mortal offence; it received indeed an answer, but such a one as I could by no means reply to; and there ended (for it was impossible it should ever be renewed) a friendship that bid fair to be lasting; being formed with a woman whose seeming stability of temper, whose knowledge of the world, and great experience of its folly, but above all, whose sense of religion, and seriousness of mind (for with all her gaiety, she is a great thinker), induced us both, in spite of that cautious reserve that marks our characters, to trust her, to love and value her, and to open our hearts for her reception. It may be necessary to add, that by her own desire I wrote to her under the assumed relation of a brother, and she to me as my sister.—*Ceu fumus in auras.*"

I think I can picture Unwin handing over the letter, with a quiet smile, to his wife. I fancy I can hear her laughing aloud, albeit in a friendly spirit, after she had read its contents, while "little John," in whose progress and education Uncle William always took a keen interest, wondered what the fun was about. For Unwin, when visiting London, had called, at Cowper's instigation, to see Lady Austen, and his opinion of her seems not quite to have coincided with Cowper's own. But, as the poet (after his reconciliation with "dear Anna") told Unwin, he "*must* have seen her to a disadvantage."

The "fracas" ended as suddenly as it had begun. By way of olive-branch Lady Austen sent Cowper three pairs of ruffles, which she had begun before the quarrel, with advice that a fourth pair would quickly follow. "Brother William," for his part, despatched to her a copy of his *Poems*, which had been promised before the *contretemps*. Peace was re-established. Lady Austen was soon visiting her sister again and sitting at the feet of Mr. Scott, and there were pleasant walks, as in the previous summer, between Olney and Clifton Hill. When the autumn rains descended, Lady Austen, not to be daunted by mere mud, made her triumphant progress to Orchard Side upon a donkey; and when the roads became impassable even for that long-suffering steed, Cowper amused himself by striking off, from a small printing press which "Anne" had herself given him, some verses wherein, as he surveyed the wintry floods, he expressed the wish that he were a Dutchman and could

> "*in a bog live well content,*
> *And find it just my element.*"

Before the floods had subsided, Mr. Jones had occasion to visit London. No sooner had he gone than Clifton Rectory, "being without a garrison," was besieged by burglars. The terrified ladies took refuge with Mrs. Unwin. Mrs. Jones and her daughter soon summoned up courage to return home; but Lady Austen, having "not quite recovered from a recent indisposition," decided to remain—until apartments were available for her at Olney Vicarage. This was not the first time she had stayed at Orchard Side, for during the summer she had ridden over one Thursday with her sister to the evening lecture at Olney, and had not long been seated in her pew before "she was attacked by the most excruciating pains of bilious colic"—a disorder, Cowper said, in describing the incident to Unwin, "to which she has lately been very subject." Nobly, however, she bore her agony—"without discovering much of what she felt even to Mrs. Jones"—until

the service was over. Cowper himself shall narrate the
sequel:

"We were just sitting down to supper, when a hasty rap
alarmed us. I ran to the hall window, for the hares being loose,
it was impossible to open the door. The evening had been a
dismal one, raining almost continually, but just at that time it
held up. I entreated Mrs. Jones to go round to the gate, and,
understanding by her tremulous voice that something distressful
was at hand, made haste to meet her. I had no sooner reached
the yard door, and opened it, than Lady Austen appeared leaning
upon Mr. Scott. She could not speak, but thrusting her other
arm under mine, with much difficulty made shift to attain the
great chair by the fireside in the parlour; there she suffered
unutterable anguish for a considerable time, till at length, by
your mother's application and assistance, being a little relieved,
she contrived to climb the staircase, and after about three hours'
agony was put to bed. At eleven at night we sent off a messenger
to Northampton, who returned at seven the next morning, and
brought a physician with him. He prescribed, and she was
better. Friday night she slept tolerably, rose cheerful, and
entertained us all Saturday with much agreeable conversation
as usual; but her spirits being too great for her strength, the
consequence was a frightful hysteric fit, which seized her just
as she was going to bed. She was alone, for her sister had been
obliged to go home; and thinking there was no need of such a
precaution, she would have nobody else to sleep with her. The
appointed signal was, that she should knock if she wanted
anything. She did so; your mother hastened to the chamber,
and I after her to know if I could be of any use. She had not
begun to undress, so I was admitted; and soon after her disorder
became quite convulsive, accompanied with most of the symptoms of the most violent fits of that sort I have ever seen. In
about an hour she grew better, rested tolerably, and was in good
spirits on Sunday, and last night well enough to return to
Clifton upon the ass. To-day we dine there."

Lady Austen's second enforced stay at Orchard Side lasted
a little longer. But the Vicarage was soon ready for her, and
there she entered into residence. The doorway in the
Vicarage wall, which had been closed since Newton left, was
opened again. Brother William and Sister Anne met each

Q

other for several hours every morning, and "a practice obtained at length of dining with each other alternately every day, Sundays excepted." In the evenings the poet read aloud, or there was a game of battledore and shuttlecock, or, while a little dog under her chair "performed in the vocal way to admiration," Lady Austen sat at the harpsichord and sang songs written for her by Cowper. Among these was "Toll for the Brave." The sea often haunted Cowper's imagination, and the wreck of the *Royal George* inevitably appealed to his passive heroism:

> "*It was not in the battle,*
> *No tempest gave the shock,*
> *She sprang no fatal leak,*
> *She ran upon no rock;*
> *His sword was in the sheath,*
> *His fingers held the pen,*
> *When Kempenfelt went down*
> *With twice four hundred men.*"

It may be that the event had also awakened echoes in the gloomier recesses of the poet's mind, and that he saw a similitude between the fate of the ship and his own imagined doom. At any rate, the poem is one of those perfectly inspired utterances which fill the reader with marvel that the simplest language—for there is hardly a line here which, isolated, is not bald prose—can, by fitting arrangement, produce so moving an effect. Hardly less successful, in its own way, is that classic of the schoolroom, *Boadicea*, written in 1780.

Cowper's correspondence from this time onwards is so plentiful that it is no longer possible for us to keep pace with the outpourings of his thoughts, moods, and fancies. Most of the letters, ranging over a wide variety of topics, are cheerful, and often merry. But melancholy continues to break in at intervals, and the writer's despairing tone about himself contrasts oddly with the combined fervour and sanity of many of his observations on religion in general. It is strange to compare letters such as that [1] which contains his reflections on a sermon by Paley with others like the following (written, however, in the month of January!) to Newton:

[1] To William Unwin, May 12, 1783.

"The new year is already old in my account. I am not, indeed, sufficiently second-sighted to be able to boast by anticipation an acquaintance with the events of it yet unborn, but rest convinced that, be they what they may, not one of them comes a messenger of good to me. If even death itself should be of the number, he is no friend of mine. It is an alleviation of the woes even of an unenlightened man, that he can wish for death, and indulge a hope, at least, that in death he shall find deliverance. But, loaded as my life is with despair, I have no such comfort as would result from a supposed probability of better things to come, were it once ended. For, more unhappy than the traveller with whom I set out, pass through what difficulties I may, through whatever dangers and afflictions, I am not a whit the nearer home, unless a dungeon may be called so. This is no very agreeable theme; but in so great a dearth of subjects to write upon, and especially impressed as I am at this moment with a sense of my own condition, I could choose no other. The weather is an exact emblem of my mind in its present state. A thick fog envelopes everything, and at the same time it freezes intensely. You will tell me that this cold gloom will be succeeded by a cheerful spring, and endeavour to encourage me to hope for a spiritual change resembling it—but it will be lost labour. Nature revives again; but a soul once slain lives no more. . . . My friends, I know, expect that I shall see yet again. They think it necessary to the existence of divine truth, that he who once had possession of it should never finally lose it. I admit the solidity of this reasoning in every case but my own. And why not in my own? . . . I forestall the answer:—God's ways are mysterious, and He giveth no account of His matters: —an answer that would serve my purpose as well as theirs that use it. There is a mystery in my destruction, and in time it shall be explained." [1]

Gloomy, indeed! Yet the literary felicity itself belies in some degree the sentiments it expresses. Moreover, even this letter slides in the end into quite cheerful references to Mrs.

[1] In the hope of comforting Cowper, Newton recalled for his benefit the story of one Simon Browne, a dissenting minister, who had suffered all Cowper's own delusions. By citing a parallel case Newton wished to disprove the poet's own imagined singularity. He failed to convince him ; but the attempt was as well intentioned as the method, surely, was sound. Who has not sought, in a similar manner, to allay the needless fears of a friend? Yet—on the principle that any stick is good enough for the beating of an opponent—certain critics have pointed to Newton's action as an instance of his supposed obtuseness!

Unwin, Newton himself, and one of his nieces, while the writer promises to send the manuscript of a new light poem *The Colubriad*, founded on the incident of a viper's recent intrusion into the garden at Orchard Side and the reactions towards "so novel an appearance" of "the old cat" and her "retinue of kittens." The letter, indeed, shows again that for Cowper, as Goldwin Smith says, "the language of despondency had become habitual, and did not always flow from a soul really in the depths of woe."

That Cowper's despondency appears most often in his correspondence with Newton is not to be denied. The simple explanation is that, while Cowper's warmth towards his various friends fluctuated slightly at different periods, Newton was, on the whole, the one to whom he addressed himself with least reserve. To him he most freely poured out his troubles. But to him also many of his happiest and most playful letters were directed. Newton, for example, was the recipient, during the years covered by our present chapter, of three of the classic examples of Cowper's epistolary art. It was to him that the poet sent the account of Puss's escape, and of the thrilling and successful hunt for him through the town. It was Newton who received the description of the visit to Orchard Side of the unctuous Parliamentary candidate. And it was Newton who was first privileged to read another letter which, familiar though it be, must be quoted yet again:

"Since our conflagration here,[1] we have sent two women and a boy to the justice, for depredation; Sue Riviss, for stealing a piece of beef, which, in her excuse, she said she intended to take care of. This lady, whom you well remember, escaped for want of evidence; not that evidence was indeed wanting, but our men of Gotham judged it unnecessary to send it. With her went the woman I mentioned before, who, it seems, has made some sort of profession, but upon this occasion allowed herself a latitude of conduct rather inconsistent with it, having filled her apron with wearing-apparel, which she likewise intended to take care of. She would have gone to the county gaol, had Billy Raban, the baker's son, who prosecuted, insisted upon it; but he good-naturedly, though I think weakly, interposed in her

---

[1] There had recently been another serious outbreak of fire at Olney.

favour, and begged her off. The young gentleman who accompanied these fair ones, is the junior son of Molly Boswell. He had stolen some iron work, the property of Griggs, the butcher. Being convicted, he was ordered to be whipped, which operation he underwent at the cart's tail, from the stone-house to the high arch, and back again. He seemed to show great fortitude, but it was all an imposition upon the public. The beadle, who performed it, had filled his left hand with red ochre, through which, after every stroke, he drew the lash of his whip, leaving the appearance of a wound upon the skin, but in reality not hurting him at all. This being perceived by Mr. Constable Handscomb, who followed the beadle, he applied his cane, without any such management or precaution, to the shoulders of the too merciful executioner. The scene immediately became more interesting. The beadle could by no means be prevailed upon to strike hard, which provoked the constable to strike harder; and this double flogging continued, till a lass of Silver End, pitying the pitiful beadle thus suffering under the hands of the pitiless constable, joined the procession, and placing herself immediately behind the latter, seized him by his capillary club, and pulling him backwards by the same, slapped his face with a most Amazonian fury. This concatenation of events has taken up more of my paper than I intended it should, but I could not forbear to inform you how the beadle threshed the thief, the constable the beadle, and the lady the constable, and how the thief was the only person concerned who suffered nothing."

It was in writing to Newton, again, that Cowper most often broke into sportive rhyme. He also corresponded very gaily with Mrs. Newton,[1] who made him the best of returns. "When I write to Mr. Newton," he told her, "he answers me by letter; when I write to you, you answer me in fish."

IV

Cowper's gloomy letter to Newton, quoted in the previous section, is dated January 13, 1784. I have, therefore, slightly anticipated events. I reproduced that letter to show that even

[1] See, for instance, the letter of June 1780, describing the misadventure of the gingerbread man, the gingerbread wife, and the runaway horse—an incident that probably helped later to provide colour for *John Gilpin*. Also the letter (entirely in verse) dated September 16, 1781.

the darkest hours when expression was possible to Cowper at all were by no means unrelieved by lighter shades. (There were, of course, the times of actual madness when his pen lay unused.) But that epistle to Newton is evidence in itself that Cowper was, during this period, hovering precariously once more upon derangement. Mrs. Unwin had first noticed the returning symptoms of his old malady in the autumn of 1782. Ten years had separated each of his preceding attacks. The same interval, therefore, would soon have elapsed again. That mere fact could not fail to disturb the poet, with his unfortunate capacity for auto-suggestion. Lady Austen, after her second brief stay at Orchard Side, had just taken up her residence at Olney Vicarage. Her vivacity had served for a time to keep Cowper's gloomy thoughts at bay. But her presence was no magic specific against his despondency. How *could* she have permanently satisfied one who, while he had so rich a fund of gaiety, was essentially and deeply serious? She did not herself lack an underlying sobriety: but a gulf lay between her mundane good sense and Cowper's spiritual fervour.

She had been a useful tonic. But a tonic, if administered too often or too long, progressively weakens in effect. It may at length become actually dangerous. The society of Lady Austen was ultimately to reach that point with Cowper. In 1782, however, it was still efficacious. Every one knows how *John Gilpin* came to be written. One October evening as Lady Austen sat with Mrs. Unwin and the poet in the parlour at Orchard Side, she told a story, remembered from girlhood, of a certain London citizen who rode out of town with his wife to celebrate the twentieth anniversary of their wedding, and who went much further than he intended. Against the drollery of the tale Cowper's mood was at first adamant. But as the narrator, undaunted, went on, his face began to brighten, and soon the parlour echoed with peals of uncontrollable laughter. That same night *The Diverting History of John Gilpin* began to frame itself in his mind. He sprang from bed and committed to paper the first draft of the ballad, which he showed to the ladies over the breakfast table. For several days, secluded in the greenhouse, he feverishly revised and polished, and sent across instalments of the poem, as he finished them, for the delight of Wilson the barber.

John Gilpin first appeared anonymously in the *Public Advertiser* for November 1782. It became so popular that it was "hackneyed in every magazine, every newspaper, and every street." In May 1784, Henderson gave a further fillip to its fame by reading it at Freemasons' Hall, though Thomas Wright conclusively disproves the legend that it was the noted comedian who originally made its fortune. As for Cowper himself, he was both delighted and a little uneasy over its success. At least he had the satisfaction of knowing, as he told Unwin, that if people were everywhere laughing at his poem,

"they do not always laugh so innocently, or at so small an expense—for in a world like this, abounding with subjects for satire, and with satirical wits to mark them, a laugh that hurts nobody has at least the grace of novelty to recommend it. Swift's darling motto was, *Vive la bagatelle*—a good wish for a philosopher of his complexion, the greater part of whose wisdom, whencesoever it came, most certainly came not from above. *La bagatelle* has no enemy in me, though it has neither so warm a friend, nor so able a one, as it had in him."

Cowper adds that "strange as it may seem, the most ludicrous lines I ever wrote have been written in the saddest mood, and, but for that saddest mood, perhaps had never been written at all." A close bond between humour and sadness there must, in the nature of things, always be. Yet the hour in which a humorous poem is actually written can hardly itself be gloomy, and I think Goldwin Smith is right when he insists that Cowper "sometimes exaggerated his own misery," and that, while he afterwards fancied *John Gilpin* to have been inspired by a mood of deepest depression, he had probably written it "in an interval of high spirits between two such moods." However that may be, the world was greatly sweetened by the ballad of the luckless linen-draper. Clean humour, as Cowper had good cause to remark, was not then too plentiful. That *John Gilpin* was immediately appreciated shows, on the other hand, that there was already an awakening of better taste. Wesley and his followers may not have made a raising of the tone of humour their prime aim: they might even have been slightly perturbed by the idea. But Evangelicalism was, incidentally, having that effect.

The January of 1783 passed without its dreaded issue. Cowper remained comparatively cheerful. If Lady Austen were responsible for diverting his thoughts during a critical month, in which otherwise he might have frightened himself into madness again, I would not withhold one jot of the credit due to her. Her helpfulness to the poet was nevertheless approaching its end: though first she was to set him to the task in whose fulfilment he became a poet indeed. In July 1783, she suggested that he should attempt a long effort in blank verse. (The moral satires had been written in rhymed couplets.) He stared vacantly at her, and said that he lacked a subject. Whether Lady Austen spoke flippantly, or whether she realised that *any* theme, if determined for him, would suffice to stir Cowper's pen and make his fancy wander at large through earth and heaven, we cannot be sure. It is probable, however, that if she had told him to write about Noah, or Mr. Wilson's parti-coloured pole, or even perhaps her own eyebrows, instead of about the parlour sofa which happened to attract her notice at the moment, the immediate effect would have been equally happy and the final result much the same.

But since "the fair" commanded him to sing the sofa, "sing the Sofa" he did. From contemplating the sofa as a boon to the gouty, his mind passed by an easy transition to the healthy who need no sofa. These in turn prompted visions of country walks: and so, with shudders at the thought of the folly and vice of cities, he turned to the praise of Nature, and then of Nature's God. Glory be to Lady Austen who set the ink flowing! She deserves, and doubtless enjoys, her reward in paradise, as she has her secure niche in the temple of earthly fame. Yet it is nonsense to say that she "inspired" *The Task*, as she did perhaps, in the strict sense, inspire *John Gilpin*. She not only gave Cowper the theme—and the story —for that ballad: her mood vitally elicited his own. There is nothing of "Anna" in *The Task*. While it abounds in playful or charming touches of the poet's own personality, and while it has many passages of ordinary "good sense," suggesting the eighteenth-century gentleman of culture, it is, in its essential aim, scope, and sense of values, both a reflection and a product of the Methodist Revival.

Poor Lady Austen! Having set "Brother William" to work, she became an impediment to its fulfilment. Soon Cowper was so engrossed in writing the poem that he lamented the loss of time involved by his morning *devoirs*. His companion must have begun to suspect that she now played second fiddle to his muse. It has been hinted also, though there seems to be no proof, that Mrs. Unwin was a little jealous of "Sister Anne." She may have been: she was, after all, human. It is true, as Southey has said, that we shall later see Lady Hesketh and Mrs. Unwin "sharing" Cowper without any ill-feeling; but perhaps the parallel hardly holds good. At all events, Solomon's "three-fold cord" to which Cowper had compared the triumviral relationship of "Mary," "Anna," and himself, showed ominous signs of breaking. Even to Cowper it must have become plain that Lady Austen would not permanently be content with the status of "sister." What precipitated the rupture we cannot tell. All we know is that in the spring of 1784 the poet sent her ladyship "a very tender yet resolute letter, in which he explained and lamented the circumstances that forced him to renounce her society." Alas! that letter, which most of all Cowper's epistles we should like to have, was destroyed by its recipient in a fit of anger. She probably regretted her action afterwards, for she admitted that it was a very good letter. There was no reconciliation this time. Lady Austen soon left Olney for Bristol, and, though she visited her sister in 1786 and 1787, she and Cowper never met again. Her heart did not break. She eventually married M. de Tardif, an accomplished French gentleman, and died in Paris in 1802.

It is impossible to withhold sympathy from Lady Austen. Cowper had little fortune to tempt her, and she must have been attracted to him, as well she might be, for himself.

And only a month or two before the final severance he had
sent her a poem entitled, "To a Lady who Wore a Lock of
his Hair Set with Diamonds":

> " *The star that beams on Anna's breast*
>   *Conceals her William's hair,*
> *'Twas lately sever'd from the rest*
>   *To be promoted there.*
>
> *The heart that beats beneath that breast*
>   *Is William's, well I know;*
> *A nobler prize and richer far*
>   *Than India could bestow.*
>
> *She thus his favour'd lock prefers,*
>   *To make her William shine;*
> *The ornament indeed is hers,*
>   *But all the honour mine.*"

The verses are, however, in the eighteenth-century tradition
of "gallantry," and that Cowper was using the convention
sufficiently proves to us that his heart was not seriously
engaged. Had Lady Austen understood him better, she too
would have realised the truth. She might have paused to
reflect, also, that her admirer, even though he *had* given her
a lock of his hair, was a staid bachelor of fifty-two. Yet a
woman of merely average insight can hardly be blamed for
having drawn false conclusions from such an address. She
could not be expected to realise that the note of intimacy was
habitual to the writer, and that the verses had been composed
with the most guileless desire to please a friend. Cowper
may—by normal, or modern, rules—have been indiscreet.
But we cannot condemn a child for not being an adult: and,
in his attitude towards women, "Brother William" was
simple as an infant.

If Mrs. Unwin *had* been jealous of Lady Austen, she need
not have been. If one wishes to appraise the gulf between
Cowper's regard for the one woman and his love for the other,
or if one would see vividly, as on a screen, his idea of relative
values, one cannot do better than contrast the lines to "Anna"
with this imperishable sonnet:

"Mary! I want a lyre with other strings;
Such aid from Heaven as some have feign'd they drew!
An eloquence scarce given to mortals, new,
And undebas'd by praise of meaner things!
That, ere through age or woe I shed my wings,
I may record thy worth, with honour due,
In verse as musical as thou art true,—
Verse, that immortalizes whom it sings!
But thou hast little need: there is a Book,
By seraphs writ with beams of heav'nly light,
On which the eyes of God not rarely look;
A chronicle of actions just and bright!
There all thy deeds, my faithful Mary, shine,
And since thou own'st that praise, I spare thee mine."

V

The gap left in Cowper's life by Lady Austen's departure
was filled by the Throckmorton family, whom he called "The
Frogs." It will be remembered that the celebrated picnic of
1781 had been enjoyed in the grounds of Mrs. Throckmorton's
ancestral mansion, Weston Hall, about a mile from Olney.
That good lady had given Cowper the key of her Park, so that
he might range it at will; now another Mrs. Throckmorton,
"young, genteel, and handsome," reigned in her stead.[1]
With her husband, John (afterwards Sir John), there lived his
brother George. When John succeeded to the estate, Cowper
had sent him a complimentary card, begging the continuance
of the privilege extended to him by the new squire's mother,
who had recently died at Bath. The request was granted, but
two years passed before a friendship began to ripen. The
Throckmortons, the poet then wrote, "are Papists, but much
more amiable than many Protestants." They seem to have
earned his tribute. It is amusing, none the less, to see how
quickly Cowper's narrow opinions gave way to his warm
regard for individuals. He was now not merely countenancing
dissent—for William Bull still came over regularly from
Newport Pagnell, no longer carrying his own box of tobacco,

---

[1] She was the daughter of Thomas Gifford, of Chillington, Staffordshire.

since his host had taken to keeping a supply of the wicked weed in stock—but consorting with Roman Catholics!

The immediate cause of his closer acquaintanceship with the Throckmortons was an experiment in flying. "A fortnight ago," he wrote Unwin in December 1783, "I received an invitation in the civillest terms, in which he [John Throckmorton] told me that the next day he should attempt to fill a balloon, and if it would be any pleasure for me to be present, should be happy to see me. Your mother and I went." Aeronautics were then, so to speak, in the air. At least that is where its votaries wished to find themselves. But on this occasion—though the endeavour was "very philosophically made"—the balloon "could not be filled." [1] Cowper enjoyed the occasion not less on that account:

"The whole country was there. . . . Our reception was, however, flattering to a great degree, insomuch that more notice seemed to be taken of us than we could possibly have expected—indeed rather more than that of any of his other guests. They even seemed anxious to recommend themselves to our regards. We drank chocolate, and were asked to dine, but were engaged. A day or two afterwards, Mrs. Unwin and I walked that way, and were overtaken in a shower. I found a tree that I thought would shelter us both, a large elm, in a grove that fronts the mansion. Mrs. T. observed us, and, running towards us in the rain, insisted on our walking in. He was gone out. We sat chatting with her till the weather cleared up, and then at her instance took a walk with her in the garden."

Cowper and Mrs. Unwin thenceforward dined frequently at Weston Hall, and the more they saw of its occupants the

[1] Though the balloon refused to ascend, it inspired Cowper to a series of characteristic letters. In one of them he assures Newton, upon personal experience, that the new method of travel is very pleasant: "I dreamt last night that I drove myself through the upper regions in a balloon and pair, with the greatest ease and security." He asks Unwin if he does not think it possible "to convey such a quantity of inflammable air into the stomach and abdomen that the philosopher, no longer gravitating to a centre, shall ascend by his own comparative levity, and never stop till he has reached the medium exactly *in equilibrio* with himself." Discussing the matter seriously with Newton, and exhibiting considerable understanding of the scientific problems involved, he assumes that the art of flying will ultimately be mastered, but ponders whether it will prove a blessing or a "judgment." He gives his reasons for believing the latter. Some of the "thousand evils" he foresaw have been tragically fulfilled. Let us hope that in the long run his prophecy will be falsified.

more they liked them. "You say well, my dear," Lady
Hesketh was informed by her cousin a few years later,

"that in Mr. Throckmorton we have a peerless neighbour; we
have so. In point of information upon all important subjects,
in respect, too, of expression and address, and, in short, everything that enters into the idea of a gentleman, I have not found
his equal (not often) anywhere. Were I asked who in my
judgment approaches nearest to him in all his amiable qualities
and qualifications, I should certainly answer his brother
George."

Mrs. Throckmorton was described to Newton as a "consummate assemblage of all that is called good-nature, com-
plaisance, and innocent cheerfulness." Cowper added that
"they have lately received many gross affronts from the
people of this place, on account of their religion. We
thought it therefore the more necessary to treat them
with respect." As for the Throckmortons' "good-natured
Padre" who was later to give help in transcribing his
Homer, the poet could positively have "hugged" him one
evening, for some humorous comment he made at the expense of his own Popery—thereby proving, of course, his
"breadth of mind."

Partridges and hares from the Hall now found their way to
the table at Orchard Side, and when Mr. Throckmorton fished
he did not, though doubly a disciple of St. Peter, forget "the
most ichthyophagous of Protestants." When, as often happened, the family were away, Cowper and Mrs. Unwin made
the contents of the Hall garden their own. As Clifton no
longer held its old lure for him, Cowper now took his favourite
walk westwards across three fields from Olney to the slight
elevation which he called "yon eminence," where

> "*our pace*
> *Has slacken'd to a pause, and we have borne*
> *The ruffling wind, scarce conscious that it blew.*"

From here he obtained his famous view of the Ouse valley,
with its scattered villages and church spires. A descent into a
hollow led him to the farmhouse which he named "The
Peasant's Nest." Rising thence he passed through a planta-

tion of yews, firs, and pines, from the end of which "a length
of colonnade," with its chestnuts, invited him. A slight
decline led to the "Rustic Bridge," and then, mounting again,
and following a path along the northern side of Weston Park,
under a canopy of oaks, he reached the quaint hexagonal
structure known as the Alcove. Another declivity, "sharp
and short," like the re-ascent, took him across a tiny channel
—"the little Naiad." He now gained the "Avenue of Lime
Trees" of which Mr. Throckmorton was specially proud, and,
having gazed his fill at the arch made by these noble trees,
"defined with such exactness that no cathedral in the world
can show one of more magnificence or beauty," he entered,
by a Chinese gate, the Wilderness, with its cawing of rooks,
its statue of a recumbent lion, and its two monumental urns,
on one of which was inscribed his own epitaph for John
Throckmorton's pointer. In the Wilderness, surrounded by
evergreens, shrubs, and elms, was the Gothic Temple, a
favourite resort of Newton when he visited Olney; while at
the end of a vista facing the Temple stood a bust of Homer.
The grounds had been laid out by that famous eighteenth-
century landscape gardener, Lancelot—or, as he preferred to
call himself, "Capability"—Brown.[1]

Weston Hall, which lay on the left side of the road from
Olney, just outside the village, was demolished in 1827.
Having been built at different times, it was odd, rather than
beautiful, in appearance. Weston Lodge, the plain stone
house which Mrs. Unwin and Cowper were later to make their
home, survives. It stands on the opposite side of the street,
which is entered through one of the old gates of Weston Park
—the reason being that the private road of the Throckmortons
is now the public road, while the former public road has long
since been disused. Various other relics of "Capability"
Brown's work still mark the site of the Park, and give a touch
of the bizarre to what is otherwise an undistinguished but
pleasant hamlet. The church, at the top end of the climbing

[1] Readers who wish to supplement their reading of *The Task* with detailed
information about its topography should turn to Storer's charming book of
engravings entitled *Cowper Illustrated by a Series of Views In or Near the Park of
Weston-Underwood, Buckinghamshire, Accompanied with Copious Descriptions and a
Sketch of the Poet's Life.* 1804. See also *The Town of Cowper.* By Thomas Wright.

village, remains indeed a haunt of ancient peace; and from
the churchyard—undisturbed, save, perhaps, by the gravedigger with whom I recently talked as he puffed at his clay
pipe—one may gaze down upon a pastoral landscape which
has changed comparatively little since it inspired the herald
of the Romantic Revival.

village retains indeed a band of morris peace, and from the backward

Chapter Eleven

THE POET AND HIS AGE

I

IN WRITING *The Task* Cowper followed Tully's rule—"Nulla dies sine linea"—which, he said truly, "will make a volume in less time than one would suppose." On some days he composed only three lines; on others he discovered "a more fluent vein." But he resolved not to "meddle" with blank verse again: "not having the music of rhyme, it requires so close an attention to the pause and cadence, and such a peculiar mode of expression, as to render it, to me at least, the most difficult species of poetry." If in the sequence of his ideas Cowper was the most spontaneous of writers, he was a fastidious—though not always an impeccable—stylist.

In October 1784, he sent the completed manuscript—"four quires of verse"—to Unwin. "In some passages," he told him,

> "you will observe me very satirical. Writing on such subjects I could not be otherwise. I can write nothing without aiming at least at usefulness: it were beneath my years to do it, and still more dishonourable to my religion. I know that a reformation of such abuses as I have censured is not to be expected from the efforts of a poet; but to contemplate the world, its follies, its vices, its indifference to duty, and its strenuous attachment to what is evil, and not to reprehend, were to approve it."

After further variations on this familiar theme, the letter concludes:

> "My descriptions are all from nature: not one of them second-handed. My delineations of the heart are from my own experience: not one of them borrowed from books, or in the least degree conjectural. In my numbers, which I have varied as much as I could (for blank verse without variety of numbers is no better than bladder and string), I have imitated nobody, though sometimes perhaps there may be an apparent resem-

blance; because at the same time that I would not imitate, I have not affectedly differed.

"If the work cannot boast a regular plan (in which respect however I do not think it altogether indefensible), it may yet boast, that the reflections are naturally suggested always by the preceding passage, and that except the fifth book, which is rather of a political aspect, the whole has one tendency; to discountenance the modern enthusiasm after a London life, and to recommend rural ease and leisure, as friendly to the cause of piety and virtue."

To Unwin, this time, was delegated the business of finding a publisher. Johnson was to be approached first; but if he stroked his chin, surveyed the ceiling, and cried "Humph!" Unwin was to anticipate him by saying that the author would certainly not wish him to undertake anything to his own disadvantage. Longman was to be tried next, and, failing him, Nichols, the printer of the *Gentleman's Magazine*. But, urged the poet, "take no pains to conquer them. The idea of being hawked about, and especially of you being the hawker, is insupportable . . . I may possibly envy authors who can afford to publish at their own expense, and in that case should write no more . . . the mortification would not break my heart." Johnson, however, did not cry "Humph!" and Cowper foolishly sold him the copyright. *The Task* brought its author little direct profit, though it paved the way for a State pension later.

It will be recalled that when his first volume was being written Cowper temporarily offended Unwin by not telling him of it, and by consulting Newton about its production. Why had he now reversed the process? Even though Newton and his wife spent three weeks at Olney while the first book of *The Task* was on the stocks, they were given no hint of what was toward. Not until the work was well advanced were tidings of it broken to Newton, who replied with "a most friendly letter indeed," but who, like Unwin on the former occasion, was naturally a little nettled. He received excuses similar to those previously offered Unwin. There was a momentary breach. Newton became somewhat "peevish," and Cowper, on his own confession, answered him in haste.

R

But the storm in a teacup quickly subsided. Newton wrote most appreciatively of *The Task* when it was printed, and Cowper replied that he had received "a like favourable report of it from several different quarters, but never any (for obvious reasons) that has gratified me more than yours."

The honours in this brief battle belong, surely, to Newton. Cowper, even if his true purpose had been that of "surprising agreeably," had shown bad taste and an uncharacteristic disregard for past favours. The plea sometimes made for him— that he was afraid Newton might wish to narrow down the scope or style of the poem—may have in it a grain of justification. But, as he had treated Unwin similarly a few years earlier, I think the main explanation of his conduct lies merely in his moodiness. He had, as I have suggested, "warmer" or "colder" fits towards particular friends. Or it might be truer to say that circumstances, during certain periods, dictated a more regular correspondence with one friend than with another, and that the friend uppermost in his thoughts *at the time* seemed to demand the closest degree of intimacy.

He was soon writing again as affectionately as ever to Newton—and again revealing his mercurial spirits. Referring to the approaching publication of *The Task*, he says: "I am even so indifferent to the matter, that I can truly assert myself guiltless of the very idea of my book sometimes whole days together. God knows that, my mind having been occupied more than twelve years in the contemplation of the most distressing subjects, the world, and its opinion of what I write, is become as unimportant to me as the whistling of a bird in a bush." This was quite honest at the moment, and it reflected the deepest side of Cowper's nature. Yet, while for "whole days together" he might be indifferent to applause or censure, there were other days when he expressed himself, with equal sincerity, thus:

"Having imitated no man, I may reasonably hope that I shall not incur the disadvantage of a comparison with my betters. Milton's manner was peculiar. So is Thomson's. He that should write like either of them, would, in my judgment, deserve the name of a copyist, but not of a poet. A judicious and sensible reader therefore, like yourself, will not say that my manner is not good, because it does not resemble theirs, but will rather consider what it is in itself. Blank verse is susceptible of much greater diversification of manner, than verse in rhyme: and why the modern writers of it have all thought proper to cast their numbers alike, I know not. Certainly it was not necessity that compelled them to it. I flatter myself, however, that I have avoided that sameness with others, which would entitle me to nothing but a share in one common oblivion with them all. It is possible that, as the reviewer of my former volume found cause to say that he knew not to what class of writers to refer me, the reviewer of this, whosoever he shall be, may see occasion to remark the same singularity. At any rate, though as little apt to be sanguine as most men, and more prone to fear and despond, than to overrate my own productions, I am persuaded that I shall not forfeit anything by this volume that I gained by the last."

He was a true prophet. *The Task* appeared in June 1785, and was immediately successful. The volume contained also *John Gilpin, Tirocinium,*[1] and *An Epistle to Joseph Hill.* Cowper had felt scruples about including *Gilpin.* Doubtless the ballad helped to win popularity for *The Task,* and perhaps, as the writer hoped, to make some thoughtless readers travel, like the linen-draper himself, though to better purpose, further than they intended!

II

"In his poems," says Humphry Ward, Cowper "has revealed himself with a winning *naïveté* that is almost without example; and when we add to the autobiographical passages in *Retirement* and *The Task* the friendly confidences of the letters, we find that there remains nothing for the critic to interpret."[2] That is one reason, perhaps, why Cowper has always been more popular with "middle class" readers than with the *intelligentsia.* Not all professors are so modest as Dr. Ward. Many of them wish to display their own prowess,

---

[1] See Chapter III.   [2] *The English Poets,* Volume III.

and like an author who offers it a subtler challenge. Nor does
Cowper give much scope for the detective of "influences."
In his simplicity and fidelity of description, though hardly in
his themes, he reveals his discipleship to Homer; while in
Retirement and elsewhere he shows, in his combination of
shrewd sense, precision, and playfulness, an even closer kinship
with Horace. The blank verse of *The Task* carries faint echoes
of Milton in his milder moods. Some of his shorter poems
reflect admiration for "dear Mat Prior's easy jingle"; while it
is evident from the earlier moral satires that the writer had
once been impressed by his Westminster schoolfellow, "the
great Churchill." Nor did he quite escape the lingering
dominance of Pope. The heroic couplet was chosen as the
metre for the satires. But in Cowper's hands the instrument
itself became as different from Pope's as were the motives
which prompted the two writers. For the rest, Cowper as a
poet was plain, homespun William Cowper. He may have
slightly underestimated the extent of his reading; but no
writer ever borrowed less from literature. He just looked at
the world about him and into his own mind and heart, and
expressed directly what he saw, thought, and felt.

What he thought was often at variance, however, with
what he felt. There are no ambiguities in his poetry: the
meaning of any isolated passage is transparently plain. But
there are, unfortunately, many contradictions; nor is their
effect lessened by a style which resembles in discursiveness
that of an essayist. The moral satires [1] and *The Task* ramble,
sometimes with a fairly obvious thread of connection, at other
times rather inconsequently, through what appears to present-
day readers a baffling medley of ideas and moods. Even *The
Progress of Error* and *Expostulation* are livened with humour
and epigram, while *Table Talk, Conversation, Retirement,* and

---

[1] Goldwin Smith, whom other writers have followed, is, I think, unduly severe
in saying that " of satirical vigour " these poems " have scarcely a semblance."
Their epigrammatic darts do sometimes hit the target. It must nevertheless be
admitted that Cowper was no Juvenal or Swift, and that he fell far short even of
his true master, Horace. I doubt, however, if his segregation from the world
whose follies and extravagances he aimed at ridiculing was, as is most commonly
alleged, the main reason of his failure. That, I suspect, lay rather in his innate
kindliness, though, as often happens when a naturally gentle person attempts to
be " very satirical," the effect is apt to seem that of a scold.

The Task are marred not merely by explicit sermonising—in itself bad enough—but by sermonising which often refutes the spirit of the context. These defects prevent Cowper's poetry from taking the highest rank, and cause it to survive in extracts rather than in the bulk. Yet it is folly to detach his work from its time, and, subjecting it to analysis in the light of modern psychology, to attribute its shortcomings to a warped personality. We happen to know, from other sources, that the man himself *was* warped to some extent by his constitutional malady; and the fact is reflected in several of his lyrics. But there are no traces of madness, few even of excessive melancholy, in the main body of his poetry; nor is there much of the introspection and self-pity which sometimes creep into his letters.

It is utterly misleading to isolate from *The Task* the passage about the "stricken deer." [1] Torn from its setting, it has, despite the poet's statement of his being made to "live," an air of pathos and defeat. *In* the context it yields a very different impression: unless we are wilfully blind or constitutionally incapable of understanding the values which are here most vitally Cowper's own. The Third Book of *The Task* opens with an address to domestic happiness. With it are contrasted the evils of prostitution and infidelity, which in a satirical interlude the poet associates, as is his wont, with city life. Then, suddenly becoming personal, he continues:

> "*I was a stricken deer, that left the herd*
> *Long since; with many an arrow deep infixt*
> *My panting side was charg'd, when I withdrew*
> *To seek a tranquil death in distant shades.*
> *There was I found by one who had himself*
> *Been hurt by th' archers. In his side he bore,*
> *And in his hands and feet, the cruel scars.*
> *With gentle force soliciting the darts,*
> *He drew them forth, and heal'd, and bade me live.*
> *Since then, with few associates, in remote*
> *And silent woods I wander, far from those*
> *My former partners of the peopled scene;*
> *With few associates, and not wishing more.*"

[1] Book III, 108-120.

Here most biographers or critics end the quotation. Let us, however, go on:

> "*Here much I ruminate, as much I may,*
> *With other views of men and manners now*
> *Than once, and others of a life to come.*
> *I see that all are wand'rers, gone astray*
> *Each in his own delusions; they are lost*
> *In chase of fancied happiness, still woo'd*
> *And never won. Dream after dream ensues;*
> *And still they dream that they shall still succeed,*
> *And still are disappointed. Rings the world*
> *With the vain stir. I sum up half mankind,*
> *And add two-thirds of the remaining half,*
> *And find the total of their hopes and fears*
> *Dreams, empty dreams.*"

The writer then examines the various types of dreamers: the millions who flit from flower to flower of pleasure, as if created only like insects, and the "sober dreamers," seemingly "grave and wise," who, with their historical, scientific, or philosophical studies, are

> "*dropping buckets into empty wells,*
> *And growing old in drawing nothing up.*"

The picture, of course, is exaggerated, and elsewhere in *The Task* Cowper corrects in measure his own perspective. It is needless, surely, to say that the passage quoted above reflected merely a mood. And who will deny that such a mood is sometimes salutary? It *is* unquestionable that many men of action, merely cancelling out one another's mistakes, and many scholars, involved in learned dust—

> "*each claiming truth,*
> *And truth disclaiming both*"—

spend their labour for that which profiteth not. And though a lofty detachment from the combat may, if long continued, become a deadly danger in its turn, who, I say, is not the better for surveying now and then the vanity of human wishes, and for drawing from the vision, as Cowper proceeds to do, a fresh satisfaction in the plain duties, simple joys, and abiding consolations open to us all? [1]

The "stricken deer" reference, however, while itself sane enough, is less typical than is often supposed. Cowper's major poems are, on the whole, remarkably objective for the work of one prone to introspection. His mind was basically critical, and the writing of verse diverted his thoughts from the pre-occupation with self which his morbid taint induced in idle hours. Even when he was mad, he did not, in his own words, lose his senses—only the use of them. He was sane when he wrote most of his poetry: sane, by contemporary standards, even in his Calvinism. It is the standards themselves which have changed. The contradictions in Cowper's poetry are the contradictions of his age, which only a great creative artist could have surmounted.

Cowper was temperamentally not a creator, but a commentator. By that generalisation I still hold. Every generalisation, it is true, needs qualification. Human nature is a tangled skein, which even modern psychology has not finally unravelled. No man is *wholly* creative or *wholly* critical. Even Shelley's genius had an intellectual admixture: a very strong admixture. If, indeed, Shelley had lived to maturity, his imagination and reason might have fused themselves into a harmony which would have ranked him among the few master poets of the world. Cowper, on the other hand, had *some* creative ability. Certain of his shorter poems, like *The Shrubbery*, have a pure lyrical note which is prophetic not only of Wordsworth but of Byron in his quieter moods:

> " *This glassy stream, that spreading pine,*
> *Those alders quivering to the breeze,*
> *Might soothe a soul less hurt than mine,*
> *And please, if anything could please.*
>
> *But fixed, unalterable care*
> *Forgoes not what she feels within,*
> *Shows the same sadness everywhere,*
> *And slights the season and the scene.*"

---

[1] " Is there any dream like the dream of life, which amuses us with the neglect and disregard of these things ? Is there any folly like the folly of our manly state, which is too wise and busy to be at leisure for these reflections ? " These

But just as in Shelley, despite his great intellectual endowment, the *fundamental* impulse was imaginative, so in Cowper, though he did not entirely lack creativeness, the *determining* motive was critical. His true "lyrics" are few in number. And though the genuine spirit of poetry animates the best portions of the satires and *The Task*, such passages are incidental and are seldom long sustained.

That Cowper was not inherently creative, and that much of his work consequently "dates," is his misfortune: it is not his shame. The Calvinism which finds expression in his longer poems was held by some of the most cultured religionists of his day. It was by no means confined to Evangelicalism. It may have lain dormant, during the first half of the century, in the Latitudinarian portion of the Church; but it slumbered merely because the Church itself slumbered. The effect of the Methodist Revival was twofold. By reawakening the Church it reawakened a theology that was still largely Calvinistic; it also set in motion new forces and ideas that were to give Calvinism the *coup de grâce*. Evangelicalism itself reflected an age divided by a sharp conflict of theological opinion.

Calvinism, as I have earlier shown, could hardly have failed to attract the rationalistic side of a nature which, because of warmer qualities in itself, could not have found satisfaction outside Evangelicalism altogether. It was inevitable, then, that Calvinistic theology should have its place in the work of one who, because he was a Calvinist, took a solemn view of the poet's mission:

> "Happy the bard (*if that fair name belong*
> *To him that blends no fable with his song*)
> *Whose lines, uniting, by an honest art,*
> *The faithful monitor's and poet's part,*
> *Seek to delight, that they may mend mankind,*
> *And, while they captivate, inform the mind:*
> *Still happier, if he till a thankful soil,*
> *And fruit reward his honourable toil:*
> *But happier far, who comfort those that wait*
> *To hear plain truth at Judah's hallow'd gate.*" [1]

words occur in the description of the death of Penitens in William Law's *Serious Call*. It provides an interesting parallel in prose to the passage I have quoted from *The Task*.　　　　　　　　　　　　　　　[1] *Hope*, 754-763.

The same idea recurs again and again, though sometimes the poet cannot help himself indulging in the very "push-pin play" which he condemns:

> "The man that means success should soar above
> A soldier's feather, or a lady's glove;
> Else, summoning the muse to such a theme,
> The fruit of all her labour is whipt-cream.
> As if an eagle flew aloft, and then—
> Stoop'd from his highest pitch to pounce a wren;
> As if the poet, purposing to wed,
> Should carve himself a wife in gingerbread." [1]

Here is yet another variation:

> "Accomplishments have taken virtue's place,
> And wisdom falls before exterior grace;
> We slight the precious kernel of the stone,
> And toil to polish its rough coat alone. . . .
> Learning itself, receiv'd into a mind
> By nature weak, or viciously inclin'd,
> Serves but to lead philosophers astray,
> Where children would with ease discern the way.
> And, of all arts sagacious dupes invent,
> To cheat themselves and gain the world's assent,
> The worst is—scripture warp'd from its intent." [2]

This last line may well provoke an ironic smile, when we recall how Cowper's mind itself interprets the Bible:

> "Man, on the dubious waves of error toss'd,
> His ship half founder'd, and his compass lost,
> Sees, far as human optics may command,
> A sleeping fog, and fancies it dry land:
> Spreads all his canvass, ev'ry sinew plies;
> Pants for 't, aims at it, enters it, and dies!
> Then farewell all self-satisfying schemes,
> His well-built systems, philosophic dreams;
> Deceitful views of future bliss, farewell!
> He reads his sentence at the flames of hell.
>   Hard lot of man—to toil for the reward
> Of virtue, and yet lose it! Wherefore hard?—
> He that would win the race must guide his horse
> Obedient to the customs of the course;
> Else, though unequall'd to the goal he flies,
> A meaner than himself shall gain the prize.

[1] *Table Talk*, 548-555.   [2] *The Progress of Error*, 417-420, 431-437.

> Grace leads the right way: if you choose the wrong,
> Take it, and perish; but restrain your tongue.
> Charge not, with light sufficient, and left free,
> Your wilful suicide on God's decree." [1]

Such a view of salvation is, to our minds, a relic of ancient magic. It represented, nevertheless, Cowper's considered belief. In one of his letters, previously quoted, there is a passage which has a topsy-turvy aspect to our modern vision. "Unless profession and conduct go together," he says, "the man's life is a lie, and the validity of what he professes itself is called in question." *We* should reverse the order, and call the man a hypocrite whose conduct does not tally with his profession. But Cowper's pen had not slipped. It *was* a rationalised tenet of Calvinism that works, while they should accord with faith, are of themselves fruitless.

We may sometimes rejoice, however, that man is not wholly a rationalising animal. Even the Calvinist could not always maintain his own logic. Indeed, though Calvinism in the vaguer sense was still a potent force in Cowper's time, its full rigour no longer survived except in theory, and not always in that. Of *pure* Calvinism there is little in the moral satires and *The Task*. There are scattered references to predetermination:

> " *All has its date below; the fatal hour*
> *Was registered in heaven ere time began.*" [2]

But such passages are not frequent; and even the relative Calvinism undergoes further modifications, according to the poet's mood, until it becomes something to which, allowing for differences in mere phraseology, any modern Christian could subscribe. Even though he took his theology more seriously than did many Calvinists, over whom it held merely traditional sway, his mind was not always in the ascendant. His sympathies were wider than his opinions, and though it was from his "reason" and from the desire to be "useful" to the cause of Calvinism that there sprang the original impulse, the sustained writing of verse itself aided the liberation of his heart.

[1] *Truth*, 1-20.   [2] *The Task*, Book V, 529-530.

The process is apparent even in *Truth*. This poem, one of the most definitely didactic, opens with the long Calvinistic passage which I have quoted. Then, still pondering upon the futility of "works" as a means to salvation, the writer asks:

> "*Who judg'd the Pharisee? What odious cause*
> *Expos'd him to the vengeance of the laws?*
> *Had he seduc'd a virgin, wrong'd a friend,*
> *Or stabb'd a man to serve some private end?*
> *Was blasphemy his sin? Or did he stray*
> *From the strict duties of the sacred day?*
> *Sit long and late at the carousing board?*
> *(Such were the sins with which he charg'd his Lord.)*
> *No—the man's morals were exact. What then?*"

One might expect the answer to be that the delinquent did not "believe" in the Calvinistic sense. The reply, however, is something quite different:

> "*'Twas his ambition to be seen of men;*
> *His virtues were his pride, and that one vice*
> *Made all his virtues gewgaws of no price;*
> *He wore them, as fine trappings, for a show;*
> *A praying, synagogue-frequenting, beau.*"

Immediately, it will be seen, we are in another world: a world no longer of theological, but of ethical, values. Cowper, the Calvinist, begins by presenting the Pharisee as an example of one who thought to be justified by works rather than by faith. Then suddenly the poet's heart takes control of his pen, and the Pharisee is condemned, not because he lacks "faith," but because his *works* are mere formalities. The original intention was to show the indispensability of "belief": the effect is to prove, or at least very clearly to insinuate, the importance of *true* works: of works, that is to say, inspired by the only vitalising impulse of love.

Cowper, in a word, has passed, by a transition from one side of his nature to another, from the Calvinistic conception of "Justification by Faith" to the Arminian. Bygone theological terms may irk modern ears; but a permanent spiritual principle underlay "Justification by Faith" as interpreted by Wesley and his followers. Wesley repeatedly said that this all-important doctrine must be guarded from abuse. He utterly rejected the idea, held by many Calvinists, that faith was itself sufficient for at-one-ment with God. Equally, however, morality by itself was not enough. Only the divine spirit of love, apprehended through the eye of faith, could make "works" vital. On the other hand, where that spirit existed the fruits would necessarily be seen.

Cowper, while theoretically denying the Arminian position, constantly shifted to it when his heart won the victory over his head.[1] His longer poems abound in lines like these:

> "Man's obligations infinite, of course
> His life should prove that he perceives their force:
> His utmost he can render is but small—
> The principle and motive all in all." [2]

Or again:

> "No works shall find acceptance, in that day
> When all disguises shall be rent away,
> That square not truly with the scripture plan,
> Nor spring from love to God, or love to man." [3]

These utterances are far indeed removed from Calvinism in any strict sense. It is true, again, that "works" without the quickening spirit are dead: but that is universal Christian truth:

> "One act, that from a thankful heart proceeds,
> Excels ten thousand mercenary deeds." [4]

And though, after a passage in which he most scornfully attacks those who would substitute morality for religion,[5] Cowper reasserts the dogma that only "Grace" can make "the slave a free man," his view of the effects of Grace

> —"humanising what is brute
> In the lost kind, extracting from the lips
> Of asps their venom, overpow'ring strength
> By weakness, and hostility by love" [6]—

contradicts the Calvinistic letter with the spirit of the Sermon on the Mount. And on many occasions when he speaks of

---

[1] In *Conversation* (605-624) he even draws a portrait of Wesley—the arch-foe of Calvinism—in words as eulogistic as they are truthful.
[2] *Truth*, 197-200.   [3] *Charity*, 557-560.   [4] *Truth*, 223-224.
[5] *The Task*, Book V, 635-687.   [6] *Ibid.*, 700-703.

Divine wrath towards individuals or nations he is merely declaring, in the semi-Calvinistic idiom which had become habitual to him, that certain errors or follies unavoidably involve certain penalties; and his ethical values, while coloured by the Evangelical fear of "pleasure," as well as by a few rather sweeping generalisations of his own, are, very often, indisputably sound.

What Cowper sometimes called the vengeance of God we should call the law of cause and effect; or, with Paul, we might say that "Whatsoever a man soweth, that also shall he reap." But beneath the poet's grim terminology there is often inspired common sense, the burden of it all being:

"Peace follows virtue as its sure reward." [1]

It is a truth which we might do well to remember to-day. Indeed, while Cowper could at times sound a conventionally patriotic and even martial note,[2] he is nowhere more sanely "Christian," as a rule, than when discussing the folly and the causes of war. He was, in this respect, far ahead of his time. His analysis of the stupefying and dehumanising effect of military training is the more persuasive for being humorously framed;[3] and his account of the origin, growth, and survival of warfare loses nothing of essential veracity because it was written by one who soberly accepted the Old Testament as history.[4]

Further examples could be furnished to show that, even when he was in a formally religious mood, Cowper often belied his own creed. One might cite his declaration that "mercy" is free to all who will receive it: an absolute denial, this, of predestination.[5] One might point to his indignant rejection of the idea that the uninstructed heathen will perish:[6]

"Charge not a God with such outrageous wrong!"

Even the non-heathen will not be penalised if their motives

---

[1] *The Progress of Error*, 42.   [2] *The Task*, Book II, 255-284.
[3] *Ibid.*, Book IV, 613-658.   [4] *Ibid.*, Book V, 187-304.
[5] *Truth*, 345-350.   [6] *Ibid.*, 515-538.

and aspirations are pure. After the beautiful description of the walk to Emmaus,[1] he says of the two disciples:

> "*Their views indeed were indistinct and dim,*
> *But yet successful, being aimed at Him.*"

And his portraits of different types of clergymen reveal, again, the conviction that belief and conduct are alike vain unless inspired by love.

I have not chiefly in mind his famous, but more superficial, indictment:

> "*Oh, laugh or mourn with me the rueful jest,*
> *A cassock'd huntsman and a fiddling priest!*" [2]

I am thinking more especially of the long passage in the second book of *The Task*,[3] in which the false minister is contrasted with the true, and in which the writer, declaring that he seeks

> "*divine simplicity in him*
> *Who handles things divine,*"

expresses his detestation of hypocrisy:

> "*In my soul I loathe*
> *All affection. 'Tis my perfect scorn;*
> *Object of my implacable disgust.*"

In nothing was Cowper more sincere than in this loathing; and, while he hints, of course, that the ideal pastor's "doctrine" should be sound, he undermines the strict Calvinistic position by his insistence that the doctrine is best judged by the life:

> "*To such I render more than mere respect,*
> *Whose actions say that they respect themselves.*"

Finally, if his own mind could acknowledge a grim enough Deity, his heart prompted the charge that

> "*When Cromwell fought for pow'r, and while he reigned*
> *The proud protector of the pow'r he gained,*
> *Religion, harsh, intolerant, austere,*
> *Parent of manners like herself severe,*
> *Drew a rough copy of the Christian face*
> *Without the smile, the sweetness, or the grace.*" [4]

---

[1] *Conversation*, 505-536.　　[2] *The Progress of Error*, 110-111.
[3] Lines, 326-498.　　[4] *Table Talk*, 610-615.

III

But Cowper's preaching is not always religious in tone. Much of it, as this next example will show, strikes the note of common debate, though the underlying impulse is still Evangelical:

> *" Mountains interpos'd*
> *Make enemies of nations, who had else,*
> *Like kindred drops, been mingled into one.*
> *Thus man devotes his brother, and destroys;*
> *And, worse than all, and most to be deplor'd,*
> *As human nature's broadest, foulest blot,*
> *Chains him, and tasks him, and exacts his sweat*
> *With stripes, that mercy, with a bleeding heart,*
> *Weeps when she sees inflicted on a beast.*
> *Then what is man? And what man, seeing this,*
> *And having human feelings, does not blush,*
> *And hang his head, to think himself a man?*
> *I would not have a slave to till my ground,*
> *To carry me, to fan me while I sleep,*
> *And tremble when I wake, for all the wealth*
> *That sinews bought and sold have ever earn'd.*
> *No: dear as freedom is, and in my heart's*
> *Just estimation priz'd above all price,*
> *I had much rather be myself the slave,*
> *And wear the bonds, than fasten them on him."* [1]

There follow the lines often quoted by Cobden: lines which perhaps derived their inspiration from the poet's Whiggism as well as from his religion:

> *" Sure there is need of social intercourse,*
> *Benevolence, and peace, and mutual aid,*
> *Between the nations, in a world that seems*
> *To toll the death-bell of its own decease,*
> *And by the voice of all its elements*
> *To preach the gen'ral doom."* [2]

Cowper's work abounds with such passages, in which he

---

[1] *The Task*, Book II, 17-36.   [2] *Ibid.*, 48-53.

surveys social customs, morals, and manners at large.   Consider, for example, his weighing of the relative rights of men and animals,[1] with its almost legalistic conclusion:

> " *The sum is this.—If man's convenience, health,*
> *Or safety, interfere, his rights and claims*
> *Are paramount, and must extinguish theirs.*
> *Else they are all—the meanest things that are—*
> *As free to live, and to enjoy that life,*
> *As God was free to form them at the first,*
> *Who, in his sov'reign wisdom, made them all.*"

This is the comment of a writer who, while looking at life from his own very different angle, was no less essentially a critic than Pope himself.   Incidentally, in the course of his reflections on the progress of poetry,[2] which characteristically leap from Homer to the Garden of Eden and thence to the Restoration drama, Cowper writes of Pope in a manner which shows, as do his letters, that he was, within his prescribed range, sound and fair in his literary judgments:

> " *Then Pope, as harmony itself exact,*
> *In verse well disciplin'd, complete, compact,*
> *Gave virtue and morality a grace,*
> *That, quite eclipsing pleasure's painted face,*
> *Levied a tax of wonder and applause,*
> *Ev'n on the fools that trampled on their laws.*
> *But he (his musical finesse was such,*
> *So nice his ear, so delicate his touch)*
> *Made poetry a mere mechanic art;*
> *And ev'ry warbler has his tune by heart.*" [3]

It must be confessed that Cowper's argumentative verse is often prosaic, though it has lines of memorable beauty and vision, as well as many proverbs which have passed into common currency—such as

> " *An idler is a watch that wants both hands,*
> *As useless if it goes as when it stands,*" [4]

---

[1] *The Task*, Book VI, 560-587.   [2] *Table Talk*, 556-771.
[3] *Ibid.*, 646-655.   [4] *Retirement*, 681-682.

or the even more famous one which Bulwer Lytton quoted in his play *Money*:

"*How much a dunce that has been sent to roam*
Excels a dunce that has been kept at home." [1]

There is a charmingly playful note in couplets like this:

"*For 'tis a rule, that holds for ever true,*
Grant me discernment, and I grant it you." [2]

It was, again, a whimsical observer of human nature who penned the description of the townsman in the country, which was being spoiled (even then!) by "suburban villas, highway-side retreats," [3] and who satirised "the reeking, roaring hero of the chase," [4] or the different kinds of bores who

"*employ their health, an ugly trick,*
In making known how oft they have been sick" ; [5]

or the malcontents whose misery is their only joy:

"*Some fretful tempers wince at ev'ry touch,*
You always do too little or too much:
You speak with life, in hopes to entertain,
Your elevated voice goes through the brain;
You fall at once into a lower key,
That's worse—the drone-pipe of an humble bee.
The southern sash admits too strong a light,
You rise and drop the curtain—now it's night.
He shakes with cold—you stir the fire and strive
To make a blaze—that's roasting him alive.
Serve him with ven'son, and he chooses fish;
With soal—that's just the sort he would not wish.
He takes what he at first profess'd to loath,
And in due time feeds heartily on both;
Yet still, o'erclouded with a constant frown,
He does not swallow, but he gulps it down.
Your hope to please him, vain on ev'ry plan,
Himself should work that wonder, if he can—
Alas! his efforts double his distress,
He likes yours little, and his own still less.
Thus always teasing others, always teas'd,
His only pleasure is—to be displeased." [6]

[1] *The Progress of Error*, 415-416. [2] *Ibid.*, 534-535.
[3] *Retirement*, 406-514. [4] *Conversation*, 405-426.
[5] *Ibid.*, 311-312. [6] *Ibid.*, 325-346.

S

As might be expected of one who combined a keen critical faculty with a warm interest in individuals, Cowper gives us many portraits. Not only did he sketch his own intimates and the leaders of his faith. Public characters in every walk of life unconsciously "sat" to him. Chatham is the modern Demosthenes; [1] Chesterfield—

> "*Thou polished and high-finished foe to truth,*
> *Grey-beard corrupter of our listening youth*"—

is the Petronius; [2] while Handel, despite the obvious Calvinistic bias of his limner, appears as "the more than Homer of his age." [3]

IV

The great creative geniuses may be free, "out-topping knowledge." Others abide our question; and it is no rare thing for posterity to reverse an author's own values. Had I been attempting a literary appreciation of Cowper, I should not have lingered so long over the preacher and the detached critic of his age. Since my chief aim, however, is to understand the man in relation to his century, it has been necessary to disturb a certain amount of dust. I have shown that his Calvinism is explicable enough in the light of his day and of his keen logical faculty, but that even he could not long maintain its doctrines at full strength. Charity and true spiritual vision break in upon his dourest sermonising, as humour and epigrammatic wisdom enliven his prosiest homilies on contemporary topics and manners. But patience is needed to disentangle what is timeless from what is outworn, and the average reader may well shirk the effort. "The faithful monitor's and poet's part" cannot, in any case, be successfully combined. It is natural, therefore, that Cowper's verse should survive mainly in anthologies by virtue of the sauce with which he garnished his message.

But while we may no longer read his duller passages, we should gratefully remember that it is to them we owe the brighter ones. His occasional imaginative fire was struck, as a rule, on the tinder of theology or reflection. But for his

---

[1] *Table Talk*, 340-353.   [2] *The Progress of Error*, 335-352.
[3] *The Task*, Book VI, 632-657.

wish to be "useful" in propagating Calvinism, Cowper would have remained a merely "occasional" poet. Not only, however, was his heart more genial than his creed. As he warmed to his task, his genuine if slight creative faculty was kindled. He had, too, the refined taste of a gentleman and a scholar, and fortunately did not scruple to use his rich fund of humour as a coating for his pill.

He would have been alarmed at the thought that his sugar would continue to be relished, while his physic would be neglected. But just as he is not the only writer whose estimate of his own work has been revised by Time, so—to look at the matter from another angle—he is not the only writer who, after all, wrought even his own purpose better than he knew. Pioneers may not appreciate the full ramifications of their own gospel. They are, at any rate, more intent upon pressing home the gospel itself than upon constructively setting forth what may seem to them but the indirect and secondary results of its application. It is less understandable that modern critics should fail to be wise after the event, and should see in Cowper's true *poetry* a revolt against Evangelicalism! It is beyond dispute that Methodism quickened the social conscience and fostered the ethical sense. To suggest that Cowper's religion, as reflected in the homiletic portions of *The Task*, had ceased to be Evangelical and had become ethical is equivalent to saying that an apple tree is no longer an apple tree when its blossom is shed and the fruit appears. Nor did Evangelicalism prompt only a new sense of duty. Even if it frowned on certain pleasures, it promoted a truer, because an inward, conception of happiness. It made a frontal attack upon vice and luxury; but it also attacked them indirectly, and with greater success, by inspiring a deeper satisfaction in the simplest joys. Cowper's poetry becomes most vital when these values are allowed to speak implicitly: but the values themselves are there. They find didactic expression in the poet's heavier style: they *permeate* his better one.

When he wrote one of his most famous passages, he may have been consciously thinking only of providing another bait for his less serious readers; or Pegasus may have run away with him, as it sometimes did. It was nevertheless a good

Evangelical who sang the homely delights of "The Winter Evening," heralded by the arrival of the post-boy:

> "Hark! 'tis the twanging horn o'er yonder bridge,
> That with its wearisome but needful length
> Bestrides the wintry flood, in which the moon
> Sees her unwrinkled face reflected bright;—
> He comes, the herald of a noisy world,
> With spatter'd boots, strapp'd waist, and frozen locks;
> News from all nations lumb'ring at his back.
> True to his charge, the close-pack'd load behind,
> Yet careless what he brings, his one concern
> Is to conduct it to the destin'd inn:
> And, having dropp'd th' expected bag, pass on.
> He whistles as he goes, light-hearted wretch,
> Cold and yet cheerful: messenger of grief
> Perhaps to thousands, and of joy to some;
> To him indiff'rent whether grief or joy.
> Houses in ashes, and the fall of stocks,
> Births, deaths, and marriages, epistles wet
> With tears, that trickled down the writer's cheeks
> Fast as the periods from his fluent quill,
> Or charg'd with am'rous sighs of absent swains,
> Or nymphs responsive, equally affect
> His horse and him, unconscious of them all.
> But oh th' important budget! usher'd in
> With such heart-shaking music, who can say
> What are its tidings? . . .
>
> Now stir the fire, and close the shutters fast,
> Let fall the curtains, wheel the sofa round,
> And, while the bubbling and loud-hissing urn
> Throws up a steamy column, and the cups,
> That cheer but not inebriate, wait on each,
> So let us welcome peaceful ev'ning in." [1]

At this point the poet cannot help contrasting *his* evening with that of the unhappy and dissolute city-dwellers: the theatre crowd out-scolding "the ranting actor on the stage"; the political orators, "bursting with heroic rage," or the placemen, "all tranquillity and smiles." There follows a characteristic tirade against mundane ambitions and vanities. Still:

> "'Tis pleasant through the loop-holes of retreat
> To peep at such a world; to see the stir

[1] *The Task*, Book IV, 1-25, 36-41.

Of the great Babel, and not feel the crowd;
To hear the roar she sends through all her gates
At a safe distance, where the dying sound
Falls a soft murmur on th' uninjur'd ear.
Thus sitting, and surveying thus at ease
The globe and its concerns, I seem advanc'd
To some secure and more than mortal height,
That lib'rates and exempts me from them all.
It turns submitted to my view, turns round
With all its generations; I behold
The tumult, and am still.   The sound of war
Has lost its terrors ere it reaches me;
Grieves, but alarms me not.   I mourn the pride
And avarice that make man a wolf to man;
Hear the faint echo of those brazen throats
By which he speaks the language of his heart,
And sigh, but never tremble at the sound. . . .

Oh Winter, ruler of th' inverted year,
Thy scatter'd hair with sleet like ashes fill'd,
Thy breath congeal'd upon thy lips, thy cheeks
Fring'd with a beard made white with other snows
Than those of age, thy forehead wrapt in clouds,
A leafless branch thy sceptre, and thy throne
A sliding car, indebted to no wheels,
But urg'd by storms along its slipp'ry way,
I love thee, all unlovely as thou seem'st,
And dreaded as thou art!   Thou hold'st the sun
A pris'ner in the yet undawning east,
Short'ning his journey between morn and noon,
And hurrying him, impatient of his stay,
Down to the rosy west; but kindly still
Compensating his loss with added hours
Of social converse and instructive ease,
And gath'ring, at short notice, in one group
The family dispers'd, and fixing thought,
Not less dispers'd by day-light and its cares.
I crown thee king of intimate delights,
Fire-side enjoyments, home-born happiness,
And all the comforts that the lowly roof
Of undisturb'd retirement, and the hours
Of long, uninterrupted ev'ning, know." [1]

This was a new note in English poetry, and one in which its

---

[1] *The Task,* Book IV, 88-106, 120-143.

originator has never been excelled. The joys it celebrated may not, as Goldwin Smith says, be heroic: "but they are pure joys, and they present themselves in competition with those of Ranelagh and the Basset Table, which are not heroic or even masculine, any more than they are pure."

Certain difficulties must, of course, be met. Recent critics have read into the whole passage—not merely into the phrase "loopholes of retreat"—an escapist's philosophy. There is, we have again been told, something in the poet's attitude of the Pharisee's thankfulness to God that he is not as other men, and a touch of hypocrisy in his denunciation of London while he enjoys reading about its activities in a newspaper printed there. That Cowper was an escapist, in the physical sense, may be true: his supersensitive nervous constitution demanded solitude. For the rest, however, he cannot be understood apart from Evangelicalism itself. A certain isolation and even a certain self-righteousness were, it may be, almost necessary to the Evangelicals in their reaction against the immorality and extravagances of their day. At least an appearance of self-righteousness was unavoidable in those who were impelled—in the circumstances with very good reason —to make a definite stand against worldliness. In the best of the Evangelicals the self-righteousness *was*, I think, apparent rather than real. But, even if genuine, it rested on a sounder basis than that of the Pharisee. Evangelicalism was not formal; nor, except very superficially, was it escapist. Its seeming other-worldliness served this world better than did any political panaceas. There is the truest practical wisdom in Cowper's claim, often reiterated,[1] that if all men were content with simple possessions and homely joys, because their treasures were laid up in the heart and mind, there would be fewer muddles for the statesman to unravel, or make worse, and fewer quarrels for the soldier to settle—or aggravate.

As for the charge of hypocrisy: let us confess that absolute consistency of thought and conduct is hardly attainable by finite beings; and, acknowledging that, let us recall the parable of the beam and the mote. But let us also use our common sense and realise that even Cowper, the most direct

[1] See, for example, *Charity*, 604-627.

of writers, can sometimes speak symbolically. It is true that
a large measure of solid conviction underlies his assertion that
"God made the country, and man made the town." But he
is not actually so foolish as to imagine that the town is either
dispensable or completely abandoned to evil. He admits that

> "*true worth and virtue in the mild*
> *And genial soil of cultivated life*
> *Thrive most, and may perhaps thrive only there.*" [1]

But he also sees that

> "*thither flow,*
> *As to a common and most noisome sew'r,*
> *The dregs and feculence of ev'ry land.*" [2]

Here, again, the *pros* and *cons* of city life are weighed:

> "*Man in society is like a flow'r*
> *Blown in its native bed: tis there alone*
> *His faculties, expanded in full bloom,*
> *Shine out; there only reach their proper use.*
> *But man, associated and leagu'd with man*
> *By regal warrant, or self-join'd by bond*
> *For int'rest-sake, or swarming into clans*
> *Beneath one head for purposes of war,*
> *Like flow'rs selected from the rest, and bound*
> *And bundled close to fill some crowded vase,*
> *Fades rapidly, and, by compression marr'd,*
> *Contracts defilement not to be endur'd.*
> *Hence charter'd boroughs are such public plagues,*
> *And burghers, men immaculate perhaps*
> *In all their private functions, once combin'd,*
> *Become a loathsome body, only fit*
> *For dissolution, hurtful to the main.*
> *Hence merchants, unimpeachable of sin*
> *Against the charities of domestic life,*
> *Incorporated, seem at once to lose*
> *Their nature; and, disclaiming all regard*
> *For mercy and the common rights of man,*
> *Build factories with blood, conducting trade*
> *At the sword's point, and dyeing the white robe*
> *Of innocent commercial justice red.*

[1] *The Task*, Book I, 678-680.   [2] *Ibid.*, 682-684.

Hence, too, the field of glory, as the world
Misdeems it, dazzled by its bright array,
With all its majesty of thund'ring pomp,
Enchanting music, and immortal wreaths,
Is but a school where thoughtlessness is taught
On principle, where foppery atones
For folly, gallantry for ev'ry vice." [1]

Parts of the indictment had special justification when they were written. There are other lines which might seem to be prophetic rather of to-day, when limited liability companies, while mainly made up of decent individuals, have no souls to be damned, and when excessive urbanisation has stimulated the herd instinct to an unhealthy degree. There is a large measure of sound sense in Cowper's picture. It is, admittedly, a caricature. But it is good caricature, and, accepted as such, it provides a mirror through which we may see an important aspect of the poet and his age. "God made the country, and man made the town" is indefensible as a serious generalisation. But even Cowper did not fully intend it as such. He was consciously over-emphasising his point. Nature was just being "discovered," and served, therefore, to show up more vividly the artificiality of the towns, where sophistication was, at the moment, ripe unto rottenness. There was manifestly a need for a return to simpler and more spontaneous standards of life. Evangelicalism preached that need, and Nature provided for Cowper an illustration of the text.

Yet intensification of feeling in one direction often has unforeseen effects in another. Cowper, basking in the sunlight of a new vision of Nature, was moved to contrast with it the gloom and corruption of cities. He saw some things out of proportion: but he was among the first to see certain things at all. He might exaggerate the evils of urban life: he was at least concerned with them. It is strange that among Cowper's many critics, Stopford Brooke [2] alone seems fully to appreciate this truth or its significance. "Unlike the town poet of the past to whom the dwellers in the country are nothing," says Brooke, "we have now the country poet deeply interested in the life of towns as well as in the life around him. It is no

---

[1] *The Task*, Book IV, 659-690.   [2] *Theology in the English Poets*. 1874.

longer classes of men which awake sympathy, nor special societies; it is no longer the passionate or the moral or the intellectual side of human nature, each alone, on which the poet dwells—it is the whole of mankind, it is the whole of human nature." We are reminded that Cowper, "not with savage bitterness, but with a gentleness which healed while it lashed," touched upon almost every phase of English society: "on the universities and the schools, the hospitals and the prisons; on cities and villages, on the statesman, the clergy-man, the lawyer, the soldier, the man of science, the critic, the writer for the Press, the pleasure-seeker, the hunter, the musician, the epicure, the card-player, the ploughman, the cottager, and fifty others." His interest in humanity, con-fined to no single type or class, outflowed into an interest in the nation, and from that into all nations as potential partners in a universal commonwealth.

Thence sprang his faith in liberty, which made him write prophetically of the Bastille:

> *" Ye horrid tow'rs, th' abode of broken hearts;*
> *Ye dungeons and ye cages of despair,*
> *That monarchs have supplied from age to age*
> *With music such as suits their sov'reign ears—*
> *The sighs and groans of miserable men!*
> *There's not an English heart that would not leap*
> *To hear that ye were fall'n at last; to know*
> *That ev'n our enemies, so oft employ'd*
> *In forging chains for us, themselves were free.*
> *For he who values liberty confines*
> *His zeal for her predominance within*
> *No narrow bounds; her cause engages him*
> *Wherever pleaded. 'Tis the cause of man."* [1]

There is nothing of the Calvinist here, or in the passage im-mediately following, in which the crime of tyranny and the tortures of imprisonment are further moralised. Then break in the well-known lines:

> *" 'Tis liberty alone that gives the flow'r*
> *Of fleeting life its lustre and perfume;*
> *And we are weeds without it. All constraint,*
> *Except what wisdom lays on evil men,*

[1] *The Task*, Book V, 384–396.

> *Is evil; hurts the faculties, impedes*
> *Their progress in the road of science; blinds*
> *The eyesight of discov'ry; and begets,*
> *In those that suffer it, a sordid mind*
> *Bestial, a meagre intellect, unfit*
> *To be the tenant of man's noble form."* [1]

Cowper's *heart* is speaking here, as well as in his subsequent expressions of patriotic pride that England, blameworthy enough in other ways, is still the home of freedom.

But what if England should ever lose the blessing "for which our Hampdens and our Sidneys bled?" The thought suddenly strikes a chill into the poet's *mind*: and his Calvinism reawakens. The future will be what it must: "all has its date below." We cannot alter God's preordained plans: the very wish were blasphemy! But, after all, there is yet

> *"a liberty unsung*
> *By poets, and by senators unprais'd,*
> *Which monarchs cannot grant, nor all the pow'rs*
> *Of earth and hell confed'rate take away."* [2]

This inward liberty is that of the redeemed in the Calvinistic sense. But again Cowper's heart takes fire, and again he moves through gradations of conflicting thought and feeling, until finally, when he declares that

> *"He is the freeman whom the truth makes free,*
> *And all are slaves beside,"* [3]

his feeling has won another victory. If those lines be examined in their context, it will be found that Cowper's values have once more become universal values, and that he touches the inward source not only of individual happiness but even of external freedom itself. He saw one ideal and remedy for all men: the Cross of Christ. "Whatever one may think of his religion, or the manner of it," Stopford Brooke concludes, "there is no doubt that it indefinitely extended his poetic sympathy, and that in this extension we find ourselves in another world altogether from that of Dryden, Pope, or Gray."

Cowper's thoughts—or rather his feelings—were his own: they were those of a recluse, who read little. Yet, in another

---

[1] *The Task*, Book V, 446-455.   [2] *Ibid.*, 538-541.
[3] *Ibid.*, 732-733.

sense, they were not original. The poet, though little aware
of the fact, was a sensitive instrument, touched by a wind that
had begun to sweep across Europe. The placid surface of the
"eighteenth century" was being ruffled, and was soon to be
violently shaken, by a ferment of new ideas. Revolt against
immediate political tyranny, as in France, or against spiritual
apathy and intellectual formalism, as in England, may have
hastened the process. The time, in any case, was ripe for a
new working of the human spirit. The movement, taking
various forms, was fundamentally one. It rose from im-
patience with constraints which had hitherto been unconsciously accepted. It was an urge to liberty: a quest, both
outward and inward, after ampler experience. It inspired
Rousseau to his vision of the noble savage and to his plea for a
social contract based on men's equal rights as children of
Nature, their universal mother. It prompted John Wesley to
a more intimate search after God; and the effect, though not
the aim, of the Methodist Revival was also to foster the
conception of human brotherhood, since men now appeared
as children of a common Father.

Cowper's delight in Nature, which admits of comparison
with Rousseau's, owed nothing, in its origin, to Evangelicalism. Cowper tells us repeatedly, both in his poems and his
letters, that he could not recall the time when he did not love
rural sights and sounds, or when the English landscape did
not colour his dreams of paradise. But to see in his affection
for Nature the one true element in him, which necessarily
became warped by Evangelicalism, is to see things wholly
awry. The new feeling for Nature which was creeping into
men's hearts, and the thirst after closer communion with
God, were twin impulses of Revolutionary stock. They
seemed independent at the time: even antagonistic. Rousseau, preoccupied with Nature, drew his line in one direction:
Wesley, concentrating upon God, drew his in another.
Actually, however, the diverging lines were arcs of a circle,
itself incomplete and therefore as yet unrecognisable as such:
a wider circle of human vision, bringing with it a new conception of the universe and of man's place in it. The arcs
were to diverge further before they began to meet. But to

meet they were surely destined. A truer love of Nature is bound, in the long run, to produce deeper thoughts of a Creator; while vital religion, in its turn, by quickening spiritual sensibility, cannot fail to give men keener eyes for the beauty of Creation.

Now in Cowper, though his controlling spirit was simple and childlike, the elements, as we have seen, were mixed. His love of Nature by itself might have made him a disciple of Rousseau; his religious devotion and warmth of heart might of themselves have made him a full and avowed follower of Wesley. His feelings were drawn both ways. But the dualism was merely superficial. There were only theoretical difficulties in reconciling two impulses which really had the same origin. Those theoretical difficulties were, at the time, inevitable; but Cowper, when his heart escaped from the Genevan cage in which his mind sought to hold him, was before his day in sensing that the theory itself must be at fault. He saw the line of Rousseau tending in one direction, and that of Evangelicalism in another. He could equally understand them both, and, though he could not actually see that they were arcs of what would one day become a circle, he intuitively knew that they ought somehow to be connected. He did connect them. He drew a straight line between the diverging arcs, and made a segment: a segment of truth: of the truth of the Creative Spirit's immanence in Nature.

This, to change the metaphor, was a step forward from the view which had hitherto prevailed. Despite unamiable qualities, Pope—"that crooked, perverse, little wretch at Twickenham," as Sarah Marlborough called him—had been genuinely devout. But, holding that the proper study of mankind was man, he saw Nature as a mere environment for man: an environment created indeed by God, but by a God who, having set the world going, like a super-mechanic, was Himself withdrawn. Such a Deity commanded worship, but, as Addison's hymn reveals, it was merely the worship of awe:

> " *The spacious firmament on high,*
> *With all the blue ethereal sky,*
> *And spangled heavens, a shining frame,*
> *Their great Original proclaim.*

> *The unwearied sun, from day to day,*
> *Does his Creator's power display;*
> *And publishes to every land*
> *The work of an almighty hand."*

Cowper saw the natural world

> *"assuming a more lovely face,*
> *Borrowing a beauty from the works of grace"*; [1]

and he protested that

> *"Who studies nature with a wanton eye*
> *Admires the work, but slips the lesson by."* [2]

The time was at hand, but had not yet come, when Nature, being detached alike from man and God, could be studied for its own sake. A truer insight was then to breed a new affection, which, though it had no formally religious impulse, engendered none the less a spirit of worship. Shelley, because he revolted against official Christianity, thought himself an atheist. He recognised an all-pervading Spirit in the World, but chose to call it, impersonally, Love or Life. Wordsworth spoke of a Presence which disturbed him "with the joy of elevated thoughts." But Romanticism, while it seemed to the orthodox religion of its time to be a disintegrating and paganising influence, had the ultimate effect of extending theology itself. Science, which haunted Victorian deaneries like a grim spectre, was, in its own way, to carry the process still further. "Christianity," as Mr. Alfred Noyes once said, "accepts, accepts, accepts." It cannot dispense with dogma, and it needs its conservers of the truths hitherto smithied upon the anvil of revelation by the hammer of experience. Equally it demands its pioneering spirits who will attempt new methods: the great creative geniuses who win fresh life for religion because they are not afraid to lose the old.

If the love of Nature had been the one true impulse in Cowper, and if he had been fundamentally creative, he would indeed have been guilty of "compromise" in not having followed the light of Nature wherever it had led him. But his love of Nature, deep and genuine though it was, reveals

---

[1] *Retirement*, 357-358.   [2] *Ibid.*, 213-214.

itself as merely one of several qualities equally characteristic and sincere. His was the many-sided temperament of the critic and commentator, not born to forge out a new approach to truth along some line of its own, but to survey life as a whole and, by the range rather than the depth of his vision, to provide his own generation with the best synthesis attainable at the moment. He belonged, intellectually, to the order of custodians of religious truth, for the religious impulse was, after all, the strongest element in him. Much as he loved Nature, he was more concerned to show that loving it was not incompatible with love of God, as revealed in Scripture, than he was to prove that loving Nature intensely for its own sake might ultimately lead to a finer conception of God. He saw the new-born love of Nature drifting away from the love of God, as he understood it; and, having a heart broad enough to embrace them both, he claimed the lesser love as an ally of the greater:

> " *The soul that sees Him, or receives sublim'd*
> *New faculties, or learns at least t' employ*
> *More worthily the pow'rs she own'd before;*
> *Discerns in all things, what, with stupid gaze*
> *Of ignorance, till then she overlook'd—*
> *A ray of heav'nly light, gilding all forms*
> *Terrestrial in the vast and the minute;*
> *The unambiguous footsteps of the God*
> *Who gives its lustre to an insect's wing,*
> *And wheels his throne upon the rolling worlds.*" [1]

Yet no man who serves his own generation really well, because he possesses the essence of eternal truth and is utterly sincere, can fail at least to point to the future. Cowper, though he was cautious by nature and though his purpose was to be a guardian of revealed religion, became sometimes a pioneer in spite of himself, and his voice was genuinely prophetic when—his heart enjoying a season of clearest shining—he no longer saw matter as " dead," but as

> "*impell'd*
> *To ceaseless service by a ceaseless force,*
> *And under pressure of some conscious cause.*

[1] *The Task*, Book V, 805-814.

The Lord of all, himself through all diffus'd,
Sustains, and is the life of all that lives.
Nature is but a name for an effect
Whose cause is God. . . .

> *One spirit—His*
Who wore the platted thorns with bleeding brows—
Rules universal nature. Not a flow'r
But shows some touch, in freckle, streak, or stain,
Of his unrivall'd pencil. He inspires
Their balmy odours, and imparts their hues,
And bathes their eyes with nectar, and includes,
In grains as countless as the sea-side sands,
The forms with which he sprinkles all the earth." [1]

V

It requires an effort of imagination to carry us back to the
time when the immanence of the Creative Spirit in Nature
was a novel and revolutionary conception. Yet it *was* so novel
that only seldom did Cowper himself see the truth clearly or
express it in terms which have value—if only the value of
truism—for us. Most of his attempts to reconcile Nature with
God, and to define man's relationship to both, now seem not
so much inadequate as supererogatory. Why, we are inclined
to ask, all that waste of labour? that needless fuss? But again,
if we are to understand Cowper and to give him his due place
in history, we must remember that for one of his critical mind
and comprehensive sympathies the fuss was unavoidable.
The problems of the eighteenth century seem to be simple
indeed in the light of later knowledge and experience. But
they were as real and puzzling then as are our very different
problems to-day: and may we tackle our problems in the
spirit in which Cowper helped thousands of his own generation to approach theirs!

Would Cowper's influence have been even stronger and
wider if he had not been a Calvinist? Certainly it would. I
have said that he erred in not more fully trusting his heart.
Yet perhaps, after all, it is the accusation itself which is at
fault. No man can be essentially other than himself; and,
on fuller reflection, I doubt if, with his temperament and in

[1] *The Task*, Book VI, 218-224, 238-246.

his circumstances, Cowper did not actually do the best of which he was capable. On one side of his nature a Whig gentleman of refinement and "reason," he was on another side, and more fundamentally, a born religious enthusiast. It was almost inevitable, therefore, that his "enthusiasm" should direct and colour his logic, and that his logic and refinement together should make him a Calvinist. It was no less natural, fortunately, that his emotions, more genial than his creed, should constantly overflow the channel of his opinion, and that, when he took to writing, his refinement, being deep-seated and permeating his feelings no less than (through his mind) it impelled him towards the more select wing of the Revival, should serve to mellow propaganda into literature. If, with full allowance for his period, it is still necessary to point to duality in him, the conflict was not between, say, his love of Nature and his Evangelicalism, but between the two aspects of Evangelicalism itself. His Calvinism, governing his intellect, kept him more narrowly within the limits of his century than might otherwise have been the case. Yet he belonged, on balance, to the Arminian side of the Revival, because his heart was even warmer than his head was hard. Nor, in assessing his contemporary importance, must we forget that even his Calvinism had its useful side. He caught the ears of the Calvinists, but sang them new tunes. It might be said that he was made a Calvinist to the Calvinists that he might make some of them Arminians.

He was essentially a bridge-builder. Many of his bridges were, in the nature of things, temporary. They were nevertheless serviceable in their day. Not only did Cowper help to revive both poetry and personal religion: he brought them, then sundered, into some sort of agreement which marked the course for a fuller unity in the future. His teaching had the effect of carrying the spirit of poetry into thousands of middle-class and poor homes which it had not previously entered. On the other hand, his poetry spread the doctrines and (what was to better purpose) the fuller implications of Evangelicalism among the sophisticated who could perhaps have been reached in no other way. His influence was widespread and, in the main, liberalising. All the new spiritual and ethical values implicit in Evangelicalism—the hatred of slavery, oppression, and cruelty, the love of Nature and of simple domestic joys, the deeper regard for women, children, the poor, and animals—found in him their first clear voice.

It is possible, paradoxically, that his historical significance would be better appreciated if, in the course of his writings, mainly directed to conserving and rekindling religion in his own time, he had not chanced to strike off certain passages of poetry which outflowed all contemporary bounds and have won immortality in their own right. Lines like the following were amazingly new when they were written: and they will be fresh so long as boys are boys and there remain a few square miles of English countryside:

> "For I have lov'd the rural walk through lanes
> Of grassy swarth, close cropt by nibbling sheep,
> And skirted thick with intertexture firm
> Of thorny boughs; have lov'd the rural walk
> O'er hills, through valleys, and by rivers' brink,
> E'er since a truant boy I pass'd my bounds
> T' enjoy a ramble on the banks of Thames;
> And still remember, nor without regret
> Of hours that sorrow since has much endear'd,
> How oft, my slice of pocket store consum'd,
> Still hung'ring, pennyless, and far from home
> I fed on scarlet hips and stony haws,
> Or blushing crabs, or berries, that emboss
> The bramble, black as jet, or sloes austere." [1]

No innovation, of course, leaps entirely out of the void. Even a writer who does not read much is susceptible to influences which are in the air; and were I mainly concerned with Cowper's poetry as such, it would be necessary to trace, again, his descent from Thomson, Gray, Collins, and Goldsmith. The fact remains that he derived little from literary sources, and that it was in his verse that the conventional Arcadian trappings—the sham idyll—fully disappeared from the description of Nature.

There is, perhaps, something of Collins in the well-known passage beginning:

> "Come, Ev'ning, once again, season of peace;
> Return, sweet Ev'ning, and continue long!" [2]

[1] *The Task*, Book I, 109-122.   [2] *Ibid.*, Book IV, 243-266.

T

Even here, however, the pupil (if such he be) already excels his master in direct vision, while in the concluding lines the domestic note is all his own. And often, as in this picture of the snow-covered landscape, he passes beyond any suspicion of discipleship at all:

> " *The cattle mourn in corners where the fence*
> *Screens them, and seem half petrified to sleep*
> *In unrecumbent sadness. There they wait*
> *Their wonted fodder; not like hung'ring man,*
> *Fretful if unsupply'd; but silent, meek,*
> *And patient of the slow-pac'd swain's delay.*
> *He from the stack carves out th' accustom'd load,*
> *Deep-plunging, and again deep-plunging oft,*
> *His broad keen knife into the solid mass:*
> *Smooth as a wall the upright remnant stands,*
> *With such undeviating and even force*
> *He severs it away: no needless care,*
> *Lest storms should overset the leaning pile*
> *Deciduous, or its own unbalanc'd weight.*
> *Forth goes the woodman, leaving unconcern'd*
> *The cheerful haunts of man; to wield the axe*
> *And drive the wedge, in yonder forest drear,*
> *From morn to eve his solitary task.*
> *Shaggy, and lean, and shrewd, with pointed ears*
> *And tail cropp'd short, half lurcher and half cur—*
> *His dog attends him. Close behind his heel*
> *Now creeps he slow; and now, with many a frisk*
> *Wide-scamp'ring, snatches up the drifted snow*
> *With iv'ry teeth, or ploughs it with his snout;*
> *Then shakes his powder'd coat, and barks for joy. . . ."* [1]

And how spontaneously humour blends with realism!—

> " *Now from the roost, or from the neighb'ring pale,*
> *Where, diligent to catch the first faint gleam*
> *Of smiling day, they gossip'd side by side,*
> *Come trooping at the housewife's well-known call*
> *The feather'd tribes domestic. Half on wing,*
> *And half on foot, they brush the fleecy flood,*
> *Conscious, and fearful of too deep a plunge.*
> *The sparrows peep, and quit the shelt'ring eaves*
> *To seize the fair occasion. Well they eye*
> *The scatter'd grain; and, thievishly resolv'd*

---

[1] *The Task*, Book V, 27-51.

> *T' escape th' impending famine, often scar'd,*
> *As oft return—a pert voracious kind.*
> *Clean riddance quickly made, one only care*
> *Remains to each—the search of sunny nook,*
> *Or shed impervious to the blast.   Resign'd*
> *To sad necessity, the cock forgoes*
> *His wonted strut; and, wading at their head*
> *With well-consider'd steps, seems to resent*
> *His alter'd gait and stateliness retrench'd.*" [1]

Well might Cowper claim that his "descriptions are all from nature: not one of them second-handed." And well might he add that his "delineations of the heart" were from his own experience: not one of them borrowed from books, or in the least degree conjectural." He saw, because first of all he *loved*, the countryside watered by his slow-winding and sinuous Ouse.   That he both loved and saw is plain not only from the sheer fidelity with which the landscape itself is drawn, but from the naturalness with which the human figures—the farm-labourer, the woodman with his dog, the henwife, the waggoner, and the rest—take their place in the scene:

> "*The sheep-fold here*
> *Pours out its fleecy tenants o'er the glebe.*
> *At first, progressive as a stream, they seek*
> *The middle field; but, scatter'd by degrees,*
> *Each to his choice, soon whiten all the land.*
> *There from the sun-burnt hay-field, homeward creeps*
> *The loaded wain; while, lighten'd of its charge,*
> *The wain that meets it passes swiftly by;*
> *The boorish driver leaning o'er his team*
> *Vocif'rous, and impatient of delay.*" [2]

Such verse is its own evidence that truer sympathy with Nature had brought a truer sympathy with man.   Cowper's peasants were neither the idealised types of contemporary pastoral nor were they vaguely merged in "the lower orders." He had obviously not only watched them, but talked with them on terms of human equality.   He would take for granted the social gulf: he would accept the affectionate title of "Sir Cowper" as his right.   But, though some men were called to

<hr />

[1] *The Task*, Book V, 58-76.   [2] *Ibid.*, Book I, 290-299.

lower mundane position, he realised, as a young Scottish ploughman was soon to proclaim, that "A man's a man for a' that." Here, as Goldwin Smith says, is the unvarnished record of visitings among the humble of Olney, showing that Cowper might have been "a more exquisite Crabbe" if his vocation had tended that way:

> " Poor, yet industrious, modest, quiet, neat;
> Such claim compassion in a night like this,
> And have a friend in ev'ry feeling heart.
> Warm'd, while it lasts, by labour, all day long
> They brave the season, and yet find at eve,
> Ill clad and fed but sparely, time to cool.
> The frugal housewife trembles when she lights
> Her scanty stock of brush-wood, blazing clear,
> But dying soon, like all terrestrial joys.
> The few small embers left she nurses well;
> And, while her infant race, with outspread hands
> And crowded knees, sit cow'ring o'er the sparks,
> Retires, content to quake, so they be warm'd.
> The man feels least, as more inur'd than she
> To winter, and the current in his veins
> More briskly mov'd by his severer toil;
> Yet he, too, finds his own distress in theirs.
> The taper soon extinguish'd, which I saw
> Dangled along at the cold finger's end
> Just when the day declin'd, and the brown loaf
> Lodg'd on the shelf, half eaten, without sauce
> Of sav'ry cheese, or butter, costlier still;
> Sleep seems their only refuge: for, alas,
> Where penury is felt the thought is chain'd,
> And sweet colloquial pleasures are but few!
> With all this thrift they thrive not. All the care
> Ingenious parsimony takes but just
> Saves the small inventory, bed, and stool,
> Skillet, and old carv'd chest, from public sale.
> They live, and live without extorted alms
> From grudging hands; but other boast have none
> To soothe their honest pride, that scorns to beg,
> Nor comfort else, but in their mutual love." [1]

This "domestic interior" still has power to move us, while the numerous passages in which the poet *discusses* the claims of the poor leave us cold. Similarly, we can delight in his

[1] *The Task*, Book IV, 374-406.

pictures of animals, though we regret that moralising so soon intrudes:

> " *Here, unmolested, through whatever sign*
> *The sun proceeds, I wander. Neither mist,*
> *Nor freezing sky nor sultry, checking me,*
> *Nor stranger intermeddling with my joy.*
> *Ev'n in the spring and play-time of the year,*
> *That calls th' unwonted villager abroad*
> *With all her little ones, a sportive train,*
> *To gather king-cups in the yellow mead,*
> *And prink their hair with daisies, or to pick*
> *A cheap but wholesome sallad from the brook,*
> *These shades are all my own. The tim'rous hare,*
> *Grown so familiar with her frequent guest,*
> *Scarce shuns me; and the stock-dove, unalarm'd,*
> *Sits cooing in the pine-tree, nor suspends*
> *His long love-ditty for my near approach.*
> *Drawn from his refuge in some lonely elm*
> *That age or injury has hollow'd deep,*
> *Where, on his bed of wool and matted leaves,*
> *He has outslept the winter, ventures forth*
> *To frisk awhile, and bask in the warm sun,*
> *The squirrel, flippant, pert, and full of play:*
> *He sees me, and at once, swift as a bird,*
> *Ascends the neighb'ring beech; there whisks his brush,*
> *And perks his ears, and stamps and cries aloud,*
> *With all the prettiness of feign'd alarm,*
> *And anger insignificantly fierce*" [1]—

and so, after equally charming glimpses of "the bounding fawn," "the horse as wanton," and the gambolling kine, we return from the fields to the pulpit again! But while we resent the recurring didacticism, we must bear in mind that, in his own age of reason, Cowper's arguments carried weight with thousands of readers who had no eye for his descriptions, and that, if the social conscience is still none too tender, it was then hardly existent. There was vital need that the *case* for the "meaner part" of humanity, and for the brute creation, should be *stated*; and it was a voice both original and bold which defended animals, and dared the opinion that "oft the beast has seem'd to judge the man." [2]

I have said that Cowper's contemporary importance might

---

[1] *The Task*, Book VI, 295-320.   [2] *Ibid.*, 478.

better be judged if he had not occasionally outsoared himself. Looking at the matter in this light—though only, of course, in this light—it is specially unfortunate that he should sometimes have clearly foreshadowed Wordsworth, as in the famous passage:

> " *And witness, dear companion of my walks,*
> *Whose arm this twentieth winter I perceive*
> *Fast lock'd in mine, with pleasure such as love,*
> *Confirm'd by long experience of thy worth*
> *And well-tried virtues, could alone inspire—*
> *Witness a joy that thou hast doubled long.*
> *Thou know'st my praise of nature most sincere,*
> *And that my raptures are not conjur'd up*
> *To serve occasions of poetic pomp,*
> *But genuine, and art partner of them all.*" [1]

Wordsworth was fifteen when these lines appeared. Verily, a voice was crying in the wilderness, preparing his way. But while it is no small title to honour to have played the Forerunner to the Romantic Revival, that title too narrowly governs the modern estimate of Cowper. He lives indeed in his own right, and as the prophet of others greater than himself. Yet he was a poet, in the stricter sense, by accident rather than by nature or design. Occasionally, as in his picture of the frost-built palace,[2] his imagination displayed really considerable power. As a rule, even in his best poetic form, when he ceases to moralise, he remains less a creator than an observer, clear and precise in vision, though imparting to his descriptions the vital glow which comes only from true feeling.

The lover of poetry for its own sake can—and must—ignore a considerable proportion of Cowper's work. The student of Cowper himself and of his century cannot afford to do so. The literary critic may deplore the large amount of dross from which Cowper's gold has to be sifted. The student of the man and his period must not fall into the error of supposing that the "dross" *was* dross—either poetically or spiritually —to eighteenth-century readers. It was the day of moralising verse; but Cowper's use of Pope's couplet was as novel as much of his actual teaching was new. Had Cowper spoken to

---

[1] *The Task*, Book I, 144-153.   [2] *Ibid.*, Book V, 107-168.

his own age *only*, he would have been awarded his due place
among its thinkers. But since he speaks also in some measure
to ourselves, we are biased by the contrast in his verse between
the imperishable and the perished. We are tempted to see
another lost leader: a potential creative artist who robbed
posterity by clutching the skirts of his time. Rather should
we see a critic who served his own era well, and who, in the
process, happened to kindle a small but unique and in-
extinguishable flame of poetry.

Chapter Twelve

"MY MARY!"

I

"I AM A whimsical creature," said Cowper; "when I write for the public, I write, of course, with a desire to please —in other words, to acquire fame . . . but when I find that I have succeeded, feel myself alarmed, and ready to shrink from the acquisition." Success, even if it would ever have brought him much satisfaction, meant relatively little now. He was fifty-four—quite elderly for his period.[1] It is true that, despite all he had suffered, he was well preserved. He told Lady Hesketh that he had not grown gray so much as he had grown bald. "No matter," he went on;

"there was more hair in the world than ever had the honour to belong to me. Accordingly, having found just enough to curl a little at my ears, and to intermix with a little of my own that still hangs behind, I appear, if you see me in an afternoon, to have a very decent head-dress, not easily distinguishable from my natural growth; which being worn with a small bag, and a black ribbon about my neck, continues to me the charms of my youth, even on the verge of age."

He completed the picture of himself by adding two items: that he was in debt to nobody, and that he grew fat. Altogether he claimed to be still "a very smart youth."

Something must be attributed to his healthy mode of life; something also to his capacity, when melancholy was in abeyance, for finding happiness in simple things. But he must, again, have been fairly robust. His hypochondria was now to make him resort frequently to doctors, who wasted, instead of husbanding, his strength.[2] Even so, his life was to cover

[1] Pope had died at fifty-six; Thomson at forty-eight; Gray at fifty-five; Goldsmith at forty-six.

[2] For interesting particulars about the poet's doctors, with their varied methods and medicines, see *The Life of William Cowper*. By Thomas Wright, Pp. 481-483.

almost the psalmist's full span. Fifteen years yet remained to him. During those years he was to revive old friendships and to form new ones. He was to write, in point of *size*, his greatest achievement, as well as a few of his most famous lyrics. He was to compose, at sixty-seven, a poem whose beauty of expression belies the unrelieved dejection which is its theme. All this, I say, is evidence of constitutional strength. Nevertheless, Cowper in his middle fifties was no longer the man he had been. When *The Task* was published, his evening, though it was to be a long one, had already set in.

It came graciously, with a promise not to be fulfilled. He was superficially gratified to find himself acknowledged the greatest living poet, and to hear that *The Task* was widely appreciated in England, America, and elsewhere. What pleased him infinitely more, however, was a revival of intercourse with old associates. Had his spirit been less simple and sweet, he might have viewed rather cynically the haste with which relatives and friends, who had apparently forgotten him, now vied with one another in declaring, with tangible tokens, their deep regard. Clotworthy Rowley returned some books which the celebrated author of *The Task* had lent him as a youth in the Temple. Walter Bagot, now rector of Blithfield, in Staffordshire, came to visit his brother at Chicheley, near Olney, and eagerly looked up the illustrious poet, his old schoolfellow. General (formerly Major) Cowper ordered sherry, brandy, and rum to be delivered at his nephew's door. Lady Hesketh sent her cousin money and arranged with other members of the family to increase his allowance. "Anonymous," who alone had never lost faith in her old lover, clinched a previous offer by conveying, through her sister, the promise of an annuity of fifty pounds. Other gifts—the forerunners of many more from Lady Hesketh and Theodora—arrived by the Wellingborough coach. They included a pocket-book, the "completest" imaginable; a watch-chain, the "most brilliant"; a snuff-box embellished on the lid with a landscape; and, best of all, "a most elegant writing-desk" of cedar, mounted in silver. "How pleasant it is," said its recipient, "to write upon such a green bank."

Cowper was specially delighted at the renewal of correspondence with Lady Hesketh. Not only did he like her
vivacity, which stimulated one side of his nature, as that of
Lady Austen had done: a host of memories flocked back to
him when, on October 12, 1785, he recognised her hand-
writing on a letter beside his breakfast plate. "This," he
replied ecstatically, "is just as it should be. We are all grown
young again, and the days that I thought I should see no more
are actually returned." There ensued a correspondence
through which Lady Hesketh's sprightliness, generosity,
and mundane good sense shine as plainly as do Cowper's
affection and joy. And when, in the following February,
the poet heard that his cousin proposed visiting him, he
became, like the fishwife expecting Colin's return, "downright dizzy wi' the thought." "I shall see you again,"
he wrote;

> "I shall hear your voice; we shall take walks together; I will
> show you my prospects, the hovel, the alcove, the Ouse and its
> banks, everything that I have described. I anticipate the
> pleasure of those days not very far distant, and feel a part of it
> at this moment. Talk not of an inn! Mention it not for your
> life! We have never had so many visitors but we could easily
> accommodate them all."

Genuine enough! Yet it is the language of one who was
habitually moved by pleasure or gratitude to lyrical fervour.
I have no wish to minimise Lady Hesketh's fine qualities or
Cowper's feeling for her. She was for a time—but only for a
time—to brighten the surface of his life. She was to show
him great practical kindness, which redounds to her eternal
credit. But she was, after all, neither less nor more than a
conventional, prosperous Georgian lady, who never had so
much as a glimpse into the deeper recesses of the poet's soul.
It is symptomatic that he often wrote to her in his most playful
mood, sometimes addressing her as "My dearest Coswoz" or
"My dearest Cuzzy-wuzzy," and signing himself, in allusion
to some old joke, as "Giles Gingerbread." It was to the Giles
Gingerbread in him that his "generous and benevolent
cousin" appealed, not to the castaway whom a light still

sometimes surprised as he prayed. Cowper might long since have abandoned the set forms of prayer, as being useless for himself. That prayer for the world at large remained the consistent attitude of his heart is manifest enough. When Lady Hesketh, during her visit, induced him to resume the saying of grace before meat, she probably thought it a gain both for him and for religion. There is nothing in her recorded utterances which suggests that, in spiritual matters, she distinguished the shell from the kernel.

She had arrived in June, with her own carriage and her three attendants—Mrs. Eaton, "Cookee," and Samuel. Cowper, who had been advised not to meet her in person, arrayed his gardener "Kitch" in blue livery and sent him on horseback to Newport Pagnell to await the travellers at the Swan. "The first man, therefore, you shall see in a blue coat, with white buttons, in the famous town of Newport, cry 'Kitch!' He will immediately answer 'My lady!' and from that moment you are sure not to be lost." Such had been the poet's final instructions. All went according to plan, and as the distinguished stranger entered Olney—probably scattering pennies, as was her wont, to the children who made an informal bodyguard—the church bells rang out a merry peal. It was, said Cowper, the first time that this compliment had been paid to any visitor (Lord Dartmouth excepted) since he had lived in the town. As Lady Hesketh declined to stay at Orchard Side, apartments had been found for her at the Vicarage, now tenanted only in part by Scott's successor, a bachelor curate named Postlethwaite, who must have felt a little nervous at the prospect of the glory suddenly to be thrust upon his hermitage. Lady Hesketh was to have all the rooms except two, at the rate of twelve guineas a year, and the local Jack-of-all-trades, a Quaker called Maurice, undertook to furnish them complete—"from a bed to a platter"—for five guineas from June to November inclusive.

So, after twenty-three years, the cousins met again. Cowper suffered a temporary reaction from the excitement of anticipation. He soon recovered, and was the more delighted with Harriet's company because she and Mrs. Unwin genuinely took to each other. Lady Hesketh lost little time in sending her impressions to Theodora:

"It proving a wet evening we had no temptation to walk, but continued sitting comfortably round one dining-room table without stirring till after supper. Our friend delights in a large table and a large chair; there are two of the latter comforts in the parlour. I am sorry to say that he and I always spread ourselves out in them, leaving poor Mrs. Unwin to find all the comfort she can in a small one, half as high again as ours, and considerably harder than marble. However, she protests it is what she likes, that she prefers a high chair to a low one, and a hard to a soft one; and I hope she is sincere; indeed, I am persuaded she is. Her constant employment is knitting stockings, which she does with the finest needles I ever saw, and very nice they are (the stockings I mean). Our cousin has not for many years worn any other than those of her manufacture. She knits silk, cotton, and worsted. She sits knitting on one side of the table in her spectacles, and he on the other reading to her (when he is not employed in writing) in *his*. In winter, his morning studies are always carried on in a room by himself; but as his evenings are spent in the winter in transcribing, he usually, I find, does this *vis-a-vis* Mrs. Unwin."

Lady Hesketh's description of Mrs. Unwin speaks well for the writer's adaptability and graciousness. On the other hand, as coming from a woman of the world who did not understand, let alone share, her new friend's Evangelicalism, it should dispel any false view of Mrs. Unwin herself:

"She is very far from grave; [Theodora was informed] on the contrary, she is cheerful and gay, and laughs *de bon cœur* upon the smallest provocation. Amidst all the little puritanical words which fall from her *de temps en temps*, she seems to have by nature a great fund of gaiety—great indeed must it have been, not to have been totally overcome by the close confinement in which she has lived, and the anxiety she must have undergone for one whom she certainly loves as well as one human being can love another. . . . When she speaks upon grave subjects, she does express herself with a puritanical tone, and in puritanical expressions, but on all other subjects she seems to have a great disposition to cheerfulness and mirth. . . . I must say, too, that she seems to be very well read in the English poets, as appears by several little quotations which she makes from time to time, and has a true taste for what is excellent in that way. There is something truly affectionate and sincere in her manner."

Lady Hesketh's carriage was the means of enlarging Cowper's world. Visits to Weston Hall became more frequent; the Wrights, the Chesters,[1] and other families of quality were now within easy range. The local gossips were not slow to take advantage of "Sir Cowper's" blossoming out, and one of them, having business in London, made it his further mission to call on Newton and tell him the latest Olney scandal. Cowper himself had previously remarked that he never knew a lie hatched at Olney to wait long for a bearer; and this particular story lost nothing in the telling. The poet was represented not merely as taking occasional innocent drives to enjoy the society of decorous people, and as sometimes donning the green livery of an archer: Newton was given to understand that his old friend was spending his time in a constant round of positive dissipation.

We may blame Newton for his apparent readiness to credit the fable: it is irrelevant to criticise his standard of values. The Evangelicals may have been narrow in their attitude toward "the world"; but Cowper, to the end, was at least as strict as the rector of St. Mary Woolnoth. When balls were held at Weston Hall, the poet and Mrs. Unwin never attended, and Cowper admired Mrs. Throckmorton's tact in not sending invitations which he would have been under the painful necessity of declining. And he once observed that the only purpose to which his card-table had never been put was that of card-playing. He allowed that what has been called Newton's "unwarrantable interference" would have been amply justified if it had been based on a true report. There was a slightly heated correspondence between Olney and Coleman Street Buildings; but harmony was soon restored.

[1] Charles Chester, of Chicheley Hall, was a brother of the Rev. Walter Bagot, but had altered his surname.

II

Newton, whose protests were softened by barrels of oysters or baskets of skate, had another complaint against Cowper, and one which, if not entirely on his own grounds, was certainly better justified. He lamented that the poet was spending his time in translating Homer instead of producing more original work. It seems that Lady Austen had put this idea into "Brother William's" head, though his admiration for the Iliad and the Odyssey, and his distaste for Pope's version of "the two finest poems ever composed by man," dated back to his Westminster days. So, finding himself idle after the completion of *The Task* and *Tirocinium*, and having developed a preference for sustained writing, he had one day taken up the Iliad, "merely to divert attention," and had translated the first twelve lines. "Every day bringing its occasion for employment with it, every day consequently added something to the work," till he reflected that, as the two poems together contained forty thousand lines, the rendering of the whole into English would furnish occupation for a considerable time. He had, therefore, set to in earnest, and this gigantic labour, begun in November 1784, almost exclusively engaged his attention during the next six years. Joseph Johnson published it by subscription in July 1791, and its success was such that Cowper received a thousand pounds—which had the effect, quite common in natures like his, of making him more careful with money than he had ever been before.

It may seem strange that Cowper, an Evangelical Christian and the gentlest of creatures, should have had anything in common with the great pagan. He shall, therefore, explain himself:

"Except the Bible, there never was in the world a book so remarkable for that species of the sublime that owes its very existence to simplicity, as the works of Homer. He is always nervous, plain, natural. . . . Homer is, on occasions that call for such a style, the easiest and most familiar of writers . . . his accuracy of description, and his exquisite judgement never, never failed him. He never, I believe, in a single instance sacrificed beauty to embellishment. He does not deal in hyperbole . . . accordingly, when he describes nature, whether in man or in animal, or whether nature inanimate, you may always trust him for the most consummate fidelity. . . . Oh! how unlike some describers that I have met with, of modern days, who smother you with words, words, words, and then think that they have copied nature; when all the while nature was an object either not looked at, or not sufficiently." [1]

Cowper lamented that this "most blameless writer" was "not an enlightened man," but drew comfort from the fact that he had "interspersed many great and valuable truths throughout both his poems."

It was easier for Cowper to see where Pope failed than it was for himself to succeed. His own version is a faithful rendering. He did not, like Pope, pervert the original in order to gain epigrammatic effects, or, like Chapman, do violence to it through excess of sentiment and fancy. Cowper, however, while he admired Homer's directness and truth, was unable to sympathise or square his conscience with the passions of a primitive world. "He knew," as Mr. Harold Child puts it,

"exactly what Homer meant to say; he appreciated, in great measure, Homer's manner of saying it; but his head was full of Milton. He believed Milton's style to resemble Homer's; and, by modelling his blank verse on Milton's, he achieves inversions, pauses, and pomposities which are wholly unlike the smooth and simple rapidity of Homer. This is not to say that there are not excellent passages in Cowper's *Homer*, or that the whole work is not a lofty achievement in scholarship and poetry. But in avoiding the cleverness of Pope, Cowper fell into the opposite extreme. Homer is grand and lively, Cowper's *Homer* is grand and dull."

"Perhaps its least disputable title to fame," says Mr. Child, "is that it kept the poet busy and happy, staving off, for a while, his persistent foe, despair." *For a while*; yes! The task was, in fact, a doubtful blessing. In its earlier stages it was unquestionably helpful; but, long before it was finished, Cowper confessed that he felt like an ass overladen with

[1] Letters to Lady Hesketh, December 1785, and January 1786.

sandbags. It was one thing to translate his three or forty lines a day when he was well and there were no distractions. It was quite another thing for a temperamental freelance to be compelled to plod on, under less favourable conditions, in fulfilment of a contract. Then there was the labour of transcribing, with which the Throckmortons' "good-natured Padre" and other friends helped, but which remained sometimes a distressing burden, rendering its bearer less fit for the incomparably greater burdens which were to come.

III

In the autumn of 1786, when he had been occupied with *Homer* for two years, the barometer of Cowper's spirits still stood relatively high. In 1784, after finishing *The Task*, he had enjoyed three days' complete respite from the conviction of his spiritual doom, and, though it had proved but an oasis in the desert, it is possible that, notwithstanding his subsequent statement that God had but given him hopes in derision and taken them away in vengeance, he derived some more lasting encouragement from the experience. Once again we must discount Cowper's gloomy references to himself. That a spectre continued to hide in a fastness of his mind is plain enough; but it remained there for long periods, and even when it stalked forth it was probably less fearsome to the poet himself than, dressed in the colours of his fluent fancy, it might seem to those who knew it only from his description. Real madness, as I have previously hinted, may provide its victim with an anodyne not extended to onlookers. Thirteen years had now passed since Cowper's last attack of insanity. His spirits had, it is true, fluctuated much, as they always did; but thirteen winters, each dreaded as it came, had been negotiated without disaster. Let Lady Austen and Lady Hesketh have full credit for what each did in turn to keep melancholy at bay. But let us not draw foolish deductions from the fact that Cowper had suffered no breakdown during the period of Lady Austen's friendship, and that his fourth derangement, presently to be recorded, did not occur until Lady Hesketh had left him after her several months' visit in

1786. If the seat of his malady did not lie beyond all human reach, it certainly lay beyond that of mere vivacity and good sense. These valuable qualities, to change the metaphor, might serve as an additional defence against the demon's exit from his den. But, at the first real alarm, the demon was ready to spring out again, crumbling such defences like paper. The simple explanation of Cowper's long immunity is, it seems to me, that there had been no major disturbance in his life for over a decade. Another was now to come.

The blow fell soon after he and Mrs. Unwin had moved to Weston Lodge. The Throckmortons had, some time previously, tendered them the refusal of this plain, substantial house. They had discussed, but rejected, the offer. In 1786, however, Lady Hesketh, while staying at Olney Vicarage, had persuaded them to reverse their decision. She had every argument of common sense on her side. Olney lay low; Orchard Side was in many ways incommodious and ill-situated, though Thomas Wright is perhaps correct in saying that it was less unhealthy than is often supposed. The village of Weston Underwood stood relatively high, amid pleasant surroundings, and Weston Lodge, in immediate proximity to the Hall, was airy and bright. It is questionable, nevertheless, if the change were a happy one for Cowper. He sometimes grumbled about Orchard Side, but he had grown attached to the gaol-like building in which he had spent his best years.

Change, in any case, disturbed him; and though Weston Lodge was situated in "one of the prettiest villages in England" and was free from the "fishy-smelling fumes of the marsh miasma," it had, with its better but fewer rooms, drawbacks of its own for the poet. He complained, to the Rev. James Hurdis,[1] of its lack of privacy:

"I wish always when I have a new piece in hand to be as secret as you, and there was a time when I could be so. Then I lived the life of a solitary, was not visited by a single neigh-

[1] Hurdis was rector of Bishopstone, in Sussex, his birthplace, and professor of poetry at Oxford. He was himself a poet of contemporary repute. An appreciative letter which he sent Cowper about *The Task* had led to a friendly correspondence between the two men. Cowper, before hearing from Hurdis, had read and enjoyed *The Village Curate*.

U

bour, because I had none with whom I could associate; nor ever had an inmate. This was when I dwelt at Olney; but since I have removed to Weston the case is different. Here I am visited by all around me, and study in a room exposed to all manner of inroads. It is on the ground floor, the room in which we dine, and in which I am sure to be found by all who seek me. They find me generally at my desk, and with my work, whatever it be, before me, unless perhaps I have conjured it into its hiding-place before they have had time to enter. This, however, is not always the case, and consequently, sooner or later, I cannot fail to be detected. Possibly you, who I suppose have a snug study, would find it impracticable to attend to anything closely in an apartment exposed as mine; but use has made it familiar to me, and so familiar, that neither servants going and coming disconcert me; nor even if a lady, with an oblique glance of her eye, catches two or three lines of my MS., do I feel myself inclined to blush, though naturally the shyest of mankind. . . ."

It is obvious that loyalty to his interrupters dictated the white lies with which the writer concludes. Cowper needed a regime in which society and solitude—with perhaps a predominance of the latter—were blended. In moving from Olney to Weston he had changed one disadvantage for another.

It was inevitable that when he had occasion to call at Orchard Side, which had not yet found new tenants, he saw in it, "deserted of its inhabitants," a "forlorn and woeful" spectacle: "no unapt resemblance of a soul that God has forsaken." But concern for others was soon to put private grievances from his mind. He and Mrs. Unwin were barely settled at Weston Lodge before news arrived of William Unwin's sudden illness and death. Unwin was travelling with Henry Thornton when he was fatally seized with typhus at Winchester. He seems to have been a thoroughly attractive character, combining the full discharge of his loving duty to his parishioners at Stock with the wider life of an eighteenth-century gentleman and scholar. He travelled often to London, Bristol, and elsewhere, and had, as Cowper's letters reveal, many "influential" friends; but there is no hint that social popularity spoiled the simplicity which had won him the poet's instant affection at Huntingdon. He was buried in

Winchester Cathedral, and an epitaph in English [1] was chosen
by his family in preference to one which Cowper wrote in
Latin.

"Poor Mrs. Unwin and Mr. Cowper!" wrote William Bull;
"I rode over to smoke a pipe yesterday, and sympathise a little
with them. They bore it better than I expected." The tone
of Cowper's letters, conveying the sad intelligence to Lady
Hesketh, Joseph Hill, and other friends, was, indeed, manly
and restrained. He dwelt mainly upon Unwin's virtues, upon
the consequences of bereavement to his family, and upon the
dispensations of Providence, which "we cannot contemplate
without astonishment, but which will nevertheless be explained hereafter, and must in the meantime be revered in
silence." Only at the end of his long epistle to Lady Hesketh
does he give vent to his own feeling: "So farewell, my friend
Unwin! The first man for whom I conceived a friendship
after my removal from St. Albans, and for whom I cannot but
still continue to feel a friendship, though I shall see thee with
these eyes no more."

Cowper had put forth a special effort for Mrs. Unwin's sake.
There was the inevitable recoil: for in truth Unwin's passing
had struck, for the time being, at his heart's core. It was not
merely that he had deeply loved him, or that his intimates
were too few in number not to be sorely missed. The fact of
death—especially when it snatched away one in the prime of
life—again disconcerted him. There was renewed the
struggle between his insatiable curiosity to know what lay
beyond the veil and the shrinking of his nervous constitution
from the physical process of dissolution. The delusion about
his own spiritual fate was reawakened: and January lay just
ahead. A letter written to Lady Hesketh in the middle of

---

[1] IN MEMORY OF THE

REV. WILLIAM CAWTHORNE UNWIN, M.A.

RECTOR OF STOCK, IN ESSEX

He was educated at the Charter-house, in London, under the
Rev. Dr. Crusius; and, having gone through the education of
that school, he was at an early period admitted to Christ's
College, Cambridge. He died in this city, the 29th of Nov.
1786, aged forty-one years, leaving a widow and three young
children.

that month was ominous. The demon was stirring, and within a few days Cowper was once more in his clutch. He made two fresh attempts at suicide. One was frustrated in the nick of time by Mrs. Unwin, the other by William Bull. The latter continued to call with devoted regularity. But the invalid declined to see him; and he compelled Mrs. Unwin, if she needed any compulsion, to reject Mrs. Newton's offer to come to her assistance. "The sight of any face, except Mrs. Unwin's, was to me," he afterwards declared, "an insupportable grievance." He spoke of the previous derangement as "the dreadful seventy-three" and of this one as "the more dreadful eighty-six." It was, indeed, attended by more harassing physical symptoms: Cowper's constitution was naturally less able now to bear the strain. Otherwise the attack followed much the same course as its predecessors. It went through varying stages of intensity, and then suddenly vanished in June. But it had left Cowper a definitely "older" and weaker man, subject henceforth to indigestion, pains in the head, and other ailments.

There was, however, another temporary brightening of the evening sky. Cowper found almost a second Unwin in Samuel Rose, who had paid his first visit to Weston before the breakdown, and who came again soon after the poet's recovery. This brilliant and sensitive boy of twenty was the son of Dr. William Rose, a schoolmaster at Chiswick, who had an interest in the *Monthly Review*. The "Bouton de Rose" —as Cowper soon came to call Samuel—was studying law at Glasgow University, from which he passed later to Edinburgh, where "young as he was," he so highly pleased Adam Smith "that as long as he resided there he was constantly invited to the literary circle of that eminent philosopher." [1] It was while returning on vacation from Glasgow that Rose first broke his journey at Weston in January 1787. His avowed purpose was to bring the thanks of the Scottish professors to the author of *The Task*. His true aim, perhaps, was himself to meet the writer whom he admired, through his work, to the point of hero-worship. The incense of youth is always fragrant to an ageing writer; but Rose's eager appreciation

---

[1] Hayley's *Life of Cowper*, 1812 Edition.   Volume III, p. 427.

sprang from clear-eyed judgment and solid character. Despite the difference in their years, a warm friendship sprang up between the two men. Their relationship, as Hayley said, resembled that of father and son.

Cowper did not resume translating until some months after his recovery. "Homer's battles," he said, "cannot be fought by a man who does not sleep well, and who has not some little degree of animation in the daytime." He spent much of his time in reading books—mostly memoirs and travel—from the Throckmortons' well-filled shelves. He found much pleasure in communicating his discoveries to Rose, who, for his part, introduced Cowper to Burns's poems. "A very extraordinary production" was the verdict, to which was subsequently added the rider that "poor Burns loses much of his deserved praise in this country through our ignorance of his language. His candle is bright, but shut up in a dark lantern."

Rose paid a longer visit to Weston in the summer of 1788, and helped Cowper with the transcription of *Homer*. Newton, his wife, and Miss Catlett, were there for some weeks at the same time. After Newton's departure, the poet wrote to him:

"I rejoice that you and yours reached London safe, especially when I reflect that you performed the journey on a day so fatal, as I understand, to others travelling the same road. I found those comforts in your visit which have formerly sweetened all our interviews, in part restored. I knew you; knew you for the same shepherd who was sent to lead me out of the wilderness into the pasture where the Chief Shepherd feeds His flock, and felt my sentiments of affectionate friendship for you the same as ever. But one thing was still wanting, and that the crown of all. I shall find it in God's time, if it be not lost for ever."

This letter should be read in conjunction with a previous one, in which Cowper, while expressing an undiminished regard for his friend, speaks of having for a time lost belief in Newton's "identity." He had had "the disagreeable suspicion," he says, that he was addressing himself to the one whom he "loved and valued so highly" in his "better days," whereas Newton was now in fact "not that friend, but a stranger." The letter is curiously worded, and reveals the distorted condition of the poet's mind at this time. But the unmistakable point is that Cowper conceives himself to be the one who has changed: and changed for the worse. He had indeed changed, but only, again, as a pupil may be said to change when he travels along a different road from his master towards the same actual, if not the same apparent, goal.

Later in the year Rose was at Weston once more, and sent his sister Harriet the following description of the daily routine at the Lodge:

"I came here on Thursday; and here I found Lady Hesketh, a very agreeable, good-tempered, sensible woman, polite without ceremony, and sufficiently well-bred to make others feel happy in her company. I here feel no restraint, and none is wished to be inspired. The 'noiseless tenor' of our lives would much please and gratify you. . . . We rise at whatever hour we choose; breakfast at half-past nine, take about an hour to satisfy the *sentiment*, not the *appetite*—for we talk—good heavens, how we talk! and enjoy ourselves most wonderfully. Then we separate . . . Mr. Cowper to Homer, Mr. R. to transcribing what is already translated, Lady Hesketh to work and to books alternately, and Mrs. Unwin, who in everything but her face is a kind angel sent from heaven to guard the health of our poet, is busy in domestic concerns. At one, our labours finished, the poet and I walk for two hours. I then drink plentiful draughts of instruction which flow from his lips, instruction so sweet, and goodness so exquisite, that one *loves* it for its flavour. At three we return and dress, and the succeeding hour brings dinner upon the table, and collects again the smiling countenances of the family to partake of the neat and elegant meal. Conversation continues till tea-time, when an entertaining volume engrosses our thoughts till the last meal is announced. Conversation again, and then rest before twelve, to enable us to rise again to the same round of innocent, virtuous pleasure."

Happy "Bouton de Rose!" His was a sanguine temperament, in spite of—or perhaps partly because of—ill health. He prospered in his profession, and became a barrister on the Home Circuit. He was, however, consumptive, and was already ailing when in 1804 he defended William Blake against a charge of high treason. Blake had become involved in an encounter with a drunken soldier, whom he ejected from his front garden. The soldier and a companion accused him of having used "seditious" language, and the magistrate —evidently allowing nothing for the influence of alcohol upon the witnesses—ordered Blake for trial at the Sussex Sessions. Rose's speech secured his acquittal, but the strain was too much for the advocate, who never recovered from its effects. He was thirty-eight when he died, serene and cheerful to the end. "Farewell, sweet Rose!" mourned Blake. "Thou hast got before me to the celestial city. I also have but a few more mountains to pass; for I hear the bells ring and the trumpets sound to welcome thy arrival among Cowper's glorified band of spirits of just men made perfect." [1]

Another new friend was Mrs. King, wife of the rector of Pertenhall, in Bedfordshire. This lady, who was described to Newton as "evidently a Christian, and a very gracious one," had been intimate with the poet's brother. John Cowper had himself been a versifier, and Mrs. King, having written in the first instance to his great namesake to express, as a stranger, her delight in *The Task*, later sent some of John's compositions which she had preserved in manuscript. A characteristic correspondence followed, and, though Mrs. King, when she visited Cowper, proved to be very different from the imaginary portrait of herself which he had sent her, he was charmed with her personality. Many of his subsequent letters were anxiously concerned, with good cause, about her health. She died, much to his sorrow, in 1793.

Meanwhile his own health and spirits had much improved. He had enjoyed a memorable day's outing to Chicheley Hall, driven with Mrs. Unwin and Mrs. Throckmorton in the latter's chaise, in November 1787. "It seemed," he wrote to Lady Hesketh,

"as if all the world were there to meet us, though in fact there was not above half of it, their own [the Chesters'] family, which is very numerous, excepted. The Bishop of Norwich was there, that is to say, the little Doctor Lewis Bagot, and his lady. She is handsome, and he in all respects what a bishop should be. Besides these, Mrs. Praed was there, and her sister, Miss Blackwell.

---

[1] *The Letters of William Blake*, edited by H. G. B. Russell, p. 154.

There might be many others, but if there were I overlooked them. 'Foresaid little Bishop and I had much talk about many things, but mostly about Homer."

Cowper must have been in specially charitable mood that day. He had little respect for bishops as a rule, and had satirised them (rather bitterly for him) in his poems. But this, it is only fair to add, he had done partly to please Mrs. Unwin, who liked mitred heads and gaitered legs even less than he did.

The *Homer* was now progressing steadily again, and the poet was "delivered" of "other brats." In the spring of 1788 he wrote five ballads of slavery, two of which appeared in the *Gentleman's Magazine*.[1] *Sweet Meat has Sour Sauce, or, The Slave-Trader in the Dumps* has a true touch of satire and a rollicking popular air. The others are more remarkable for the writer's imaginative identification of himself with the slaves than for the quality of the verse. But again Cowper served his own age well. It was a bold voice which then dared to proclaim that

> "*Skins may differ, but affection*
> *Dwells in white and black the same.*"

Another new movement of the period was that of the Sunday School. It had been started before 1780, but had been given its first real impetus in that year by Robert Raikes, the proprietor of the *Gloucester Journal*; and it spread so rapidly that it reached even Olney nine years later, when James Bean, the new (and resident) vicar, a friend of Newton's, asked Cowper to write a hymn for the children. There resulted the stanzas beginning:

> "*Hear, Lord, the song of praise and pray'r,*
> *In Heaven, thy dwelling-place,*
> *From infants made the public care,*
> *And taught to seek thy face!*"

That would hardly pass muster to-day. Cowper, no more than Wesley, knew how to approach the child mind, though

[1] A number of Cowper's more famous short poems appeared in the *Gentleman's Magazine*, including *The Poplar Field* with its beautiful couplet:

> "The poplars are fell'd, farewell to the shade
> And the whispering sound of the cool colonnade."

he loved children no less intensely. Children, indeed, were then little understood. The early Sunday Schools helped to bridge a gulf. They spread the rudiments of Scriptural and general knowledge among many youngsters who would otherwise have lacked instruction altogether: they served at the same time, in an atmosphere less formal than that of the day schools, to teach adults the alphabet of child psychology.

When writing his hymn for Mr. Bean, Cowper observed: "I am somewhat in the case of Lawyer Dowling in *Tom Jones*, and could split myself into as many poets as there are muses, and find employment for them all." He wrote some verses on the King's recovery in 1789, which happened just in time to silence the dispute between Pitt and Fox about the regency. Cowper at the moment was so much relieved that the dissolute Prince of Wales was not to become his father's deputy that he saw George III in a more flattering light than he normally viewed him or kingship itself. Even a month later we find him telling Newton, who was less censorious of the Prince because of the temptations inseparable from his elevated situation, that "the expense which attends a Kingly government is an argument which millions begin to feel the force of."

Cowper's advanced political ideas are well seen in a letter addressed to Lady Hesketh, whom he teased for her conventional Toryism, nearly two years later. Though he had, as we have seen, prophesied and welcomed the fall of the Bastille, he had recoiled with horror from the excesses of the French people after the execution of Louis XVI. Fear, however, did not make him betray his faith in liberty. While many of its own friends in this country were yielding to panic, he wrote calmly:

"The French are a vain and childish people, and conduct themselves on this grand occasion with a levity and extravagance nearly akin to madness; but it would have been better for Austria and Prussia to let them alone. All nations have a right to choose their own mode of government, and the sovereignty of the people is a doctrine that evinces itself; for whenever the people choose to be masters they always are so, and none can hinder them. God grant that we may have no revolution here;

but unless we have a reform we certainly shall. Depend upon it, my dear, the hour is come when power founded in patronage and corrupt majorities must govern this land no longer. Concession too must be made to dissenters of every denomination. They have a right to them, a right to all the privileges of Englishmen, and sooner or later, by fair means or by force, they will have them."

Cowper's loyal address to the King may have helped to bring him an offer of the laureateship on the death of Warton in 1790. He was in fact asked to fill the office only after William Hayley, his future friend and biographer, then at the zenith of his rocket-like reputation, had declined. Cowper, in his turn, begged to be excused. "I could neither go to Court, nor kiss hands," he said, "were it for a much more valuable consideration." To Lady Hesketh, who wished him to accept the honour, thereby showing again how little she understood him, he wrote: "Heaven guard my brows from the wreath you mention, whatever wreath beside may hereafter adorn them! It would be a leaden extinguisher clapped on all the fire of my genius. . . . To speak seriously, it would make me miserable, and therefore I am sure that thou of all my friends wouldst least wish me to wear it." So Henry James Pye became the richer by ninety-odd pounds a year; while Cowper doubtless consoled himself with the reflection that, if he were not made for royal favours, he was at least the graveyard-laureate of All Saints' Church, Northampton.[1] "A fig," he was able to say, "for poets who write epitaphs on individuals! I have written *one* that serves *two hundred* persons."

Cowper had now grown accustomed to the arrival of strangers at Weston Lodge. He was probably not surprised, therefore, when, on a day in January 1790, another undergraduate, colt-like in his high animal spirits combined with bashfulness, turned up without any previous introduction, as Samuel Rose had done. Whatever annoyance Cowper may have felt at being disturbed instantly yielded to pleasure at

---

[1] See the whimsical letter to Lady Hesketh (November 27, 1787) in which he describes the circumstances which led to his accepting this onerous position, which he held for six years.

the sight of this engaging youth, whose shyness soon made
him forget his own; and pleasure became inexpressible delight
when the newcomer announced himself as the grandson of
Roger Donne. Twenty-seven years had now passed since
there had been any intercourse between Cowper and his
Donne (or "Norfolk") cousins. Now from John Johnson of
Ludham, who was Catherine's son, he learned that Elizabeth
had married Thomas Hewitt of Mattishall, that Harriet had
become Mrs. Balls, that Ann was the wife of Thomas Bodham
of Mattishall, and that Castres was Vicar of Ludham. We
may imagine with what keen interest the poet, who said that
there was more of the Donne than of the Cowper in himself,
listened to this information as it spluttered from the lips of
his young visitor. Little did he then see in this droll, good-
natured boy, whom he afterwards called "Johnny of Norfolk,"
a figure of destiny! Little did Johnny imagine that his own
name would come to be immortally linked with his illustrious
kinsman's!

At the moment, Johnson, who had broken his journey to
Cambridge, where he was studying at Caius College for holy
orders, was more concerned with the literary ambition he
cherished for himself. He had written a poem called "The
Tale of a Lute," the scenes of which were laid at Audley End.
Anxious to have Cowper's opinion, yet fearful and coy, he
resorted to subterfuge. He represented the manuscript as
being the work of Lord Howard, who had sent it by him,
desiring a verdict from the author of *The Task*. Cowper read
the poem, praising some points, but rather severely criticising
others. On the next day, as the two men walked in Kilwick
Wood, Johnny's conscience smote him. The confession of his
guile met with gracious and tender response; but several
months later he was still burdened by the remembrance, for
we then find Cowper writing to him:

"Give yourself no trouble on the subject of the politic device
you saw good to recur to when you presented me with your
manuscript; it was an innocent deception, at least it could harm
nobody save yourself—an effect which it did not fail to produce;
and since the punishment followed it so closely, by me at least
it may very well be forgiven. You ask how I can tell that you

are not addicted to practices of the deceptive kind? And certainly, if the little time that I have had to study you were alone to be considered, the question would not be unreasonable; but in general, a man who reaches my years finds

> ' *That long experience does attain*
> *To something like prophetic strain.*'

"I am very much of Lavater's opinion, and persuaded that faces are as legible as books, only with these circumstances to recommend them to our perusal, that they are read in much less time, and are much less likely to deceive us. Yours gave me a favourable impression of you the moment I beheld it, and though I shall not tell you in particular what I saw in it, for reasons mentioned in my last, I will add that I have observed in you nothing since that has not confirmed the opinion I then formed in your favour. In fact, I cannot recollect that my skill in physiognomy has ever deceived me, and I should add more on this subject had I room."

Cowper loved Johnny the more because he saw in him certain reflections of his own character. "You are a scatterbrain," he tells him.

"I made the discovery perhaps the sooner because in this you very much resemble myself, who, in the course of my life, through mere carelessness or inattention, lost many advantages: an insuperable shyness has also deprived me of many more. . . . You will do well to guard against both, for of both, I believe, you have a considerable share as well as myself."

Had ever a young man a franker, yet kindlier, mentor? How tactful, again, is the reply to his question whether, as one training for the Church, he ought not to cultivate a staider manner!—

"Yours, my dear Johnny, are vagaries that I shall never see practised by any other; and whether you slap your ancle, or reel as if you were fuddled, or dance in the path before me, all is characteristic of yourself, and therefore to me delightful. I have hinted to you indeed sometimes that you should be cautious of indulging antic habits and singularities of all sorts, and young men in general have need enough of such admonition. But yours are a sort of fairy habits, such as might belong to Puck or

Robin Goodfellow, and therefore, good as the advice is, I should be half sorry should you take it. This allowance at least I give you;—continue to take your walks, if walks they may be called, exactly in their present fashion till you have taken orders! Then indeed, forasmuch as a skipping, curvetting, bounding divine might be a spectacle not altogether seemly, I shall consent to your adoption of a more grave demeanour."

It would be pleasant to linger over Cowper's letters to his "son," who visited Buckinghamshire repeatedly, bringing his fiddle with him, since he was assured that the poet liked a little music and that no serious competition was to be feared, there being only two fiddles at Weston—"one a gardener's, the other a tailor's: terrible performers both!" Johnny was, of course, set to transcribing Homer. He confessed that he had never read the Odyssey; but that apparent difficulty was overruled. He was told that he was the more "to be envied" for the pleasure now to come.

Meanwhile Johnny had spread glowing accounts of Cowper among the members of the Donne clan. The poet, it seems, had not struck him as being in any way abnormal, apart from his genius, for Mrs. Bodham had no inkling that Cowper was a recluse, subject to moods of grave melancholy, when she broke her long silence by asking him to visit her. She might as well, he said, have invited the house in which he dwelt. He was delighted, however, to hear from cousin Ann —the "Rose" whom he nursed as a boy; and as for the gift with which her letter was accompanied—the gift of his mother's portrait—it opened all the floodgates of emotion:

"My dearest Rose [he replied] whom I thought withered and fallen from the stalk, but whom I find still alive; nothing could give me greater pleasure than to know it, and learn it from yourself. Every creature that bears any affinity to my mother is dear to me, and you, the daughter of her brother, are but one remove distant from her. I love you therefore, and love you much, both for her sake and for your own. The world could not have furnished you with a present so acceptable to me as the picture you have so kindly sent me. . . . I kissed it, and bring it where it is the last object that I see at night, and, of course, the first on which I open my eyes in the morning."

The sequel is well known. The portrait moved Cowper to one of his most passionate and tender poems, which, for the light it throws upon his childhood, has already been quoted.[1] By a fitting coincidence it was written a month or so after the sonnet, equally noble, *To Mrs. Unwin*.[2] Cowper told Mrs. King that he had never found greater joy than in writing these two poems: the one on the parent whom he remembered so clearly, though she died when he was a child, "and the other to a lady whom I expect in a few minutes down to breakfast, and who has supplied to me the place of my own mother these six-and-twenty years."

IV

Alas! Mrs. Unwin was now ailing. On Christmas Eve, 1787, she had narrowly escaped being burned to death after lighting her own bedroom fire. Her preservation had certainly all the appearance of being providential, and Cowper ascribed it to the fact that, at the moment of conflagration, she was engaged in prayer. The shock, however, left its effects, which were accentuated by a fall, some time later, upon a frozen gravel path. She was crippled for some months after this second accident, and never fully regained her former strength. Cowper's growing anxiety for her health is pathetically apparent from now onwards, as also is his jealous concern for her in other matters. Typical is his gentle reminder to Johnny Johnson: "By the way, had you a letter from Mrs. Unwin? I am witness that she addressed one to you before you went into Norfolk; but your mathematico-poetical head forgot to acknowledge the receipt of it."

Mrs. Unwin's care of Cowper had been its own reward. "Duty" cannot have been associated in her thoughts with a service wholly based upon love. Only love in its truest form could, indeed, have adequately equipped her for the task. For while Cowper's manifest affection for herself, as well as his charm and courtesy, often rendered her burden light, at other times, even when he was comparatively cheerful, he must unconsciously have made heavy demands upon her.

[1] See p. 50.   [2] See p. 251.

Man—"especially man that is born to write verse"—is notoriously impatient of the chares of life. He is quick to grumble if there be any neglect of those duties on which depend his comfort and his own capacity to work; he usually takes them for granted when they are silently and efficiently performed. Nor must we forget that in Cowper's winsome personality there was yet a more than average share of irritability: hints of it constantly appear in his letters for those with eyes to see. I believe he strove, and strove nobly, to make his habitual temper consort with his religious profession. Yet Mrs. Unwin, utterly self-effacing as she was, cannot have found him easy, at the best, to live with. And when madness overtook him, when he sat for weeks or months together staring vacantly before him, and when he turned suspiciously even against his guardian angel, her cross could have been carried only by one who had deep inward resources upon which to draw.

Blessings are never more clearly apprehended than when their continuance is threatened. While Cowper had never been blind to the debt he owed Mary, I think he saw it far more clearly now that she showed signs of failing. And it bespeaks his own fundamental unselfishness that, instead of wringing his hands in panic, as many far less sensitive men might have done, he braced himself for an undertaking from which every inch of his physical nature must have shrunk. What Mrs. Unwin had been to him, that, so far as might be possible, he resolved to be to her. It is true that his melancholy had to find an outlet: the more so because his own health had deteriorated since his last breakdown. And so, fortunately for himself and for Mary, he found a safety-valve in Samuel Teedon, the Olney schoolmaster. Cowper had known this semi-educated, self-opinionated, unctuous, and irrepressible character for some years. At first he had seen the ridiculous side of him; but later, having come to pity him for his poverty, he had taken delight in entertaining and "stuffing" him. Even after *The Task* was published, good-natured fun still mingled in its writer's references to "poor Teedon," whose solemn and excessive flattery made it difficult for the poet to restrain his mirth in the schoolmaster's presence. A few years later, however, by gradual or sudden stages, Teedon had established suzerainty over Cowper's mind, and was accepted, with his dreams and visions, as the oracle he thought himself.

One of the first occasions on which the poet sought his advice was in the autumn of 1791. In the summer of that year the *Homer*, which had gravely overtaxed his strength, had been successfully launched, and its translator was now asked by Joseph Johnson, the bookseller, to undertake the arrangement of a magnificent edition of Milton, comparable with Boydell's Shakespeare. Much as Cowper loved Milton, he had had little experience of annotation and lived remote from libraries. On the other hand, he needed occupation, and part of the proposed task—the rendering of the Latin poems into English—strongly appealed to him. In two minds about his answer, he consulted Teedon, who, after laying the matter before the Throne of Grace, declared it to be God's will that Cowper should accept his publisher's offer. The task was therefore begun. It was never finished, and long before its editor was compelled to relinquish effort, it had become a "trap" from which he yearned to be free.

For the moment, however, he took Teedon's ruling not only on *Milton*: he turned to him for "revelation" on other points, as well as for the interpretation of his own visions and "voices." It is estimated from Teedon's manuscript diary that, before his influence on Cowper began to wane, as his prophecies lacked fulfilment, nearly a thousand letters passed between the two men, while the schoolmaster constantly visited "the Esqr." and "Madam" at Weston.[1] Yet it is unfair to speak of Teedon's "malign" effect upon Cowper. Teedon's mind was itself disordered on one point, but he does not seem to have been a conscious charlatan. He probably believed as sincerely in his unique share of divine favour as Cowper did in his unique share of divine disapproval. Nor, in the worst sense, did he tyrannise over the poet. He spoke mostly comfortable words to him, and appears to have been honestly concerned for the welfare of one whose genius cast

[1] For details of Teedon and his diary, see *The Life of William Cowper*, by Thomas Wright, pp. 375–379, 587–594.

a reflected glory on himself. Teedon had played no part in driving him mad; nor did he aggravate what was probably an ineradicable taint. He was, on the contrary, the means of canalising the flow of Cowper's gloomy thoughts.

The poet, even in his letters to Teedon, records moments of spiritual hope and times when he was permitted by God "once more to approach Him in prayer." This proves, again, that his obsession was not unrelieved. And even when he speaks of a "settled melancholy" overclouding everything, he has to admit that, "miraculous" as it may seem, he is "not absolutely incapacitated for the common offices of life." The chances are, indeed, that he was the better able to continue those offices because, by writing to Teedon, he worked the dangerous excess of morbidity out of his system. He was, in my opinion, no more responsible for the poison being originally in his system than a baby is responsible for being born with a hare-lip. All the circumstances of his early life, moreover, had tended to spread the malady through his whole nature. That it remained relatively localised shows how sound in every other respect his constitution must have been, and how successfully his spirit withstood the danger from the mind.

Even now, while pouring out his misery to Teedon, and relieving himself the better through the exaggeration to which he was prone, he remained quite sane at every point save one. He continued also to have many cheerful moods: notwithstanding the fact that, soon after he had started on Milton, there had fallen the shadow of the calamity which in this world he most dreaded. In December 1791, Mrs. Unwin had suffered a paralytic stroke. She had suddenly called on "Mr. Cowper" not to let her fall, and, even as she spoke, he had caught her helpless figure. She soon rallied, however, and writing to Rose a few days later, the poet was able to say that she seemed in all respects better. "She has been my faithful and affectionate nurse for many years," he added, "and consequently has a claim on all my attentions. She has them, and will have them as long as she wants them; which will probably be, at the best, a considerable time to come." His spirits now rose and fell as Mrs. Unwin's condition fluctuated,

and we may be sure that, in whatever tones of despair he
wrote to Teedon, he showed *her* a cheerful face. His letters
at this time were full of his love and concern. Within a
month or two she was relatively well again. Cowper resumed
his Milton, and the old whimsicality broke out once more in
his letters to an ever-widening circle of correspondents.

His newest friend, and the one destined with Johnny of
Norfolk to preside over his and Mrs. Unwin's closing years,
was William Hayley. Born at Chichester in 1745, and
educated at Eton and Trinity Hall, Hayley, having private
means, had early abandoned law for a life of "books, retirement, and friendship." After abortive attempts at the drama,
he wrote essays in verse on painting, history, and epic poetry,
addressed respectively to Romney, Gibbon, and Mason. His
next poem, *The Triumphs of Temper*, was among the great
successes of its time. Pseudo-romantic and flamboyant,
Hayley revealed in his work more of the sensibility than the
sense of his age, and his domestic relations were hardly such
as Cowper, had he been less preoccupied and worried, would
lightly have condoned. For Hayley, having found his wife's
morbidity insupportable, had formed an irregular connection
from which proceeded the son, Thomas Alphonso, whom he
idolised. Mrs. Hayley, who may have been morbid but was
certainly not jealous, adopted the child as her own. A few
years later, however, she and her husband separated "upon
amicable terms," while Tom's mother was settled in a cottage
just outside the patrimonial estate at Eartham, in Sussex,
where her lover had retired in 1774. Here Hayley devoted
himself not only to literature but to building and gardening,
until Gibbon, his constant visitor, proclaimed the result "a
little Paradise."

Hayley may seem a little absurd to modern eyes. But his
verse suited the taste of the time, and there is general agreement that his manners were winning, his conversation delightful, and his heart genuinely warm. Lion-hunter though he
were, his relations with Cowper do him credit, for it was *The
Task* which first damped the reputation of *The Triumphs of
Temper*. It was, indeed, out of rivalry that the friendship
between the two men arose. Hayley was himself working on

the Life of Milton when he heard that Cowper was somewhat similarly engaged. Attempts had been made in the Press to foment jealousy between the competitors. Hayley, however, wrote to Cowper in friendly terms, and enclosed a complimentary sonnet. Cowper was so touched by this magnanimity that a correspondence, which waxed very genial on both sides, was opened. Hayley was then invited to Weston.

He arrived in April 1792. "Everybody has fallen in love with him," Cowper declared; "wherever he goes everybody must." Hayley, for his part, accounted Cowper "the chief acquisition" that his own verse had ever procured him. "My host, though now in his sixty-first year," he told Romney, "appeared as happily exempt from all the infirmities of advanced life as friendship could wish him to be." He described Mrs. Unwin as "a muse of seventy." "Their reception of me," he continued, "was kindness itself. I was enchanted to find that the manners and conversation of Cowper resembled his poetry, charming by unaffected elegance, and the graces of a benevolent spirit. I looked with affectionate veneration and pleasure on the lady who had devoted her life and fortune to the service of this tender and sublime genius." Cowper was described as being of middle stature, and rather strong than delicate in the form of his limbs; he had light brown hair, bluish-grey eyes, and a ruddy complexion. His favourite attire was a green coat turned up with black, and buff waistcoat and breeches.[1] "Green and buff are colours in which I am more often seen than in any other," he himself said, "and are become almost as natural to me as to a parrot." These were the colours of the Hesketh Archery Club in the days of his youth.

If anything were needed to cement the happy feeling immediately established between the "rivals," it occurred while Hayley was still at Weston. Mrs. Unwin had a second seizure. The news was broken to the two poets as they returned from a walk. "My agitated friend," wrote Hayley,

"rushed to the sight of the sufferer; he returned to me in a state that alarmed me in the highest degree for his faculties—

---

[1] Indoors he now wore the linen cap made by Lady Hesketh.

his first speech to me was wild in the extreme—my answer would appear little less so; but it was addressed to the predominant faculty of my unhappy friend, and, with the blessing of Heaven, it produced an instantaneous calm in his troubled mind. From that moment he rested in my friendship with such mild and cheerful confidence, that his affectionate spirit regarded me as sent providentially to support him in a season of severest affliction."

The second stroke had affected Mrs. Unwin's eyes and speech. She had also lost the use of her right hand and arm. Hayley, who prided himself on some medical knowledge, sent a résumé of the case to his friend Dr. Austen in London, and at the same time secured an electrical machine. Lady Hesketh offered to come, but Cowper declined her help, his declared reason being that he associated his cousin with pleasant times and would prefer having her society when she, Mrs. Unwin, and he could form, if it were God's will, "a happy trio" again. In what degree Dr. Austen's skill deserved the tribute it received in a sonnet from Cowper, or to what extent Hayley's electrical treatment was responsible for the quick improvement in Mrs. Unwin's condition, we cannot judge. Mary, at any rate, was sufficiently better within a few weeks for Hayley, ere taking his leave, to suggest that she and Cowper should visit Eartham during the summer.

To Cowper the proposal was startling. He had taken no journey of any length since settling at Olney twenty-four years ago. Hayley, however, assured him that nothing could prove more restorative to Mrs. Unwin than the Sussex air, and, as Hayley had won his complete confidence, his hope for Mary put all his own fears into the background. It did not, of course, dispel them. He saw "a thousand lions, monsters, and giants in the way"; but "perhaps," he said, "they will vanish, if I have the courage to face them." This strain breaks out repeatedly in his letters to Hayley during the next months; but he has far more to say about Mrs. Unwin herself, who, though her condition fluctuated, was making good progress on the whole. He was cheered by another visit from Johnny, whom he asked leave of Hayley to bring with him to

Eartham when Mrs. Unwin was well enough to travel.[1]
Johnny had brought Abbot, the painter, and Cowper sat for
his first—and, as many think, his best—portrait. He told
Hayley that Sam Roberts's boy bowed to the picture, and that
his dog Beau walked up to it, wagging his tail and "thus
acknowledging the likeness to his master."

On June 5 the poet was able to report "a noble day with
us—speech almost perfect—eyes open almost the whole day,
without effort to keep them so—and the step wonderfully
improved." The sedan chair had been exchanged at last for
"two elbows." There was no more "carrying or being
carried." Mrs. Unwin now walked boldly upstairs, with one
hand on the balustrade and the other under his own arm.
The provisional arrangement for the journey to Sussex in July
had to be revised, for Mary was still not quite able to walk
alone and feed herself. Soon, however, her nurse was able
to tell Hayley: "Returned from my walk blown to tatters—
found two dear things in my study—your letter and my
Mary! She is bravely well, and your beloved epistle does us
much good." He concluded: "I know not how you proceed
in your *Life of Milton*. I have literally done nothing since
I saw you. Nothing, I mean, in the writing way, though a
good deal in another; that is to say, in attending my poor
Mary. In this I have hitherto succeeded tolerably well, and
had rather carry this point completely than be the most
famous editor of *Milton* that the world has ever seen."
Johnny continued to brighten the anxious days, and a welcome new friend was Catherine,[2] the young wife of George
Courtenay, who had changed his name and had succeeded his
brother John Throckmorton at the Hall. But Cowper declined all invitations to dine there. "Though I should offend
the whole world by my obstinacy in this instance," he said,
"I would not leave my poor Mary alone. Johnny serves me
as a representative, and him I send without scruple."

The journey to Eartham was now planned to start on
August 1. Cowper's heart nearly failed him several times

[1] John Johnson had recently met Hayley—as also had Lady Hesketh—in
London.
[2] *Née* Stapleton.

during the final week of waiting; but he wrote to Hayley that prayer had opened a passage for him at last, though he was still haunted by "spiritual hounds" at night. And so, on the appointed day, the coach with four steeds drove off from Weston with William, Mary, Johnny Johnson, Sam, and Beau, the famous spaniel. The first night was passed at Barnet, where Samuel Rose met the party. The General dined with them at Kingston, and at Ripley, where they spent the second night, they found themselves the only guests at the inn. On the third night they reached their destination. Cowper had felt a little alarmed at the height of the Sussex hills, but the lions, monsters, and giants of his imagination had happily failed to materialise. It is easy for us, who speed comfortably along good highways, with garages and telephone call-boxes at frequent intervals, to smile at his fears. But hardship and dangers, not to be lightly faced by the least sensitive, were then inseparable from travel: and in Cowper's case there was the further risk of conveying along rough and lonely roads, where no medical attention could be summoned if necessary, an elderly lady but partially recovered from a second attack of paralysis. If courage is to be judged by the effort and self-control demanded, I think Cowper's "frisk into Sussex" deserves recording in that long overdue "Book of Moral Heroes." [1]

At Eartham the visitors received the kindest welcome "that it was possible for friendship and hospitality to contrive." Among their fellow-guests were Romney, who drew the famous portrait of Cowper; Charlotte Smith, the novelist, who was then writing *The Old Manor House*, portions of which she read aloud; and James Hurdis, with whom Cowper had corresponded, and in whom, save for a depression of

---

[1] On returning from Eartham Cowper broke his journey at Kingston in order to visit the General at Ham. "The struggles I had with my own spirit," he said, "labouring as I did under the most dreadful dejection, are never to be told. I would have given the world to be excused. I went, however, and carried my point against myself with a heart riven asunder." In the same letter to Hayley he suggests that "there is sometimes more true heroism passing in a corner, and on occasions that make no noise in the world, than has often been exercised by those whom the world esteems her greatest heroes, and occasions the most illustrious: I hope so at least; for all the heroism I have to boast, and all the opportunities I have of displaying any, are of a private nature."

spirits due to the clergyman-poet's loss of a favourite sister, he saw a striking resemblance to William Unwin. Hayley's son and a youth named Sockett became Mrs. Unwin's "pair of young griffins." With Cowper or Johnny pushing behind, they drew her each day in a four-wheeled chair round the garden, which occupied three sides of a hill and commanded an extensive prospect, with the Isle of Wight in the distance. Mary, who had stood the journey from Weston remarkably well, reaped solid benefit from the change. As for Cowper himself, he was as happy as one "so unaccountably local" could be anywhere away from home. "This is," he informed Lady Hesketh,

> "a delightful place. More beautiful scenery I have never beheld, nor expect to behold; but the charms of it, uncommon as they are, have not in the least alienated my affections from Weston. The genius of that place suits me better; it has an air of snug concealment . . . whereas here I see from every window woods like forests, and hills like mountains—a wilderness in short, that rather increases my natural melancholy, and which, were it not for the agreeables I find within, would soon convince me that mere change of place can avail me little."

Already he was counting the days till he could "re-conduct Mrs. Unwin to the Lodge with her health considerably mended." He said that her speech and powers of walking were much improved, but that her sight and hand still failed her.

The return journey was begun on September 17. Anxious as he was to be home, Cowper felt keenly the parting from Hayley, and when he bade farewell to Tom, who accompanied the travellers some distance upon their road, the tears gushed from his eyes. The first night was spent at Kingston. Breakfast was taken on the following morning at Rose's house in Town. Edward Williams, the Welsh stonemason-bard, was there. But Cowper, miserably conscious of being in London, stared into the fire, listening politely to Williams' conversation, but himself remaining silent. Rose accompanied the party to St. Albans. Their progress thence was unimpeded, though it was not until eight at night, "in the dark, and in a storm," that they found themselves at their own back-door.

For a time Mrs. Unwin seemed better. But the poet, on resuming work, found himself nervously prostrate. How, he asked Teedon, could he concentrate on *Milton* when he was haunted with the fear of Mrs. Unwin's approaching and sudden death? "I feel myself," he said, "the most unpitied, the most unprotected, and the most unacknowledged outcast of the human race": while he told Newton that he seemed always to be "scrambling in the dark, among rocks and precipices, without a guide," but with an enemy ever at his heels. "Thus," he went on, "I have spent twenty years, but thus I shall not spend twenty years more. Long ere that period arrives, the grand question concerning my everlasting weal or woe will be decided." It was not only to Teedon or Newton that he wrote in this manner. Gloom now increasingly characterised all his correspondence: though there were still gleams of the old playfulness, as when he informed Lady Hesketh that she knew not what she lost by not being at Weston at the moment. "We have just received from Johnny a cask of the best Holland gin, and in a few days I shall receive from Charlotte Smith a present of her novel. . . . How happy wouldst thou find thyself in the enjoyment of both articles at once."

Lady Hesketh was at Bath, unwell. She suspected that the servants at Weston Lodge were imposing on Mrs. Unwin and Cowper in their enfeebled state. The poet, in his reply, made light of what was, unhappily, the truth. Hannah Wilson, the daughter of Dick Coleman's wife by a former husband, was, like Dick himself, a cause of much anxiety and expense. Mrs. Unwin had adopted Hannah in 1781, when she was still a child. For some years she had given excellent service, but she had now grown extravagant, vain, and frivolous. Lady Hesketh said that Cowper and Mrs. Unwin were to blame for having indulged their protégées.

Mrs. Unwin was soon able to resume her walks, and Cowper's barometer rose a little again. He was now asked by Joseph Johnson to revise and annotate his *Homer* for a new edition. He laid *Milton* aside, but found the new task hardly less of a burden. His attendance upon Mary left him small leisure. Consequently he formed the habit of rising at six, and, though his eyes were seriously troubling him, of studying by candlelight. Often he did not breakfast until eleven. Overwork helped anxiety to undermine his constitution. In October 1793, Rose brought Thomas Lawrence, then a young man, who painted the poet in the muslin cap whose "ribbon-bound tassel" seemed "ambitious of brushing the sky." The visit passed pleasantly; but by November, when Hayley came again, Mrs. Unwin was much worse. Cowper himself contrived to be fairly cheerful, but Hayley was not deceived by appearances. In order to distract his friend's thoughts, he suggested Cowper's collaboration with him in a poem. "No," was the answer; "I shall never do, nor attempt, anything of consequence more, unless my poor Mary gets better."

He had, indeed, just produced something of capital consequence: the lines *To Mary* herself. Had he written nothing else, he would have immortalised himself and her. That exquisite poem could have been inspired only by truest love. It is well, nevertheless, to remember that it was written when, in every material way, Mrs. Unwin had ceased to be his comfort. Not only was she now the captious and exacting invalid; she was rapidly becoming feeble-minded. She insisted on Cowper's serving and carrying her, and grumbled at him the while. He remained her cheerful slave until at last his own nerves reached breaking-point. He now imagined that God demanded penance. He therefore abstained from food, and sat inert for hours together. The climax of pathos came when the doctor decided that the only possible chance of rousing him lay in getting Mrs. Unwin, who had by this time sunk almost into a stupor, to make some fresh demand of him. It was with great difficulty that she was made to understand what was required. Eventually, however, she was moved to remark that it was a fine morning, suitable for a stroll. Cowper immediately rose and offered her his arm, and—two tottering figures—William and Mary took their last walk together.

At length, in November, Lady Hesketh arrived. Cowper must have been relieved and soothed by her presence; but cheerful, except for brief periods, he no longer was. In January he fell into almost utter despondency, which, though

he rallied somewhat in July, he was never fully to shake off.
In April Hayley paid his third visit. Cowper manifested little
pleasure at his coming, and Tom, brought from boarding-
school, failed only less slightly to arouse his host. Even when
news arrived that, through Hayley's efforts, the King had
decided to grant Cowper a pension of three hundred a year,
payable to Samuel Rose as trustee, the poet himself evinced
no sign of pleasure. It was, indeed, a doleful household for
which Lady Hesketh had assumed responsibility. She remained at the Lodge, however, encouraging her cousin to
amuse himself with netting, putting maps together, and play-
ing with the solitaire board, throughout 1794. She was still
there in the following May, when she wrote to John Johnson
about Hannah. "I have told her," she said, "that the
daughter of a man of five thousand pounds a year would not
be allowed to dress as she does; and when one considers that
all this finery is to dine in the *kitchen*, it makes one sick. . . .
All he [Cowper] is worth in the world would not half keep
Hannah, taking finery and idleness into the account."

In April Mrs. Unwin had had another attack, affecting her
face and voice. "She is a dreadful spectacle," Lady Hesketh
wrote; "yet within these two days she has made our wretched
cousin drag her round the garden; though even Samuel can
scarce support her." Lady Hesketh's own health was rapidly
breaking under the strain.[1] In despair she summoned
Johnny. He proposed that Cowper and Mrs. Unwin should
be removed to Norfolk, where they could be under the super-
vision of his numerous kinsfolk. So, in July, Lady Hesketh
retired to Bath, and Johnny took command.

V

Johnny—of Norfolk! Some years previously, Cowper, if
he had not shrunk from travel, would have thrilled at the
thought of seeing again his mother's native country. Now

[1] Her nervous system never quite recovered, though she lived till 1807. In
her last years she took keen pleasure in helping Hayley with material for his *Life*
of Cowper.

he was indifferent: almost too weary even to dread the journey. Mrs. Unwin, for her part, was beyond having any say
or care in the matter. The scheme was represented as being
but a temporary expedient: but the poet knew instinctively
that he would never see Weston again, for secretly he wrote
on a panel of the window-shutter in his bedroom:

> "*Farewell, dear scenes, for ever closed to me;*
> *Oh, for what sorrows must I now exchange ye!*"

With less of terror than of vague foreboding, he waited again
the arrival of the coach.

His spirits temporarily brightened when, at the end of the
first day's progress, the party came to Eaton Socon, near St.
Neots. Here, while walking in the moonlit churchyard, he
discoursed with Johnny about Thomson's *Seasons*. On the
third day North Tuddenham, their destination, was reached.
Accommodation had been prepared in an untenanted parsonage, where Johnson's sister and her friend Miss Perowne
played hostesses. There were walks and drives through the
surrounding country, and Mrs. Bodham was visited at Mattishall Rectory. August was spent at Mundesley, on whose
sands the poet had raced as a child. Now, spellbound, he
gazed across

> "*the water that grows iron round the Pole,*
> *From the shore that hath no shore beyond it set*
> *in all the sea.*" [1]

The waves, the cliffs, the lighthouse: these inevitably supplied him with symbolism for the ill-fated voyage of his own
soul. Yet there was joy in his sadness. The sea had always
gripped his imagination: how could it fail to fascinate one as
moody as itself? The sight of the breakers, save when the
sun shone upon them, made him shudder; but, as Johnny
soon discovered, there was something inexpressibly soothing
to him in their sound. The sea spoke to his disordered brain:
it spoke also to his spirit. Surface called to surface; but deep
called unto deep: and in the depths there was peace. But the
mortal in him still longed for Buckinghamshire. "Gratify me

---

[1] Swinburne: *A Midsummer Holiday*.

with news of Weston!" he wrote to a friend. "Tell me if my poor birds are living! I never see the herbs I used to give them without a recollection of them, and sometimes am ready to gather them, forgetting that I am not at home."

In October, Johnny, still thinking change good for the invalids, moved them to Dunham Lodge, near Swaffham. Cowper was weaker, and his eyes had assumed a yellow cast. Nevertheless, like an injured war-horse hearing a renewed cry to battle, he rallied again a little on learning that Gilbert Wakefield had been comparing his *Homer* with Pope's. Falling into a trap carefully laid by Johnny, he started on another revision of his own text. For some time he wrote nearly sixty lines a day; but the spell was broken when he was taken again to Mundesley in September 1796. The sea air—*such* sea air!—was now too strong for him. In October, therefore, the party left the coast and settled at Johnson's own house fronting the market-place at East Dereham. Once again the poet, with occasionally beneficial results, was able to play Peeping Tom, as at Olney: till, on December 17, it became obvious that the event dreaded hourly for several years was actually at hand. Mrs. Unwin was sinking. Soon after noon she died. Cowper heard the news "not without emotion," but then asked Johnson to resume his reading aloud of Miss Burney's *Camilla*. A few hours later, he was convinced that Mrs. Unwin "was not actually dead, but would come to life again in her grave, and then undergo all the horrors of suffocation, for he was the occasion of all that she or any other creature upon earth ever did or could suffer." He accompanied Johnson to Mrs. Unwin's room. He gazed at the dear, cold face; gave one passionate cry; and then, calmly going downstairs, ordered a glass of wine. He never spoke of Mary again.

For some months he was listless. With the coming of spring, however, he resumed his walks, and benefited during the summer from a course of asses' milk. Hayley, ever optimistic and resourceful, thought that his friend's spirits might be improved if, in addition to the large correspondence which now reached him from admiring readers, he received a number of tributes from public characters. The scheme, though no possible or impossible stone was left unturned,[1] met with little success; and even though the Bishops of London and of Llandaff were prevailed upon to send letters, the pressure of Cowper's malady "had made him deaf to the most honourable praise." More successful was a new ruse by which Johnny Johnson tempted him to resume his revision of *Homer*. The work, now taken up again, served more than anything else to alleviate his suffering. Also, at the instigation of Johnson, he translated some Latin and Greek epigrams: while suddenly, on March 20, 1799, he wrote his last original poem.

He had paid several more brief visits to Mundesley, and it was, doubtless, as he gazed upon the cold North Sea under leaden skies that an incident in Anson's *Voyages*, read many years ago, had recurred to him:

> "*Obscurest night involv'd the sky,*
> *Th' Atlantic billows roar'd,*
> *When such a destin'd wretch as I,*
> *Wash'd headlong from on board,*
> *Of friends, of hope, of all bereft,*
> *His floating home for ever left.*"

There follows an account of the swimmer's battling with the waves, and of the vain efforts of his shipmates, afflicted by his cries, to save him by throwing out casks, coops, and cords. Then, after the climax, comes the obvious application:

> "*I therefore purpose not, or dream,*
> *Descanting on his fate,*
> *To give the melancholy theme*
> *A more enduring date:*
> *But misery still delights to trace*
> *Its semblance in another's case.*
>
> *No voice divine the storm allay'd,*
> *No light propitious shone;*
> *When, snatch'd from all effectual aid,*
> *We perish'd, each alone:*
> *But I beneath a rougher sea,*
> *And whelm'd in deeper gulphs than he.*"

---

[1] See the essay on "Cowper and William Hayley" in *Essays, Modern and Elizabethan*, by Edward Dowden. 1910.

Lord David Cecil sees here "the accumulated anguish and despair" of Cowper's life, blazing up in "a last towering flame of poetry." But Goldwin Smith is surely truer when he says that "the despair which finds vent in verse is hardly despair," and that "*The Castaway* ought to be an antidote to religious depression, since it is the work of a man of whom it would be absurdity to think as really estranged from the spirit of good, who had himself done good to the utmost of his powers." I have said that in the depths of Cowper there was peace. An hereditary mental taint often kept the subconscious from being consciously realised. Not, indeed, that Cowper's hypochondria is necessary to explain the relatively settled gloom of his last years. It is common enough for the end of life to be clouded, when the mortal faculties decay and bereavements accumulate. Many a perfectly normal person would have broken down completely under the burdens Cowper had been carrying. So much the greater marvel is it that he did *not* completely break down. *The Castaway* proves otherwise. His brain gave to the poem the superficial colour of despair. That he wrote it at all shows that his spirit was still alert and responsive to the world outside himself. A man cannot write a beautiful poem who has lost his joy in beauty; nor is it ultimate misery which

> "*still delights to trace
> Its semblance in another's case.*"

Cowper's *mind* might be full of pity for himself: his *heart* overflowed with compassion for Anson's sailor. There was love in the depths of his being: and, where love is, peace, however ruffled be the surface of things, remains.

In December he was moved to a larger house in the town, and amused himself by translating into Latin the fables of Gay, which he had recited as a child for the entertainment of company at Berkhampstead Rectory. In April 1800 he was seized with dropsy. Johnson[1] and the good Miss Perowne, who had done her best to take Mrs. Unwin's place, attended him with ungrudging affection. Lady Hesketh, still an

---

[1] The Rev. Dr. John Johnson—" Johnny of Norfolk "—died in 1833 and was buried at Yaxham, near Dereham.

invalid, was unable to come, and poor Hayley was watching by his dying Tom. In March Dr. Lubbock of Norwich visited East Dereham, and to his enquiries Cowper answered: "I feel unutterable despair." During the following month, Samuel Rose visited his old friend, who was now confined to bed. Soon after he left, there was a change for the worse. Johnny spoke to the poet of his approaching dissolution, and of the "unspeakable happiness" prepared by "a merciful Redeemer" for all His children. Cowper listened to the first part of the sentence, but, on hearing the second part, entreated Johnny to say no more. The disordered mind was putting up its last fight. On the evening of April 24, Miss Perowne, seeing the invalid much exhausted, offered him some refreshment. He replied: "What can it signify?"

He never spoke again. At five the next morning he became insensible, and thus remained until the afternoon. He died so peacefully that Johnny did not know he had passed until he saw that his expression had settled into one "of calmness and composure, mingled, as it were, with holy surprise." The grand question of the poet's everlasting weal or woe had been decided: unless we assume that the look of serenity and wonder were but a cheat, a reflex of expiring mortality. Had Cowper found peace merely in extinction? Or was the spirit freed at last from the tyranny of the mind? Had God indeed been His own interpreter and made it plain: made it plain, as the greatest figure of the eighteenth century had realised while in the flesh, that no Scripture can mean "that His mercy is not over all His works; that is, whatever it prove beside, no Scripture can prove predestination"?

INDEX

SOME PRESS OPINIONS

"It has remained for Mr. Gilbert Thomas to show us Cowper related to his century, and in particular to the Evangelical movement, to gather up threads left by previous biographers, and to give us what may prove, in the absence of additional evidence, to be the last word on the subject. . . . Mr. Thomas writes delightfully. . . . He is consistently fair, though firm, and carries the reader successfully through an immense amount of material without losing his thread. . . . His analysis of Cowper's poetry is excellent."—*The Observer.*

* * *

"Mr. Thomas brings to his study of Cowper a knowledge of the Evangelical movement in the eighteenth century, and a sympathy with its aims and achievements, which previous critics have not always shared . . . a very useful work . . . it will certainly be of value, even to those who do not share all his enthusiasms or are not convinced by all his arguments."—*The Times.*

* * *

"Displays a considered appreciation of character and a rare skill in the use of material. His book is both explicit and entertaining; it is a book to be read with pleasure and retained with gratitude . . . a work of enduring value . . . there is no distortion or prejudice. . . . Mr. Thomas has effected a very necessary adjustment of ideas. . . . The chapter on the Evangelical movement of John Wesley is remarkably well considered. . . . His account of the Olney period is particularly entertaining, vivid, and perspicuous . . . an honest, reliable piece of work."—C. E. Vulliamy in *The Spectator.*

* * *

"Mr. Thomas is as accurate as Mr. Wright, and as pleasant in style as Mr. Fausset and Lord David Cecil, while he shows on every page what they lack—a profound understanding of the Evangelical point of view."—Edward East in the *News-Chronicle.*

* * *

"Here at last is a consistent and convincing portrait of a singularly elusive temperament, and it emerges from a setting of rich and lifelike detail. Mr. Thomas has immersed his imagination in the spirit of the age, and his panorama of the Evangelical revival is a notable contribution to literary and religious history."—Arthur Waugh in the *Fortnightly Review.*

"Mr. Thomas describes not only Cowper's life but the lives and characters of many of his contemporaries, together with many of the circumstances of the world in which he lived . . . a very useful work. His book is one which no student of Cowper would wish to neglect."—*Times Literary Supplement.*

* * *

"A biography which for learning, original insight, and charm of style well deserves to become the poet's lasting monument. . . . Mr. Thomas's study of Newton's character and work reminds us of Macaulay's vivid prose."—*British Weekly.*

* * *

"No one can refuse to recognize the sincerity and ability, the sympathy and imaginative tenderness which Mr. Thomas has brought to his study of Cowper. . . . To understand properly his poetry or his letters the reader should have a clear idea of that England in which he lived; and he could not find a better account of it than in this book."—*Church Times.*

* * *

"His book is rich in the imagination which has fed scrupulously on facts; rich, too, in independent judgment. And it is as readable as it is precise in all its references."—Hugh I'A. Fausset in *The London Mercury.*

* * *

"Beautifully and arrestingly written. . . . It is massive, humane, and intensely interesting; and the vivid pictures given of Cowper's pre-industrial England have probably never been surpassed."—Herbert Palmer in *The Dublin Magazine.*

* * *

"Of all the books [on Cowper] that have recently appeared, Mr. Thomas's is by far the most satisfying. It is a remarkable achievement."—Professor H. B. Charlton in *The Manchester Guardian.*

* * *

"A book that must take its place in the history of the English poets."—*Church of England Newspaper.*

* * *

"Both from the literary and the religious points of view this full-length study of Cowper has great attractiveness and importance."—*Christian World.*